TERRORISM AND SEPARATISM IN NORTH-EAST INDIA

TERRORISM AND SEPARATISM IN NORTH-EAST INDIA

Chandra Bhushan

KALPAZ PUBLICATIONS
Delhi-110052

Terrorism and Separatism in North-East India
(International Studies)

Rs. 690

ISBN: 81-7835-261-3

Published in 2007 in India by
Kalpaz Publications,
C-30, Satyawati Nagar, Delhi-110052
E-mail : Kalpaz@hotmail.com

Laser Typesetting at : Shree Vaishnavi Creations, Delhi
Printed at : Mehara Offset Press

Contents

Preface

In Search of Light

Complete North east region of India has seven states. They are Assam, Meghalaya, Manipur, Nagaland, Mizoram, Tripura and Arunachal Pradesh. The inhabitants of this area belong to more than 1500 castes and tribes. They speak more than 400 different languages and follow different religions. These North Eastern states have such a multiplicity of historic, geographic, social, cultural, religious and linguistic activities that any other state in India, perhaps, may not have.

It is a fact that social, economic and cultural activities of any community depend to a large extent on its social and communal structure. The same way their social, economic and cultural activities always have an impact of the race to which they belong , their specific qualities, ambitions, communal identity, self respect and awakening, faiths, mutual relations, religions, public common beliefs, literature, etc. If we study these activities of North East region we come to a conclusion that the communities in this region have some wonderful specialities that can hardly be seen in original course in rest of the country.

The region is divided by forming small states. But the administrators of these states could not stand to the expectations of the people. They were totally unsuccessful in shouldering the heavy responsibility of public welfare, which was entrusted to them. On the other hand, they remained busy with self welfare rather than public welfare. Benefits of number of economic packages given by the Centre did not at all reach the people in general for whom they were intended and the claims of development made by publicity agencies, in turn, proved to be false and futile. Naturally the wave of terrorism and separation started blowing in this context.

The K. K. Birla Foundation selected me for undertaking research in Social , Economic Structure and Separatism / Isolation, in 2001 in North East region which I accepted as a challenge. My experience of journalism during the Nineties, in adverse circumstances and my mailing of information and news to various newspapers and periodicals came to my help in conducting the research. Though the period of one year for this work is very short, I put my utmost efforts in giving an equitable look at all the seven states and have tried to study the structure and separatist wave in the region.

There is a long list of personalities from whom I got co-operation. Even then I mention my heartfelt gratitude to senior journalists Rajendra Ranjan, Omkareshwar Pandey, Dinkar Kumar, Ratnesh, Ravishankar Ravi, local editor of Pooranchal Prahari, Guwahati , Shri Satan and Pathak, Outlook correspondent Nitin A Gokhale, Ranvijay, Samir Tanti and others for their valuable co-operation and encouragement given to me from time to time to complete the project. I express my sincere thanks to my guide Shri Rajendra Awasthi - editor of 'Kadambini' and Shivday Prakash Bharati - editor of 'Nandan' who always provided me the encouragement. Proof reading of the book was done by Laxmikant Upadhyay. I am thankful to Shri Anjani Kumar who put his day and night efforts in composing the book on computer. My life partner 'Kalpana Bhushan' was always with me during the tour of North East and helped me from time to time without which this difficult task could not have been completed.

I, once again, express my thanks to honourable director of K.K. Birla Foundation Shri Bishan Tandon and assistant director Shri S. K. Sethi who always guided me every now and then during the research. I am thankful to all those persons , institutions, etc., who directly or indirectly helped me during the project.

Chandra Bhushan

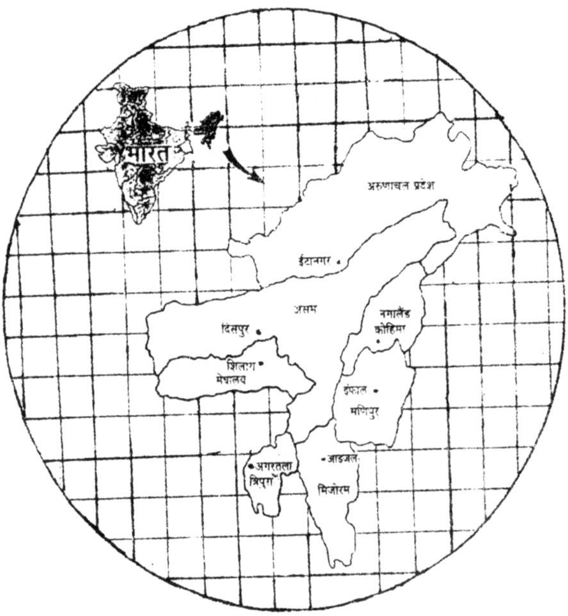
भारत
अरुणाचल प्रदेश
ईटानगर
असम
दिसपुर
नगालैंड
कोहिमा
शिलांग
मेघालय
इंफाल
मणिपुर
अगरतला
त्रिपुरा
आइजल
मिजोरम

Chapter 1

North East India

Seven Sister States

The seven states of Arunachal Pradesh, Assam, Meghalaya, Tripura, Nagaland, Manipur and Mizoram situated in far North East land of India are colloquially known as seven sister states. Actually, Himalayan ranges protect this area from North and East. South is surrounded by chitgaon and China mountain ranges whereas Western side is surrounded by hills originating from Bangladesh. The whole region covering 2 lacs 55 thousand 83 square kilometres of land and accommodating a population of 3 crores 84 lacs 95 thousand 89 (2001 census) is actually the North Eastern part of India (see table 1).

Uneven and hilly land, rivers creating sweet music, dense forests added by attractive natural beauty has been the source of attraction for centuries. Because of its situation, the complete North East region remained cut off from rest of India for a pretty long period. Access to this region in olden days was possible only on foot or by boats.

Table 1.1 Area and Population of North East States

States	*Area (sq.km)*	*Population*	*Density*
Meghalaya	22,429	23,06,069	79
Arunachal Pr.	83,743	10,91,117	10
Assam	78,438	2,66,38,407	286
Manipur	22,327	23,88,634	82
Mizoram	21,081	8,91,058	33
Nagaland	16,579	19,88,636	73
Tripura	10486	31,91,168	263
Total	2,55,083	3,84,95,089	123

But with the development of culture this region gained importance in the eyes of rest of the world. We are going to see, in the following paragraphs, information of all these seven states, but in short.

Pragjyotishpur-Kamrup i.e. Assam

Assam has its own importance in whole of the North East region. It has common boundaries with Bhutan, China, Myanmar (Burma) and Bangladesh. The name of the state 'Assam' has come up out of many wonderful things. The Historians also had given a long thought to find out the origin of this name but could not reach to a final conclusion. At the end it is accepted that the name Assam has come from a community name "Ahom". This Ahom dynasty ruled this region for about 600 years prior to British entry in the region, and therefore people started calling it Ahom's land which further was abridged as "Assam". This region was known as 'Pragjyotishpur' in ancient days. This region was ruled by 'Danavas' in that period. According to 'Kalki Puran' the Brahma created the planets (Naxatras) in this area only. As such this area surrounded by hills started to be known as 'Pragjyotishpur. During the course of time astronomy and astrology were developed in this area. Its proofs are available today also in the form of 'Nav Graha Mandir" Temple of Nine Planets. A place of strength (Shakti Peeth) 'Kamakhya mandir' must also have been erected in those days only.

Assam, in Sanskrit based language is A + Sam i.e. unequal or incomparable. As it is, the complete land in this region is uneven. There are mountains at some places whereas valleys at other places. Some places shower natural beauty whereas some places are covered with dense forests. Any way there are no two opinions regarding the nomenclature of the area.

According to a Chinese research scholar, Assam had trade relations with other countries even before 100 B.C. He further wrote that Assam had a silk trade with Egypt and Rome in those days. Archeological survey has discovered from the dug- out footprints that Assam existed right from the stone age. People of Mongol race came to this area during 'Veda Era'. The tribes of original residents of this area are known to be belonging to Mongol race who were then known as 'Kirat' in Veda era. As per 'Kalki Puran' and 'Vishnoo Puran' the area was known as 'Kamaroop'. Its area was spread up in a radius of 450 miles from Kamakhya Temple. This temple is situated on Nilanchal mountain in Guwahati. It is said that the Dunavaking Narakasur, named Bhagawati fought from the side of 'Kouravas' in Mahabharatta war at 'Kurukshetra' with full flavour and bravery. But he was killed at the hands of 'Bhima' from Pandavas. A Chinese traveller Huentsang visited Assam when it was ruled by Bhaskar Burman (594-650) and described Assam with details. The King Bhaskar Burman had friendly relations with Harshavardhan. And as such Assam was flourishing in those days. 'Slastanbha' dynasty rose after Burman rule in Assam. It ruled Assam till 10th century. Shri. Vanmala Vermandeo from this dynasty spread its rule to North Bangal. After this rule followed Brahmapal of founded the Pal dynasty which ruled Assam till early 12th century. Another important ruler 'Prithu' returned successfully the Muslim attack by Mohammad Ibne-Bakhtiar. But was defeated in 1228 by Muslims.

During 1228 itself, Ahoms from Burma entered this area by crossing 'Patkui' mountain ranges, under the leadership of 'Chukaka'. The Ahoms took many intelligent and important decisions and appointed many local persons on important posts. They founded 'Kamta' state. Koch state in Kamroop was established by Vishwa Sinha in 1515. His son 'Narnarayan' was an efficient and intelligent ruler (1540-1584). He joined north Bengal with quite a large land of Assam. He ruled Tripura Kachhar, Khasi and Jayantiya hilly areas also. The Ahom kingdom was extended to Manas river in the West by 17th century. But from 18th century Ahom rule started falling. Frequent attacks by the Mughals, internal clashes added by frequent attacks from Burma finally defeated the Ahoms in 18th century. The region then came under the rule of Britishers in 1824. The British government signed the Yadambu agreement on 24th February 1826 and compelled the Burmese to leave this region. Thus,, the Britishers captured the complete region.

The region was attached to Bengal and was ruled accordingly between 1826 and 1874. But finally in 1874 this region was declared as a province. Gwalpara, Kachhar, Silhet, Khasi, Jayantiya, Naga, North Kachhar, Mikir, Garo and Lusai (all hilly areas) were joined to Assam and were made its parts. But at the time of division of India during independence struggle the district of Silhat was given to Eastern Pakistan (todays) Bangla desh. Gradually, Nagaland, Meghalaya, Mizoram, etc., were made separate states severing them from Assam. This is the reason why

Table 1.2 Sexwise Population of North East India

States	*Male*		*Female*		*Total*	
	1991	2001	1991	2001	1991	2001
Meghalaya	9,07,687	11,67,840	8,67,091	11,38,229	17,74,778	23,06,069
Arunachal Pradesh	4,65,004	5,73,951	3,99,554	5,17,166	8,64,558	10,91,117
Assam	11657989	13787799	10756333	12850608	22414322	26638634
Manipur	9,38,359	12,07,338	8,98,790	11,81,296	18,37,149	23,88,634
Mizoram	3,58,978	4,59,783	3,30,778	4,31,275	6,89,756	8,91,058
Nagaland	6,41,282	10,41,686	5,68,264	9,46,950	12,09,548	1988636
Tripura	14,17,930	16,36,138	13,29,275	15,55,030	27,57,205	3191168
Total	16387229	19874535	15160085	18620554	31547314	38495059

all the north eastern states are known as seven sister states.

Meghalaya - Scotland of East

The state of Meghalaya was formed by severing the hilly areas of Garo, Khasi and Jayantiya from Assam on the 21st January 1972. The 22,06069 population of this state occupying the area of 22,429 square kilometres in (2001). Southern and half of the western border of this state is with Bangladesh. On all remaining sides it is surrounded by Assam.

Actually there is no historical background for the name and state of Meghalaya. The state has heavy rains during the period from April and September. The sky of this state is always full of clouds during the said period, spreading eye soothing and attractive natural beauty. It is therefore known as 'Meghalaya' Megh (clouds) + Alaya (home) i.e. Home of clouds.

Some historical information about the three important tribes of the state-Khasi, Garo and Jayantiya, is available. According to researches the Khasi tribes belong to Mongol race. It is apparent from their face cuts that they have come from outside. But their eyes are quite different from Mongolians. Another tribe 'Khasi' people came from south east Asia via Burma and Burasta or directly via Burma and settled in Khasi and Jayantiya hills. But it is a fact that they belong to Mongol and Austrian races. Secondly they came to this area during 4th century AD and before the Aryans came. There is no specific mention of these people in ancient Sanskrit literature also. There is a reference to Kirats belonging to Mongol race. We can get the references of Khasi tribals in the 'Bhagwat Purana' penned by Shankar Deo in 1500 AD. Information about these tribes was not available for a pretty long period upto 19th century. But the

'Buranji' (history) of Jayantiya has information of Hindu King 'Khayrim'. According to Koch Buranji (history) Koch king Narnarayan defeated the Jayantiya king in a battle. The king Khyrim then mediated and made both of them to leave war and resolve the problems by way of talks.

According to Ahom Buranji, the Ahom kings established marital relations with Jayantiya king in early 17 th century. Accordingly the Ahom king asked the Jayantiya king to establish a market at Fulwari near Kamroop. Their friendship lasted till early 18th century. But since the Jayantiya king arrested the Kachhari king, the then Ahom king Ramsing was annoyed. Actually the Kachharis were under the protection of Ahom king Ramsingh, that time. As a result the Ahoms killed hundreds of Jayantiya tribals.

The king Khayrim had also established friendly relations with the Ahoms during 17th century. By 18th century the Ahoms established trade relations with the people in planes.

The Britishers captured Silhat in 1765. The Khasis used to come to Silhat border for trading in silk, wax, cotton textiles, iron-ore, honey, etc., at Pandua. In return they used to take Rice, Salt and dried fish. Limestone from Khasi area was being carried to Bengal. In a short period the British traders started a trade in limestone with the Khasi tribals. Thereby they came in contact with the Khasis.

In 1824 the Burmese attacked Kachhar and pierced themselves upto the Jayantiya hill borders. The Britishers took benefit of this and sent one platoon for the help of Jayantiya king. An agreement was signed on 10th March 1824 between Jayantiya king and the Britishers under which the Jayantiya king accepted the protection of Britishers. The same way the Khasi chief also allowed the Britishers to enter their area with a view to have protection from Burmese attacks and invasion.

Later on when the possibility of Burmese attack was removed, the Britishers requested permission to construct a road joining Assam valley and Surma valley through the hilly area of Khasi and Jayantiya. This was accepted by majority of Khasi chiefs and the road was completed by March 1829. But U. Tairot Sinha had opposed this. Later on in 1862 the Jayantiyas revolted against the Britishers under the leadership of U. Kiyang Nangwah.

Specific information concerning history of Garo-tribals is also not available. But it is accepted on the basis of some proofs that these people came to this area from Tibet in ancient days and settled in Garo Hills. They had to face resistance from the king of the area when they crossed the Brahmaputra and proceeded to Assam valley. But in a short period they got a Garo girl married to a prince and in return they settled in the area. Later on the prince was displeased with the Garos for some reason. Eventually the Garos had to leave that area. Finally they settled in the southern hills of Kamaroop district. Even today the Garos consider Tibet to be their origin. This may be the probable reason why their language has nearness to Tibeti language. But their traditions, rituals at the time of birth and death and marriage have no similarity with those of Tibetians. On the other hand they are nearer to Kachhari and Naga tribes.

A large number of people belonging to western China came to Burma via Tibet in 400 A.D. But some strong tribes living in Chindwin vally of Burma pushed them to Assam. These Chinese travellers might have probably accepted some traditions and rituals from Naga tribals while travelling through their area.

Human hunting was a main tradition of Nagas. Some Garos also accepted this tradition even till today.

North-Eastern population and birth rate 1991-2001

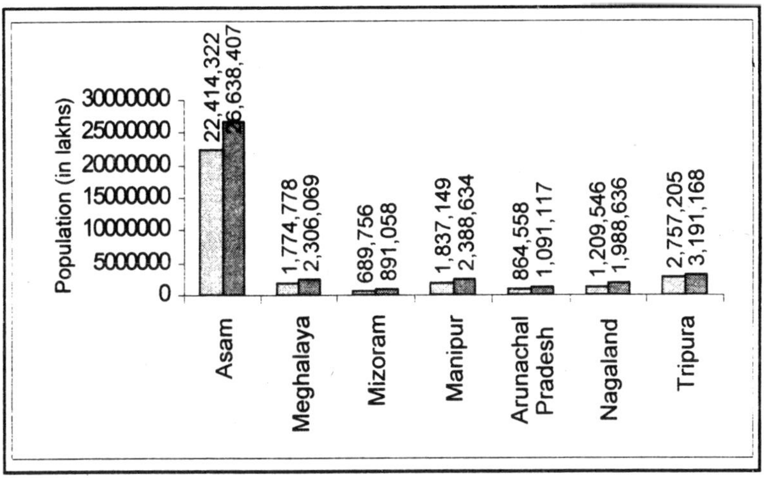

Fig. 1.

There are no historical facts available pertaining to Garo hills area for the period up to early Mughal Rule. According to history of Mughal period some landlords from plains used to recover share (tax) from the local people in hills. These landlords came under the control of Britishers when they captured the region in 1765. Naturally these landlords started paying the tax collected by them to the British government instead of Mughals. But since the clashes between these landlords and the local people increased the British asked Mr. David Scott to investigate and submit a report on the situation. Later on, landlord's rights of recovering tax was declared as illegal. After this David Scott was appointed as commissioner of this area. Then the local people accepted British control and started paying taxes to them. There existed three types of Garos that time -

1) landlord Garos 2) Tax payer Garos and 3) Independent Garos. First two Garos came under British control in the beginning. But in 1866 the British appointed an officer at Tura for bringing the independent Garos under their control. Eventually a number of independent Garo villages came under the purview of taxation. Assam was made a province in 1874 and the Garo hill district was included in Assam.

Mizoram - A state in the arms of Mountains

A larger piece of land having an area of 21,081sq kms and population of 6,89,756 people mostly Christians was separated from Assam and made a separate state on the 20th February 1987 as the implementation of an agreement of Govt. of India with Mizo National Front, signed on the 30th June 1986. The state of Mizoram has common border with Myanmar in the east and south and with Bangladesh on the west. It is connected with rest of India through its North border with Assam and Manipur on those directions. A smaller part of western border is with Tripura. As it is bordered along 630 kms by Myanmar and Bangladesh it has a strategic war importance.

As a matter of fact there is no specific mention of Mizoram and its people in the history. But according to traditional beliefs the Mizos have their origin at Chinlang in Sichun province of China. According to some historians these people came to Burma in 900 A.D. and gradually came to this area in three stages. Mizo means person living on higher lands or mountain man. These people in first stage came to Mizoram from Burma before 16 century and then to Tripura and settled in Western part of Tripura. In the second stage these people came to Kachhar and Manipur in second half of 17th century and settled there. Finally in third stage i.e. during the 17th and 18th century they finally got settled in this area. As this area is

on all sides except East by Bangala Desh. It's eastern border is with Assam and Mizoram.

Historical proofs are nowhere available as to how this area was named as Tripura. But peoples belief is that the area was named after the name of the son of 39th Daitya king of this area (Durhya). A part of popular believe that Tripura is the combination of two words Tui+Para. Tui means 'water' and Para means 'nearness'. Thus, the land which has water resources very near is Tripura. History of this area for the period upto 15th century is written on the basis of public beliefs and their traditions. Accordingly historian 'Rajmala' has opined on the basis of these beliefs and traditions. Another historian Mohmedan has different version. He says that Trilochan was the king of Tripura during Mahabharata era. There was a war between Tripura and Kachhar king during the period of king 'Prateeta' the 69th king of Tripura. Prateeta was defeated in this war and he was compelled to leave the area of Kholongma and had to shift his headquarters to Dharamnagar on the banks of river Jusi. During this rule the river Barak divided Tripura and Kachhar from each other.

Modern history of Tripura starts from Veerchandra Manikya (1862-96). The Jayantiya tribes revolted against Tripura Rule in 1863 under the leadership of Parikshit. Maharaja Veer Vikram Kishor Manikya was the last king of Tripura (1923-47). He was a versatile and efficient administrator and therefore was very popular amongst the people. He implemented a number of projects for allround development of Tripura. Construction of roads and buildings around Agartala, establishment of Rural University, etc., are some of his achievements. He also worked for development of trade and commerce. That is why he enjoys a special mention, in the history of Tripura. His minor son Kirat Vikram was throned as the king after the death of Maharaja Vir Vikram Kishor. Efforts were made to join Tripura to East Pakistan immediately after independence. King mother Maharani Kanchan Prabha Devi approached the then Home Minister Sardar Vallabh Bhai Patel and requested him to protect Tripura. In return the Government of India took immediate initiative and saved Tripura from going to Pakistan. This marked the end of empirical rule of 1300 years. Tripura was finally included in India on 15th October 1949. A recommendation was made during 1954-56 to join Manipur and Tripura to Assam. But the C.P.I. (M.) opposed this for the apparent reason of protecting the culture and rights of Jayantiyas. Thus,, it was brought under Central Territory on 1st November 1956.

Nagaland - Land of strong tribals

The land with an area of 16,579 sq. kms metres and a population of of 23,88,634 was (Census 2001) given status of Indian State on the 1st December 1963. It has Myanmar on the Eastern border ,Arunachal Pradesh on North Eastern, Assam on Western side and Manipur on the South. Specific historical Information regarding Nagas is not available. Their origin is based on the traditional beliefs and history is penned on this basis only. As a matter of fact Nagas are related to Indo-Mongol race. It is still a mystery as to how the name Naga came up. There are number of folk tales regarding this. Some say that 'Naga' comes from the word Noke, which means people. Some say that it is derived from the word Nanga, but according to Sanskrit Naga means person living in mountains.

Because of Non-availability of information it is assumed that Nagas are original Kirats. As per the folk tales based on *Mahabharata,* Naga Queen Ulupi fell in love with Arjuna and she brought him to Naga Lok. Both lived together for a period. Later on Arjuna went to Manipur. Traditional beliefs say that Nagas were on thc side of Kaurvas in the Kurukshetra War. Even this history is silent as regards to Nagas right up to 12th century. Ahom king Chukafa Verma met the Nagas while coming to India in 1228. It is believed that there was a war between Nagas and Ahoms. The Konyak Nagas defeated the Ahoms in 1536 and seized their guns. But afterwards the Konyak Nagas were defeated by Ahoms and they were compelled to enter in to treaty where under the Nagas had to return the earlier seized guns to Ahoms along with a large sum. It is further believed that this area was under Ahom rule till the end of 17th century. But it started weakening in the early 19th century. By 1816, after the invasion of Burma the Ahoms lost their hold over this land.

Relations between Nagas and Britishers can be divided in three periods. First period is taken as 1832-1850. During this period the Britishers sent their soldiers to Naga Mountains. Secon period is 1851-1863. The Britishers followed the policy of Non-interference with Nagas. But later on the Britishers left this policy. Third period starts from 1866 when the Britishers captured the Naga Mountains in toto.

The Britishers first time came in contact with Nagas when it was decided to have a road between Manipur and Assam. Captain Jenkins and Demberten proceeded to Naga Mountains with a troop of 700 Manipuri soldiers in 1832. The Nagas were quite angry and disturbed because of this move.

The Britishers recruited Nagas in their army during First World War. The Naga mountains got flared up during Second World War. The Japanese succeeded in reaching Kohima. The warfare continued for 64 days. This tale can not be complete without short discussion about Rani Gaidulu and her Khampai disciples. Rani Gaidulu staged a long opposition to the Britishers. But finally in 1950 she was captured by the soldiers of Assam Rifles. The Britishers sentenced her for life imprisonment. She was released in 1946, just one year before Indias independence. Revolt and opposition of Rani Gaidulu against the Britishers is taken as a part of freedom struggle. She went underground in 1960 and joined the movement run by Fizo. At the end in 1966 she appeared in Kohima and declared her belief and faith in the policy of Government of India.

In short, this area was made a ' Naga Mountain District' within Assam in 1881. The district was given autonomy in 1951. Finally it was given the status of Indian state with reorganisation on 1stDecember 1963.

Manipur-The land with culture

Manipur was given the status of Indian state on the 21st January 1972. This state is spread on a land measuring 22327 sq kms with a population of 23,8864. Nagaland is on North while Assam and Mizoram on West side. Its total Eastern boundary is joined with Myanmar along with more than three fourth boundary on south. Rest of the Southern boundary is joined with Mizoram.

Manipur has 90 per cent of its land as mountainous land. This is the second state alongwith Assam in North East which has maintained its cultural relations with rest of India. Majority of the population in this state belongs to Hindu religion who are known as 'Maitei'. Actually Manipur is geographically cut from rest of India. Even then cultural heritage of India is deep-rooted in this state. Although specific historical information regarding

Manipuris is not available it is believed that the Manipuris were quite rich culturally. Two-third of Manipuris population resides in the valley. They call themselves as Aryas, but their physical structure identifies with that of Mongols. Around 29 main tribes of this state reside in mountain areas.

Chapter 2

Social Structure of North East India

4 crore population of North East region consists of Aryas and Dravids. Apart from these races, a number of tribes and sub-tribes belonging to Mangol Race and Moth and Khwameth tribes belonging to Austrian race, live in this region. Along with influential and developed Aryans (majority) comparably a smaller number of backward and minority tribes are the inhabitants of this area. Large and wide differences are apparent in these tribes. About 70 % of North East population belongs to these tribes. Every tribe has it's own language, living style, traditions etc. But with the development in all areas, changes are also apparent in these tribes. Impact of western culture is more in Mizoram, Nagaland and Meghalaya. Whereas Assam, Manipur, Arunachal Pradesh and Tripura have an impact of Hindu culture. It is observed that education and other developments are greater in the tribes which are converted to Christianity in comparison to the tribes who opted to remain Hindus. But it is noticeable that these Hindu Tribes have bondage with rest of

Table 2.1 Population of North East India (Caste wise) (1991)

State	Scheduled caste	Scheduled tribes	Others	Total
Meghalaya	9072	1517927	227779	1774778
Arunachal Pradesh	4052	550351	310155	864558
Assam	1659412	2874441	17880469	22414322
Manipur	37105	632173	1167871	1837149
Mizoram	691	653565	35500	689756
Nagaland	-	1060822	148724	1209546
Tripura	451116	853345	1452744	2757205
Total	2161448	8142624	21243242	31547314

India. This is actually the outcome of ancient Indian traditions and beliefs.

Table 2.2 Number of Districts Cities etc. of North East

States	Districts (1991)	Density (1995)	Cities (1997)	Houses (1991)
Meghalaya	07	5780	12	327371
Arunachal Pr.	15	3649	10	175448
Assam	23	25590	93	3844370
Manipur	09	2212	31	296680
Mizoram	08	785	22	120994
Nagaland	08	1225	09	216982
Tripura	04	856	18	526659
Total	71	39946	195	5508513

Percentage of literacy in Mizoram is highest (80%) in this region. Even then there are some equalities in the people of this region. They are 1) Habituated to live in hilly area. 2) Consume fish (people of Mizoram are non-vegetarians they even consume dog flesh) 3) weave there own clothing at their homes. 4) there is less castism. 5) ladies are more hard working than gents and 6) they love dance and music. Apart from these there is an awakening of regional spirit which is very strong.

Social Structure of Mizoram

Mizo people belong to Mangol Race. It is believed that these people came in this region from upper Burma in 17th or 18th century. Mizo means people living in mountains. As far as physical structure of Mizos they have yellow skin flat nose, broad face, long and straight hair, short or medium height. Their upper body (above waist) is longer than the lower. Their language is related to Tibetee and Burmese. Language of every tribe is different from that of the other. Even then it is related to each other. Their language is called as Lusai which is also known as "Duhaliya- Twang". Now it is known as Mizo Twang - This language is now an official Language of Mizoram after English. Mizo tribals came under missioneries influence and got converted to Christianity during 19th century. These missioneries laid utmost stress on spread of education. Mizo Twang Language does not have it's own script. Now Roman script is accepted as authorised script for this language, as the missioneries used this script for education.

According to 1991 census 95% of 6.8 Lacs population, is Christian and 88% of Mizos are literate (Census 2001). Mizoram stands at second place after Kerala in Literacy. Mizo people are well cultured, ever smiling and social. They do not believe in casteism and classes. Because of this the social conditions of Mizoram are quite different from rest of India. The Mizos love music and dance from their heart. There is a great change in their social and professional attitude as an impact of western culture. They have adopted western living style.

Table 2.3 Literacy in North East States (%)

States	1991			2001		
	Total	M.	F.	Total	M.	F.
Meghalaya	49	53	45	63	66	60
Arunachal Pr.	42	51	30	55	64	44
Assam	53	62	43	64	72	56
Manipur	60	72	48	69	78	60
Mizoram	82	86	79	88	91	86
Nagaland	62	68	55	67	72	62
Tripura	60	71	50	71	81	65
Total	58	66	50	69	75	62

Before converting to Christianity they were known as and were the 'moving tribes'. They used to go from one place to other for their livelihood. Wherever they were going they used to establish a village. All the families in the group of tribe were strongly bound with each other. The total group used to live like one family and everyone belonging to the group was always ready to help the other. Today also there is one common quality in Mizo people which in their language is known as 'Tiawmngaihna'. There is no English or Hindi synonym to this. Literary meaning is 'Selfless', caring for others, and determined. All these are the best qualities that everyone should adopt. But now, it is not that all the Mizos possess this quality. They have defined this quality in other manner.

In olden days all the unmarried were made to live together, but not with their families in towns and villages. The elderly persons used to encourage them to act according to the above qualities. But it is a things of the past now. There is a great social and cultural change in the Mizos. This could happen as they came in contact with higher strata people, as well as political and educational development. But the same time the young Mizo association is busy with efforts to preserve old original Mizo culture. It's head quarters is at Iswal. It has it's branches in almost all places in Mizoram. Only because of that the Mizo people always share happiness and sorrows every time together whether it is a marriage, child birth or a death.

There is no restriction on the meetings of boy and girl. Male and Female children live and play together right from childhood. The grown up girls generally stay at homes and the same age group boys visit their places either individually or in groups. But such meetings do not indicate that there is a love affair between the boy and girl. They gather together to enjoy. Whenever there is love between a boy and girl they get married in a short period.

Unrestricted mixing of boys and girls is, now-adays, giving birth to free sex. This is again the influence of western culture. Females right from school going girls to grownup females smoke and consume wine. There is an increase in the number of AIDS affected youths probably because of spread of free sex. There is another reason for this and that is drug addiction. Such drugs include Charas, Ganja, Heroin, Hashish, etc. The drugs come to Mizoram by smuggling from Myanmar and other neighbouring countries. These drugs are consumed by way of smoking or by injecting. This is also an important reason for rise in AIDS patients. (See table 2.6 and 2.7) A number of diagnosis and treatment centres for these patients are opened in the state.

In olden days marriages in Mizo community were very expensive. But the churches have now put restrictions and made rules for restricting heavy expenses. Mizo Youths have freedom of choosing their life companion. Even then the Mizos observe the tradition of marriages in same caste or community.

But this tradition also is being shelved. These people do not agree to have more than one wife or one husband. In olden days more than one wife was allowed to the chief of the group. But now this tradition is also banned.

Table 2.4 Tribes of Mizoram Scheduled and Unscheduled (Census 1991)

Scheduled Tribes		
1) Lushai	6) Hamar	11) Jou
2) Lakhar (Mara)	7) Paiti	12) Kooki
3) Pavi (Poi)	8) Gangte	13) Mang
4) Vaifei	9) Wado	14) Riyang
5) Ralte	10) Simate	15) Chakma
Other Tribes		
1) Awajiya	11) Jansen	21) Rangkhol
2) Baiti or beti	12) Kelma	22) Raite
3) Chongthar	13) Khwalring	23) Rithlei
4) Chawangathu	14) Nagante	24) Sailo
5) Chakchhuak	15) Pam	25) Vlao
6) Darlong	16) Pangs	26) Banchhia
7) Fanai	17) Pachhuau	27) Tochhwang
8) Hashel	18) Pautu	28) Jawangle
9) Halam	19) Pante	29) Jahaus
10) Hualango	20) Lalong	

Because of patriarchy parental wealth is distributed within the male children . But in majority of cases the wealth is given to the youngest son. But because of implementation of new hierarchy Act, parental wealth is now distributed equally between the sons and daughters. Mizo families are named after the male persons. In olden days the father was the sole authority in the family. All the family members were to obey his orders. But now, because of changing conditions the Mizo ladies are also awakened. The Mizo ladies enjoy better position in community and Government in comparison with Mizo Males. The Mizo women resolve the family problems very easily.

The number of persons living below poverty line is very low (25.66%). (See table 2.5) The state had very small number of schools. But the Missionaries have started many schools and educational institutions. Many Mizos are now working in the offices of State as well as central Government. This could happen because of spread of education. Some have joined I.A.S., I.R.S., I.P.S. i.e. Civil services also.

Table 2.5 North East Population Living below Poverty Line 1993-94

States	*Rural (in lacs)*	*Urban (in lacs)*	*Total (in lacs)*	*%*
Meghalaya	7.09	0.29	7.38	38.92
Arunachal Pr.	3.09	0.11	3.73	39.35
Assam	94.33	2.03	96.36	40.86
Manipur	6.35	0.47	6.80	33.78
Mizoram	1.64	0.30	1.94	25.66
Nagaland	4.85	0.20	5.05	37.92
Tripura	11.41	0.38	11.79	39.01

Clothing of Mizos are simple but with a difference. Their nature of clothing is also changed by the Western impact. Gents have adopted pant-shirt-boot whereas ladies go for Blouse and Mizo Clothes. Nowadays the girls are turning to Skirts

Table 2.6 AIDS cases in North East (31-12-99)

State	*AIDS cases*
Assam	67
Arunachal Pradesh	02
Manipur	362
Mizoram	12
Meghalaya	08
Tripura	0

Table 2.7 H.I.V. (+) cases in North East (31-12-99)

Status	*No. of cases Examined*	*No. of HIV(+)*
Assam	34374	290
Arunachal Pradesh	495	—
Nagaland	8852	449
Manipur	40744	6325
Mizoram	39985	135
Tripura	602	11
Meghalaya	14250	60

Table 2.8 Drugs seized in North East (1989)

States	*Total cases*	*Charas*	*Heroin/ Ganga Kg.*
Assam	12	74939	1562
Arunachal Pr.	740	1750	—
Manipur	144	2646	15062
Mizoram	44	—	3137
Meghalaya	07	—	5858

(Regular or mini) and Blouse. Women use in ornaments also. In olden days Mizos were wild nature but now the Christianity and Churches have brought tremendous change in their nature. Mizos are non-vegetarian. They do not have any objection to eating flesh of any animal. They eat the flesh even of dogs, pigs, monkeys, snakes and frogs, etc., along with fish. Main festival of Mizos is 'Chapchar cut' (Cut here means festival). It is celebrated in February and March every year. The Mizos enjoy this festival by music, dance and merry making. All these are done jointly by males and females. Main and important Mizo dances are. Cherao (Bamboo Dance), Khulalaum and Chiyalam.

Being situated in far East of India the sun sets early (according to Indian Standard time) in Mizoram. Therefore other people may wonder that the markets

,shops as well as other establishments are closed by 5 p.m. and people start returning to their homes. The Mizos always want to be in their homes before it gets dark. This system is attributed by the Mizos to frequent curfew orders during Mizo movements. This has now become their habit. People do not move out on roads and even lanes after it gets dark. Eventually the lanes roads markets, etc., gather a solitary look. As a matter of fact, the gradual rise in terrorism is the reason for this. According to outsiders living in Mizoram, the local Mizo youths come out from evening and collect money from the shopkeepers and other establishments, by which they get drunk and create violence. That is why the people do not want to come out after evening.

According to 1981 census 6.5 % population is of outsiders. These include Nepalis, Bengalis, Asssamese Biharis, Punjabis, and South-Indians. All these people have come here as government employees, traders, contractors and mainly the Jawans of Assam Rifles and C.R.P.F. The Mizos have very little intimacy with these people in comparison to North India.

Thus, the specialities of Mizos can be stated as under :

1) These people belong to Mangol Race.
2) They are under the impact of western culture because of Christianity.
3) 95% of the population is Christian
4) 88 % of population is literate.
5) Mizo is a open community and does not have differentiation between males and females.
6) They love music and dance.
7) Mizo is a Patriarchic community
8) Almost all are non-vegetarian and lovers of wine

9) The Mizo females work more than males
10) Divorce is very easy and they are not required to go to court for this.

Social Structure of Assam

Assam is a museum of number of various castes, tribes, races, and so on. The history emphatically tells us that people belonging to number of races and areas have come in this state and accommodated themselves with others. People from all directions i.e. Austria, Dravid, Tibet, Burma, Mangolia and Aryas have made this area as there permanent living place. The Austrians came first to India and settled first in Brahmaputra valley. But afterwards other invaders pushed them to mountain area. It is said that the Khasi and Jayantiya tribes of Meghalaya belong to these Austrian races. The Dravids came after them. They are known as Kaibarta and Bania in Assam. Then came the Mangolians. These people are recognised to belong to Tibet-Burmi family under Indo China group. These people are now known as Kachharis. Bodo, Rabha and Lalung tribes and are living in mountain area of present Assam.

The physical structure of hilly tribals of Assam is quite different from that of others in Assam. They have round face, a little flat nose, eyes rose up, risen cheek bones and dry hair. Whereas people living in upper Assam have a light yellow skin, flat nose and long and straight hair. The ladies are neither short nor tall. The males in tribes put on dhoti and the females Mekhala (Chaddar) and blouse. Because of western impact they are now turning towards modern dresses. At present there are 23 tribes and 16 schedule castes. The proposal for the inclusion of number of castes from Assam in the list is pending with the central Government. The population of Assam can be divided in two categories. 1) Those living in

Brahmaputra and Barak valley 2) those living in Kachhar, Karbi and Anglang districts., The first category can further be divided in four parts. 1) Assamese from Brahmaputra valley and Bengalis in Barak Valley. 2) The Bodos 3) The Mising and 4) Outsiders. Koch, Kachhari, Lalung (tiwa) Dimacha, Rabha, Mekh, Chutiya, Musan and Bodo come under 2nd category. The "Bodo" people speaking Assamese and Chinese language came in 13 th century. They were called Ahoms. Khamiang Pakhiya Honia speaking "Tai" language come under "Ahom". Apart from these, people belonging to Nepal can be seen in urban areas and remote hilly areas also. The tea garden labour community has its own importance in Assam. Apart from various tribals, Bengalis, BiharisMarwadis and Sikh people are also included in Assamese group. (See table 2.9) In 1947 when East Pakistan was separated from India a number of Hindu refugees came to Assam. Again during the Indo East Pakistan War of 1971-72 a number of Hindus as well as Muslim families entered Assam and settled here.

According to historian Shri. B.N. Das, the Muslims came to Assam first in beginning of 13th century when Mohammad Bin Baktyar invaded Assam with his forces. But actually he was defeated every time. Because of this most of the Muslims were either captured or they did not like to go back. Gradually these Muslims married the Assamese women and got themselves mixed with the local people. Presently 4 districts of Ghubadi, Gwalpara, Barpeta, and Helakanti have majority Muslim population. But according to 2001 census the Muslims have formed majority in the districts of Marigaon,Navgaon and Karimganj also. The same way tea gardens came up in Assam and then came the labour class belonging to Santhal, Uraon, and Munda communities.

Table 2.9 Scheduled tribes and Sub-tribes of Assam

1) Bodo	11) Sonowal kachhari	21) Yeton
2) Bodo khachhari	12) kachhari	22) Mekh
3) Rabha	13) Miri	23) Matak
4) Sonowal	14) Barman kachhari	24) Hajong
5) Karbi(Mikir)	15) Deuri	25) Hojai
6) Dimach kachhani	16) Chutiya	26) Rajwanshi
7) RengManga	17) Moran	27) Turung
8) Jiminaga	18) Mising	28) Man
9) Kooki	19) Fakhiyal	29) Tai-Fakhe
10) Tiwa (Lalung)	20) Khamiyang	

Thus, formed the Assam society which includes Aryas and Anaryas, Tribals and Non-Tribals, original residents and outsiders. Majority of population living in plains is Hindus and speak Assamese language. These Hindu Assamese call themselves Aryas. Other belong to Mangol race. There is a very faint border line between tribals and non-tribals. They are a bit different from Hindus. They do not follow casteism. Untouchability, atrocities on schedule castes, dowry system, etc., undesirable traditions along with dowry deaths do not exist in these communities. The Assamese belonging to Brahmins and Vaishnavas do not eat flesh but eat fish. There are no communal clashes between Hindus and Muslims and this is the speciality of Assamese people. Even the Muslim ladies do not use Burka. The poems and music of Muslim saint Shah Dalal alias Ajan Fakir have the impact on Assamese Muslim groups. This saint initiated a movement for rebuilding the Muslims. Contributions by Shankardeo towards Assamese society can also not be sidetracked. He induced the Assamese society to become sober. For this he organised the Vaishnav Bhakti Movement. This way he was not only the person awakening the social attitude of Assamese but the preacher of Arts, Education, Drama and Music and brought a great change in Assamese society. This movement was further run by Madhao Deo. Today's Assamese society prefer to follow the path shown by Shankar Deo. This is because the Assamese have their own identity in Arts, Dance, Music and culture. There existed blind beliefs towards Tantras and Mantrs. People all over India were coming to Kamakhya temple to learn this. Today also this tradition of Tantra -Mantra learning still exists in the area of Kamakhya temple.

Another Hindu cult 'Vaishnav' had it's impact on Assam. This impact came from the 'Satra' which were established by Shankardeo. This satra is known as a centre for Arts and other constructive activities. There are hundreds of such *satras* and their branches in Brahmaputra valley. Alike the satras the 'Namghars' (Prayer places) are established in almost all towns of Assam. These are the existing proofs of social and cultural development of the state. Some main and important Satras are situated near Nawgoan district and Bardova which is the birth place of Shankardeo and other places. But some Satras with difference are still in the place Majuli in Jorhat district.

The Bouddhas came to Assam from Bhutan and Myanmar i.e. from North and East. A temple called Madhao Mandir is unique temple where people belonging to Hindu as well as Buddhas perform worship. Assamese and Bengali and Hindi are main languages spoken in Assam. Apart from these three Bodo, Karbi. Mising Raba, are other languages which are spoken by various tribes. Bodo is recognised in

Bodo area whereas Bengali is recognised in Barak Valley. As a matter of fact every tribe in the state has it's own language. They have adopted Assamese as contact language. Hindi (not pure) is also spoken by the people. The Assamese love music and dance. Many prepare their own musical instruments and play music on them which they like most.

According to 2001 census 64% of Assam population is literate of which 72 % are male and 54 % are female. A number of schools and colleges are started in the state after independence which are engaged in educating the Assamese people. Because of spread of education there is wave of awakening in these people. The Assamese society alike other North -Eastern states is interested in sports. They participate in many sports. Assam has also given players of international quality and repute.

Almost all festivals of India are celebrated in Assam. Even then the Assamese have three Agriculture based festivals. They are 1) Rangalibihu (Bohag Bihu) 2) Bhogali Bihu (Magh Bihu) 3) Rangali Bihu (Kali Bihu). The first one that is Rangali or Bohog Bihu is celebrated on Assamese new year's day which falls in April. The Bihu, but in some what changed nature, is celebrated by other tribes also. The Bodo society perform Kharai Pooja. Above all the fare at Kamakhya Mandir in Abubachi has more attraction. This fare takes place in June and July every year. The famous Umanand Mandir is situated in the centre of Brahmaputra. Its Shivratri festival is also important.

The Assamese also could not avoid the impact of changing society. As a result drug addiction is on an increase in the youth. Till recent past the tribals and non-tribals were open to each other. But this openness has gradually vanished. Disbelief in each other and terrorism have drawn a line between them.

Generally Assamese is a 'Patriarchic' society. But the females are given proper place also. Young girls, women dance and sing jointly with the males on the occasion of various festivals. There is no child marriage in this society. Marriages are mostly performed society-wise. But it is also changing. There is a tradition of marriages in which the boy and the girl run away from their homes and get married. Previously the Assamese preferred to have a joint family. But education and industrialisation has brought a change in this also. There is a tradition of mutual divorce. But the marriage system is so strong that divorces are seldom.

Social Structure of Manipur

Residents of Manipur belong to traditional Hindus with Vaishnav cult. These people are very clean and tidy along with their homes The Manipuris are supposed to be one of the most clean and tidy societies of the world. Females are more hard-working than males. Manipur has its own importance and identity in sports. It is said that the game of Polo was discovered in this state only. Manipuri Dance is one of the four classical dances of India. Manipuri is the main language. But every tribe has its own language. But Manipuri is adopted as contact language. These people are mainly vegetarian. But they eat fish which is their liking.

As a matter of fact Manipuri culture is very near the Indian culture. Various tribes and sub tribes are also residents of Manipur wherein Maitei, Naga and Kookie are important. Angom khumal, Maring, etc., groups come under Maitei society. Maitei is firmly established and a closed society. Their written history right from the first century is also available. Maitei are Hindus and they have their roots in this area from earlier than 18th century. They are Vaishnavas and they have an impact of Krishna Bhakti. Dance and music is inherent in these people. Eventually it has become a part of their culture and society.

Table 2.10 Scheduled Tribes and Sub Tribes of Manipur

1) Aimol	12) Lamgang	23) Tankhul
2) Anal	13) Mao	24) Vaifehi
3) Angami	14) Maram	25) Jaoo
4) Chiru	15) Monsang	26) Hamar
5) Chothe	16) Moyon	27) Mizo
6) Gangte	17) Paiti	28) Tarao
7) Kabui	18) Puram	29) Angom
8) Kachha naga	19) Ratte	30) Khumal
9) Koyrao	20) Sahate	31) Luwang
10) Koireng	21) Sema	32) Maring
11) Kom	22) Simate	

The Manipuri tribes are mixed with each other to such an extent that differentiation between them is very difficult. Kabvi, Tankhul, Mao, etc., Naga groups live in eastern, north eastern, and western mountain areas. They always have clashes with the Kookies for border. Kooki tribes came to this place from Myanmar quite early. They live in south eastern mountain area. It is said that Maitei rule allowed them to live there and protect the population in the plains. Social distance is quiet apparent between Maiteis and non-Maiteis. It is also said that Maiteis adopted Hinduism 300 years ago. But now some of the tribes have adopted.Christianity. This reduced Hindu Maiteis to minority. This has in turn disturbed the social structure of the Maiteis.

The third large group of Manipur population belongs to Muslims. But contrary to Muslims in other areas the Manipuri Muslims got themselves mixed with the rest of the communities. They have adopted Maitei language and culture also to the extent that their names are similar to Maiteis names. Thus, Manipur put-forth an example of unity in diversity. Inter-caste marraiges are very common in this society. Even then the Maiteis prefer to marry in the same society. In past the Manipuris were supposed to be dare devils and fighting masters. They were enjoying a special place during the battle with Myanmar and other mountain areas. Probably the same fighting instinct is inherited in Manipuri sportsmen.

Manipuri ladies have special identity. Rest of the world see them dancing and wearing shawls. Whenever there was a war or political movement in Manipur these ladies had sizeable participation in that. But the changing time has misled the Manipuri youth. They are geting more and more addicted to drugs. All these drugs are smuggled from Myanmar. Manipur is, nowadays, defamed as heaven of drugs trafficking. But this has increased the number of AIDS patients in the state. According to statistics of 1991 Manipur had highest number (362) of such AIDS patients. Accordingly 6,325 persons out of 40,744 persons examined were found to be HIV positive. (See table 2.6)

Social Structure of Meghalaya

There are three major tribes in Meghalaya. They are 1) Khasi, 2) Jayantiya and 3) Garo. The Khasi tribes live in Eastern area. They also are in Jayantiya hills. Those who live in Jayantiya hills are called Jayantiya tribes. They are known as Pharas also. Garos live in Garo Mountains.

Some of the Garos live in Shivsagar in Assam and Karbo Aglang district. But their number here is very small.

All the three tribes of Meghalaya are now converted Christians. Matriarchy is followed in these tribes. That means the mother has sole right over the family wealth. This right passes to the youngest daughter and from it a part of wealth is given to elder daughters. Till recent past the mothers were managing all the family affairs and the fathers used to discover resources for maintenance. The maternal uncle manages all the social and religious functions in joint family. Khasi male does not have any right on wifes wealth. But he can purchase or create his own assets. Khasis prefer, according to their tradition, to have marriages within the same 'Gotra' or 'Vansh' Divorce process is also very elastic. But there is now great change in their living style because of the Christian impact. There is peculiar similarity in these three tribes. That is all the three tribes like to eat rice, fish and flesh. They do not have any objection to any type of food except dog flesh. They observe the tradition of consuming wine extracted from rice.

The Garo tribes have three Kaiches They are 1) Marak 2) Sangma 3) Momin. They name the children after the rivers, animals and caves The Garos were observing Hinduism before converting to Christianity. They worship a number of deities as is done by Hinduism. They are revered in the form of : the dieities. 1) maker of the land 2) Protector of the crops. The Garos believe in the soul of the dead and create memorials in their memory. Garo males wear 'Jimfong' which is coat without collar. Garo females wrap their bodies with number of cloth pieces. Most of the females now wear shirts. Even then they wear black cloth around their waist. Garo males wear skirts along with Jimfong (a long coat). Garos do not have any objection in eating or drinking any thing except milk or anything made from milk. They consume wine daily. Garo tribes do not mix with others easily as Khasi and Jayantiya tribes. They bury the dead in presence of relations and friends. In olden days the unmarried youth had separate places to live where the elders used to train them in various aspects. At present this system is existing in some remote places. Garos do not have their own script. But now they have adopted 'Roman' as their script after the arrival of the Britishers. Alike other tribes the Garos like music and dance. Present Garo generation seems to be mad after western music They produce their own clothing themselves. Apart from this they manufacture earthern wares and articles from cane and bamboo.

'Bangla' is the main and important festival of Garos. 'Bangla' means a festival of 100 drums. This festival is celebrated after reaping the crop. Apart from this, Doregata is another festival which the Garos celebrate. The Khasis celebrate two festivals 1) Nangcrem dance and 2) Shadsuk Minsiame. Nangcrem dance festival is celebrated for five days to show their gratitude towards the god for good crop. Behding khwalaa is the important festival which is celebrated in July. Laho dance is another celebration of Jayantiya.

Credit of spread of modern education in Meghalaya goes to the British Missioneries. First primary school was started in 1841 in the joint district of Khasi and Jayantiya Thence many schools and colleges are started in Meghalaya. Khasi and Garo languages are included in the list of recognised Indian languages. The Khasi language is taught upto the post graduate level and the Garo language upto graduation level. The Ramkrishna mission has also started school in the rural areas of Khasi mountain district.

Social Structure of Arunachal Pradesh - About 110 tribes and subtribes are living in Arunachal Pradesh (Table 2.11). Seventy nine percent of the

Table 2.11 Scheduled Tribes and Sub Tribes of Arunachal Pradesh

1) Abor
2) Adi
3) Adi Gelang
4) Adi Minyang
5) Adi Padam
6) AdiPasi
7) Aka
8) Apatani
9) Ashing
10) Bangi
11) Banghi
12) Bangro
13) Bogum
14) Bokar
15) Bolak
16) Bomdo
17) Bori
18) BatMompa
19) Dafla
20) Darok Tangsa
21) Deori
22) Digru/Tarim mismi
23) Dirang Mompa
24) Gelang
25) Haisa Tangsa
26) HabiTansa
27) Hil Mini
28) Hotang Tangsa
29) Idu/Chulikata Mismi
30) Jambo
31) Kaman/ Miju Mismi
32) Kaska
33) Katin Tangsa
34) Kansing Tangsa
35) Khalim Tangsa
36) Khamba
37) Khamiyang
38] Khampati
39] Khowa
40] Khodeng bangni
41] Komkar
42] Kongbo
43] Korang Tangsa
44] Langkai tangsa
45] Libo
46] LichiTangsa
47] LijuNokle
48] Longchang Tangsa
49] Langim Tangsa
50] LanginTangsa
51] Langfi Tangsa
52] Longasi Tangsa
53] Loangsang Tangsa
54] Loang Tangsa
55] Meyar
56] Miji
57] Mikir
58] Milang
59] Milang Ebor
60] Minyang
61] Mising/Miri
62] Mismi
63] MoglumTangsa
64] Momba
65] Monpa
66] MorangTangsa
67] Mosang Tangsa
68] Muktum
69] Namsang Tangsa
70] Nimang Tangsa
71] Nishang
72] Nissi
73] Nokte
74] Nanang
75] Padam
76] Pailibo
77] Pandnen Monya
78] Pangi
79] Pasi
80] Fang Tangsa
81] Pongkong
82] PonthariNakte
83] Ramo
84] RangaiTangsa
85] Rongrang Tangs
86] SaskeTangsa
87] Sherdukpen
88] Simong
89] SimsaTangsa
90] Singfo
91] Siram
92] Sulung
93] Sulungwangni
94] Tangin
95] TanginBorrghi
96] TaisanTangsa
97] Tangs
98] Tangag
99] Taram
100] Tarang Monya
101] WaiKampati
102] Tikhak Tangsa
103] TakhaNokte
104] Namko
105] YanuBangni
106] Watong
107] Yabin
108] Yangkuk Tangsa
109] Yaugli Tangsa
110] Jakhin

population of Arunachal Pradesh is made up of these tribes. There are a large number of tribes having individual language. That means the number of languages spoken and the number of tribes in this state are equal. Above all they have a common language also which is known as Nefamiz This language is very near to Assamese language. Every tribe has got its own culture and traditions whereby they are separated from each other.

Major population of Arunachal Pradesh follow Buddhism. But because of impact of Christian missioneries some have converted themselves to Christianity. Their number is gradually increasing. Hindus, Muslims, and Sikhs also live in this state. These tribes have a system of marriage in same Gotra. But more than one marriage is prohibited, though previously they allowed such marriages. Every tribe in this state produces own clothing, arches and arrows as well as baskets.

Ladies in these tribes enjoy higher position. They work jointly in agriculture with males. But the women do not have the right on family's wealth. Unmarried girls can earn and create their own assets. These tribes consume fish as well as flesh

Moupa tribes are the residents of Twang and west Kameng district. Generally the tribes in Arunachal Pradesh are calm, sober, cultured and believers of friendly relations. They love music, dance and art. The boys side is required to pay some amount to girl's side before getting married. The people of Arunachal Pradesh had economic and social relations with the people of Bhutan and Tibet. As such their clothing and social behaviour matches with that of Bhutanese and Tibetians. The population living in southern part of Arunachal Pradesh specially the villages have similarities in their economic and social behaviour with the Assamese.

Social Structure of Tripura

East Pakistan was created along with India's independence. A large number of Bengali Hindus fled from that region and came to Tripura. The same way in 1971 during the Bangladesh war Bengali Hindus as well as Muslims left that area and came to Tripura. The number of these Bengaliese was so high that the majority of original residents became minority. There are 19 major schedule tribes in this state. Apart from these tribes a number of other tribes also live in Tripura. (Table 2.12)

The "Tripuris" are the original tribe of this state, whose present percentage is 16% in comparison to 57% of other tribes. These tribes have good relations with the Bengaliese who came from outside. As such the language, culture, etc., have a great impact of Bengaliese. We find a number of educated persons in these tribes. As there is no original script, the Bengali, (Deonagari) script is used in this state. The Bengali language enjoys

Table 2.12 Scheduled Tribes and Sub Tribes of Tripura

1) Bheel	10) Lapcha	19) Tripuri
2) Bhutiya	11) Lushai	20) Tripura
3) Chaimal	12) Mang	21) Tippera
4) Chakma	13) Munda	22) Udhai
5) Garo	14) Kaur	23) Rupini
6) Halem	15) Noatiya	24) Darlang
7) Jamatiya	16) Uraon	25) Halam
8) Khasi	17) Riyang	26) Noatiya
9) Kooki	18) Santhal	

the status of official language of Tripura. Majority of Tripuris speak and understand Bengali. They belong to Hindu community.

Another important tribe of the state is "Riyang." Which forms 14% of the population. They also belong to Hindu and followers of 'Shaktacult.' A part of Tripuri tribe is known as Jayantiya. These Jayantiya people are strongly built and of fighting nature. "Chakma" is the fourth tribe of Tripura. These people fled from Chatgaon Hills and came to this state and settled here. These Chakma people live mainly in Kelashahar, Udaypur, Amarpur, Sabrum, and Belonia. Majority of these are followers of Buddhism. and are very sober and peace lovers. Halam tribes came from North West Manipur and settled in Tripura. They are Hindu by religion. About 80% of people speak and understand Bengali. Another language spoken and understood by these people is Tripuri. It has similarity with Bengali. Tripuris speak Tripuri language whereas all others speak Bengali.

Unmarried youths belonging to Tripuri, Riyang and Halam tribes are required to stay with the would be father in law. If and when the girl's family gets convinced about his behaviour as well as social and practical activities, of the boy, the marriage is performed. This system is nowadays not followed as was in past. Marraiges in Chakma community are settled by the friends and well wishers of the families. Jayantia community has dowry system. The Riyang and Navolia tribes allow widow marriages. Halam ladies can give divorce but the children if any, is the responsibility of husband and have to stay with father.

The Tripura people celebrate "Kharchi Pooja" festival along with others. Bengaliese celebrate Dussehra. Alike other tribes, the Tripura tribes also love dance and music. The majority of Tripura people eat fresh-fish, boiled vegetables and masala dal in their meals. The ladies enjoy high position in the society and get respect like the males. They do not have any right over the parental wealth. The parental wealth is distributed equally in the sons after the death of father. In short Tripura has a mixed population of tribals and non-tribals and this influences their cultural and social life.

Social Structure of Nagaland

The Nagas belong to Indo Mangol race. They were known as "Kirats" in Mahabharat era. A number of tales are in vogue regarding their origin and from where they came to this area. In olden days majority of Naga tribes used to live on high mountain areas. It is a common fact that the Nagas are strongly built and possess fighting nature. Even today one Naga group fights bloody battles with other groups only to establish supremacy. This system is gradually abandoned. But it is a fact that these Nagas were known as human hunters. Specially in Konyak Naga group a Naga youth could not get married unless he possessed at least one human scull.

Table 2.13 Scheduled Tribes and Sub Tribes of Nagaland

1) Angami	8) Fom
2) Aoo	9) Pochuri
3) Chakhesang	10) Rengma
4) Chang	11) Sangtam
5) Khemugan	12) Sema
6) Konyak	13) Imchunger
7) Lotha	14) Jiliyang

There are differences between any two Naga tribes specially on village level. Angami, lotha, Rengma and Aao tribes adopt democratic system at village level. Whereas Sema tribes do not have this system. There were special places for the youth to live and females were not allowed to either go or enter such places. Such places were called Morang. Today also one can find the Morangs in some villages.

In 19th century when the Britishers came here

the Christian missioneries started the activists aimed at the development of Nagas. They inspired awakening towards education and health in them. About 95% of Naga are now Christians. Their main food includes cows, pigs, chicken, buffaloes, dogs, cats, birds and rice. Flesh and vegetables are cooked together but rice is cooked separately. Their loved drink is wine extracted from rice. Some undesirable and bad customs still exist in Naga society. eg. Child hunt, Slavery and Prostitution. One can find Western impact on Naga society. Addiction to drugs and free sex in the youth have caused the increase in AIDS patients (Table2.5).

Majority Nagas feel pleasure in inviting others on dinner or lunch parties on various occasions. Alike other tribes the Nagas also have given higher position to women. The family of bride groom is required to pay some amount to brides family along with buffaloes before the marriage. Angami Nagas believe in single wife. On the other hand, the Sema tribe has allowed to have as many wives as one can afford. Konyak Nagas also have the same system. Divorce is very easy in all the Naga tribes and they can give divorce from each other whenever they feel. The Nagas are very conscious about self respect. This is why they do not like to be ruled by others. Clothing of Nagas include shawls. Every Naga tribe has its own type of shawls. Nagas have sentimental relation with weapons. Though every Naga tribe has its own language they have adopted 'Nagamiz' as a common language after the missionaries came here. They have also adopted Roman script. Official language of the state is English. Almost all Naga festivals are related to agriculture. Of these 'Motsu' is important which is celebrated at the time of sowing the seeds. Main festival of Angami tribes is 'Sekerenial' which they celebrate in February and December. As in other tribes the Naga tribes also love dance and music.

Chapter 3

Economic Structure of North-East India

Whole of the North East India has plenty of Natural Resources. Valuable forest yield and wood. Petroleum, coal, natural gas., etc., are some of them. This area has ample potential for production of hydro-electricity. It is rich in tea production also. North east India has a special identification in the areas of spinning and weaving and handicraft. Because of its rich and lovely natural beauty there is tremendous scope for tourism. In spite of richness of natural resources, this area is still backward as these resources are neither properly exploited nor used. 45% of the population of this area is still living in poverty. Small and cottage industry people do not get proper returns. In most of the cases middle-men swallow the profits. Spinning and weaving is a part and parcel of the lives of the people in this area. One can go to the extent by saying that 80% of the population in North-East belongs to weaver community. These people produce cloth for themselves. In addition they, very efficiently, weave furnishing cloth, carpets and shawls. These help them in improving their financial condition. Because of various reasons these shawls, carpets, furnishing cloth can not reach outside markets and can not fetch good, even sufficient returns. Naturally people here are gradually doing away with this skilled industry. Handicraft also has an important place in the culture of North-East.

Sericulture plays an important role in improving financial condition of North-Eastern people. Jute is grown in Assam, Meghalaya and Tripura. This jute is used for preparing traditional gunny bags, etc.

Economic Structure of Meghalaya

After Assam in North-East Meghalaya not only has plenty of natural resources but so many other fields also from which Meghalaya is earning financial profits. If these areas are properly exploited and economically used Meghalaya can earn large financial gains.

Natural Resources - Meghalaya is one of the important states of India which have natural resources in plenty. These include forest yields, wood, various minerals and hydro- electricity potential. 69.8% area of Meghalaya (about 8510 sq. km.) is occupied by forests. About 993 sq. km. of forest area is either reserved forests or National Parks. This reserved forest and National Park area is under the control of state Government. Rest of the forest is controlled by Zilla Parishads. Importance of forest in the mountainous state like Meghalaya is very significant from the environmental point of view and for restricting land slides. It is still more significant for improving economic condition of Meghalaya.

As far as valuable wood is concerned Meghalaya forests are full of trees like Sagon, Bela, Gogra, Totachat, Holak, Palash, Birch, Tun, Chitawani, Shirish and Mehagony. Pine trees are grown at the height of 1500 meters in hilly areas of Khasi and

Jayantiya. These are known as Pinous Keshia or Khasi Pine. These pines stand in the high quality category of pines in the world. There are 'Saal forests' in Garo hills. Meghalaya ply-wood is supposed to be one of the best ply-woods of the world. This ply-wood is used in different industries, Trade centres and household also. Bamboo and cane trees are in plenty in Garo as well as North Khasi hills These are used in manufacture of various cane articles like furniture, baskets, etc. These are always in demand internally as well as externally in the state These provide and create employment also.

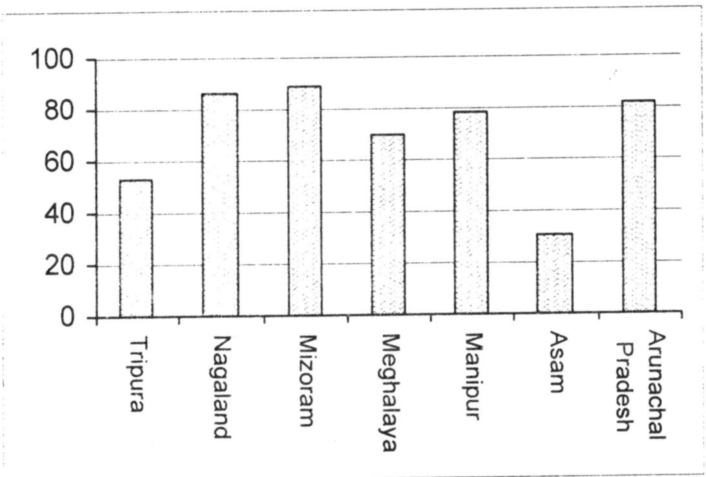

Fig. 3.1

There are various medicinal plants in Meghalaya forests which provide many opportunities to establish different medicines manufacturing units. Availability and existence of Tun trees provide ample scope for sericulture and if the forests are properly developed in this direction sericulture can become an important industry in Meghalaya. This will create number of employment whereby poor rural population can be benefited. Coffee and Rubber industry are live examples of this. There are so many types of mosquito and small creature expellent plants in these forests. They should be properly and commercially exploited. In addition honey, wax and sealing wax are traditional forest products also.

But trees in these forests are mercilessly cut in a large number. This tree cutting is destroying the forests. Apart from this, forests are being converted into plains for Zoom Agriculture, road building also. Increasing population is also one of the important reasons for cutting the forests as plain areas are required for providing residence to increasing population. This tree cutting is causing the decrease of greenery on the hill tops and slopes. (Table 3.1). This has other disastrous effect like frequent landslides, conversion of earth in sand decreasing the fertility of earth. Absence of obstruction by trees and natural slopes, rain waters carry valuable fertile earth with them making the land barren. The trees are also cut for preparing cooking coal which is used in winter as protection from cold.

As a matter of fact social forestry programme is undertaken as a remedial measure to stop forest cutting. The state government has undertaken plantation programme on Government as well as private vacant land and has been trying to work very hard for making this programme successful. The government is also providing every help to autonomous Zilla Parishads for this programme. Plantation of Sagon, Plywood, Saal and fast growing spice plants is included in this programme. This is being done while implementing Ninth Plan. Prior to this during eighth plan a programme for keeping a reserve forest for every town was implemented. A law was also passed in 1991 and implemented for this .

Hydroelectricity - Next to Arunachal Pradesh

Table 3.1 Loss/gain in forest Area Upto 1997
(Sq. Kilometers)

States	*Loss*			*Gain*			*Total Change*
	Converted To Agriculture	*Other Reasons*	*Total*	*Natural Increase*	*Other reasons*	*Total*	
Arunachal pradesh	75	-	75	56	-	56	- 19
Assam	257	159	416	163	16	179	-237
Manipur	603	-	603	463	-	463	-140
Meghalaya	75	2	77	20	-	20	-140
Mizoram	292	-	242	491	-	491	-57
Nagaland	573	-	573	503	-	503	+199
Tripura	-	3	3	4	7	11	+8
Total	1875	164	2039	1700	23	1723	-316

Meghalaya has highest Hydro-Electricity potential. As per North East council, the North East India has a potential of producing thirty thousand Megawatts of Hydro-Electricity. This is about one third of total Electricity production of India. Meghalaya alone has a potential of producing 1200 Megawatts. But presently only about 126.71 Megawatts electricity is being produced in Meghalaya. The production of electricity is now increased to 186.71 Megawatts after commissioning the fourth project at Amiam Kmbu during 8th plan Electricity to the tune of 30 Megawatts is expected to be produced from Thermal Power station established at Nangalviwara in Garo Hills. In addition to this a new Hydro Electricity project of 150 Megawatts capacity is established in Hilly districts of Jayantiya on the Assam Meghalaya border.

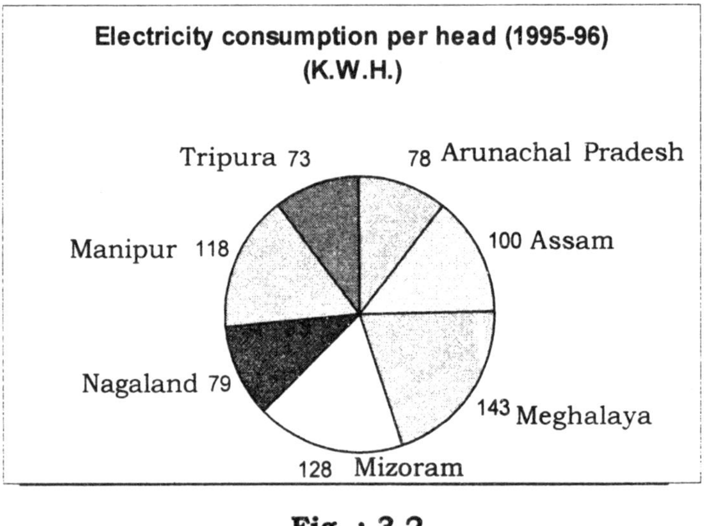

Fig. : 3.2

Presently Meghalaya has extra electricity. About 50 % of electricity produced in this state is being sold to other states. Per capita electric consumption in Meghalaya was 131.56 Kwh. in 1989-90. 46.32%

villages in the state were having electricity till the end of March 1991. The state Govt. has a plan to provide electricity to 1500 more villages during 8th Plan. This will bring 50% of Meghalaya villages under electrification.

Minerals - Meghalaya has huge deposits of different minerals. This includes coal, Limestone, China clay glinimite, etc. These are used in many industries of the country. In addition coal and limestone are being exported to Bangladesh and earn foreign exchange for the country. Almost all the districts in the state have Coal Deposits. Highest quality coal mine is also in this state. But these coal deposits contain stones in more quantity. It is therefore that the coal here is considered as Sub-bituminous type. This coal is used more in industries than in household,for examples electricity production, fertilizer industry, Cement industry cloth industry, paper as well as rubber industry etc. This coal is also used in brick ovens. A large part of coal extracted in this state was used in cement production units and brick ovens in the state upto 1970. Coal of this area was being used in 1.5 megawatts thermal power plant situated in Nangalviwara. Its results were also satisfactory. But this thermal power plant is closed because of some technical disturbance.

Some of the areas where coal deposits are discovered are as follows; Western Dadengiri, Seju, Balpakadam, Pindengiri, Lamgtin, Mavlang shell, Laitryingue and Bapung. Coal deposits to the tune of 640 million tons are discovered in this state. Garo hill area alone has coal deposits of about 359 million tons.

Deposits of high quality limestone are available in a 200 km. Southern boundary of the state. Some important areas of limestone are Cherapunji, Mavlong,

Table 3.2 Coal Deposits in North East (1998-99) (Million tons)

States	*Deposit (Million tons)*
Meghalaya	460
Arunachal Pradesh	90
Assam	520
Nagaland	19
	1089

Isamati, Komora, Shella, and Bodsora situated in Khasi hill area. Apart from this, limestone deposits are found in Seju in Garo hills Nangalviwara as well as in Lumsnong, Sutanga Nangakhalis, Sindai and Lakadung in Jayantiya hills area. It is estimated that limestone deposits of about 5 thousand million tons are with the state of Meghalaya. Apart from the use of this limestone in cement industry it is used in steel, fertilizer and chemical industries. Presently this limestone is used in cement plants (public undertaking) at Cherapunji in Khasi hill area as well as by a private cement plant at Damas in Garo hill area. It is as well used by new cement plants started recently in Garo and Jayantiya hill areas. Both these plants are public undertakings.

China clay is found in different areas of the state. This china clay is used in ceramic, paper and rubber industries. In addition this China clay is used in brick production and other like industries. This clay is of two types. These clay deposits to the tune of 85.5 million tons are discovered in this state. Best quality celemenite deposits are also discovered in the Western Khasi Hills Area. Celemenite deposits of about 0.045 million tonnes are located in this state. It is found in Sona Hills and Mavpomblang areas. As a matter of fact these deposits are about to be finished.

Phospherite (Mineral) is also available in Kopali area of the state. It is available in Sunghatti area of Khasi and Jayantiya Hills and at Rivak in Garo Hill area. According to the estimates of geological department 5 million tonnes of Phosphate ore is still lying under the earth. Glass sand is available in various areas of Khasi Hills. Existence of Iron contents in this glass sand is it's speciality. But because of this, it can not be used for production of first class glass. Even then it is used in the production of bottle glass, coloured glass, sheets, etc. This sand is useful in the production of sodium silicate. There is still a deposit of 3 Million Tonnes of Glass sand. This sand is used by Assam Glass factory at Guwahati

In addition to the above main mineral deposits, there are deposits of Quartz, Felspar, Gypsum, Copper, Zink, Nickel, Cobalt etc. Gold ore, Iron ore, and crude oil deposits are also available but in smaller quantities.

Agriculture and horticulture - About 81.95% Meghalaya population lives in villages i.e. Rural Areas and naturally is fully dependant on agriculture though only 10 % of total Meghalaya land is cultivable Land. Double harvest is taken only on 19% of agricultural land and only 1/5th of such land is irrigated. Heavy rains and vanishing forests cause landslides also. Mainly Zoom Agriculture along with forest cutting and landslides are responsible for less agricultural production. Zoom Agriculture means to "cut the forest, convert it into plains, cultivate it once, and leave the land barren". The forests are removed from the land either by cutting trees or by burning them or both. This is also one of the main reasons of vanishing forests in the state. The Meghalaya government is trying its level best to stop "Zoom Agriculture" and promoting continuous cultivation of permanent nature.

Table 3.3 Zoom farming (Shifting Cultivation) in North East (1983)

States	Area Under zoom farming (Sq.K.M.)	Period (year)	Minimum area under Zoom Farming at a time. (Sq.K.M.)	Families Engaged in Zoom Farming
Arunachal	700	3-10	2100	54000
Assam	696	2-10	1392	58000
Manipur	900	4-7	3600	70000
Meghalaya	530	5-7	2650	52290
Mizoram	630	3-4	1890	50000
Nagaland	190	5-8	1913	116046
Tripura	223	5-9	1115	43000

Important agriculture produce in this valley state of Meghalaya is rice and maize. Pulses and oil seeds are also grown here. Cotton and potatoes are also cultivated on large scale. About 1,54,000 tonnes of potatoes were produced in 1986-87. This was mainly in Khasi Hill area. Potatoes which are cultivated on a large-scale are exported to other states also. In order to boost potato production and improvement in the quality a "Central Research Laboratory for Potatoes" is established in Shillong. Garo Hill area produces Wheat also.

Cotton is considered to be the main cash crop of this state. It is grown mainly in Garo Hills area. As a matter of fact Meghalaya is the only North Eastern State where cotton is grown on large scale for a pretty long time. Jute is also grown in southern parts of Garo Hills area. Coffee, rubber, pepper, ginger, turmeric are also produced in this state.

Meghalaya has its own identity in horticultural products (See table -3.4) There are a number of Orange orchids in this state where 'Silhat' and 'Chatak" oranges are grown. Oranges grown in this

Table 3.4 Horticulture Production in North East (1998-99)

Fruits		*Assam*	*Arunachal*	*Manipur*	*Meghalaya*	*Mizoram*	*Nagaland*	*Tripura*	*India*
Pineapple	(a)	13997	6633	9950	8793	1033	1805	5025	71300
	(b)	207838	29922	69650	77202	71202	44170	44470	1071200
Oranges	(a)	5895	5566	830	-	1071	1265	4484	133900
	(b)	68527	11842	3320	-	28068	18031	21000	1161700
	(a)	7367	2717	965	6961	964	-	2710	643100
	(b)	40639	3981	5888	32980	2787	-	3520	559700
Bananas	(a)	41337	2645	1410	5370	2814	1505	4927	433000
	(b)	595258	9495	10718	63967	14871	23360	33630	13095100
Mangoes	(a)	1360	76	160	-	478	168	5027	1283000
	(b)	7811	64	880	-	2555	455	41270	10811000
Guaveas	(a)	3084	683	700	-	339	445	-	7000
	(b)	40817	2607	2100	-	1324	3227	-	139000

(a) Area in Hectars

(b) Production in Metric tonnes

Lichi	(a)	4063	181	-	-	79	55	5420	48600
	(b)	17563	251	-	-	270	171	2790	364600
Papaya	(a)	7482	457	1850	482	296	285	-	60900
	(b)	110389	1943	10175	3928	2426	2475	-	1329700
Kathal	(a)	18369	124	260	-	216	225	8125	-
	(b)	160200	708	1040	-	1391	912	214580	-
Seape	(a)	-	2369	-	-	32	83	-	217100
	(b)	-	5405	-	-	31	451	-	1214700
Nashpati	(a)	-	579	-	-	93	750	-	-
	(b)	-	1668	-	-	444	2455	-	-
Alubukhar	(a)	-	730	610	-	184	930	-	-
and Satalu	(b)	-	1896	3965	-	517	3425	-	

state are sent to Guwahati and Kolkata markets. Because of excessive orange production they are exported to nearby states and Bangladesh also. Apart from oranges, bananas pineapples are another important fruits are grown in this state. Apples are also grown in some areas of the state. Bananas, lichhis, jack fruit (kathal) and guava are also produced in Northen and Southern areas of Khasi Hills. Fruit preservation and processing units are established in this state. This shows the economic growth of the state.

The state government is trying hard for improvement and development of agriculture. The government is encouraging the farmers for production of maize and pulses. The farmers are being trained for the use of modern agriculture techniques and for using better quality of seeds. The government is also training and encouraging the farmers for triple crops in a year. Considering the high quality and quantity of fruits and flowers, horticulture industry has good potential in the state. This will also provide employment to the people of the state and improve economic condition of the state also.

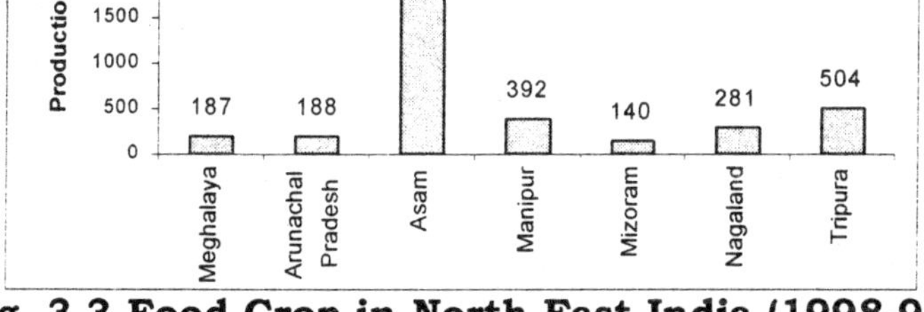

Fig. 3.3 Food Crop in North East India (1998-99)

Sericulture and Handloom - There is need to

encourage and develop sericulture in the state specially in rural areas. Presently about more than ten thousand persons are engaged in this industry. Atmosphere of the state is very congenial and useful for sericulture. Erri, Muga, Rasbhery, and tassar are also produced in the state.

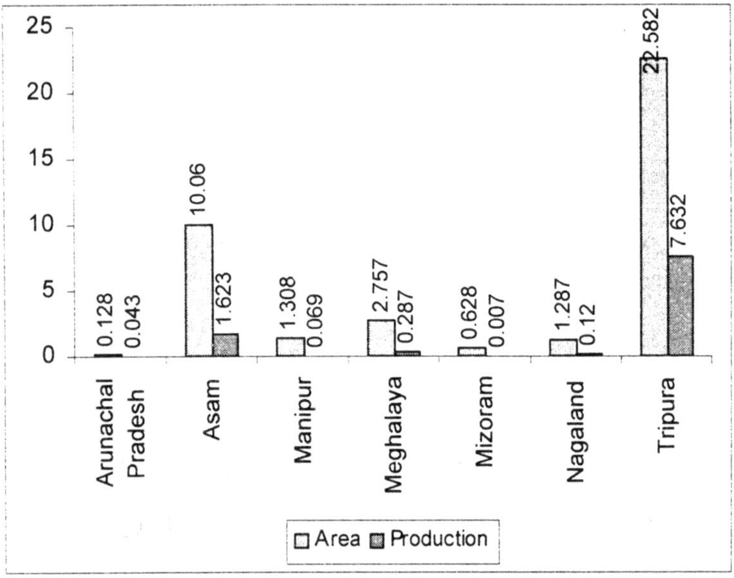

Fig. 3.4 Rubber area and Production in North East (1997) 1000 Hectares

Meghalaya people are expert in spinning and weaving. Bedsheets, silk sarees, etc., are most important handloom products. A number of centres of silkworm production can be seen in the state. Regional foreign race seed stations are established in the area of Jayantiya hills. In addition, sericulture in hot water area is also undertaken. There are more than four thousand handlooms in the state of which majority looms are indigenous. 25% of these looms are in cooperative sector. More than three thousand families got employment in handloom industry during seventh plan, whereas more than 4900 other families got employment in sericulture sectors. As a matter of fact these sectors can still be developed in fast speed.

Industry and Trade - The state has ample potential for establishing many industries as coal and hydro electricity potential is in plenty. This is over and above the development of agriculture and forestry Even after easy availability of almost all ingredients this state is still backward in the industrial sector. Main reason for this is want of willpower of the state government added by scarcity of transport and communication network and entrepreneurs. But slowly this state is coming up and secured a place in industrial map of India.

Efforts of industrialisation were started after independence and acquiring state-hood by the state. Meghalaya industrial development corporation was brought into existence in 1971. As a result some joint sector industries are established in this state Some of them are the Komora limestone Mining Co. Ltd., The Meghalaya Essential Oils and Chemicals Ltd. and The Meghalaya Fighto chemicals Ltd. In addition to this MIDC has helped in establishing Meghalaya

Table 3.5 Cotton Production and Handloom industry in North East (1997-98)

States	*No. of Looms*		*Consumption of Thread 1000 Kg*	*Cloth Production 1000 Meters*
	House hold	*Commercial*		
Arunachal pradesh	44967	653	3073.3	279.6
Assam	1251930	201803	17754.4	74875.6
Manipur	265302	283808	111012.2	582874.6
Meghalaya	11030	575	814.0	3430.9
Mizoram	41041	5944	594.0	3689.0
Nagaland	1750	2170	231.6	1852.8
Tripura	95592	23480	5638.0	35250

Plywood Ltd. and Associated Beverages Private Ltd. The state has only one large industry i.e. Mamlu Chera Cement Factory. 1.65 lac tonnes of cement is manufactured by this public sector cement factory. Another small unit of manufacturing cement at the rate of 100 tonnes per day is established in private sector at Damas in Eastern Garo hills area. One more cement factory producing 100 tonnes of cement per day is established in Jayantiya hills area i.e. The Jayantiya hills cement factory Ltd. in 1992. Limestone from Nangakhedi is used in these factories. Meghalaya has three more small scale cement units which produce 20 tonnes of cement each and per day. One of them is at Ansing and rest two are situated at Noorshala in eastern Khasi hills area. Other mineral based industries are also working in Meghalaya.

Table 3.6 Medium and Large Industries in North East (31-3-1998)

States	*Number of Units*	*Percentage*
Arunachal Pradesh	17	9.6
Assam	128	72.3
Manipur	12	6.8
Meghalaya	10	5.6
Mizoram	01	0.6
Nagaland	07	4.0
Tripura	02	1.1
Total	177	100.0

Forest based industries in Meghalaya include a ply-wood factory being the biggest in North East India This is the first medium scale industry of Meghalaya where 250 workers are presently employed. Production capacity of this factory is 20 lacs sq. meters of plywood a year. Fighto chemicals Ltd. produces sithorda oil under the head of required oils. Same way associated Beverages factory at Barnihat manufactures cold drinks like Limca, Goldspot, etc. It is planned to establish a processing industry by Coitz Ltd. of India in collaboration with Mine engineering of Yugoslovia to process the fruits like oranges, etc. Two more fruit processing units are working in this state at Shillong and Dainadulal. In addition Meghalaya Jute manufacturing industry manufactures Jute goods. Meghalaya steel and concrete products Private Ltd. manufactures steel sheets as well as electric poles. Shillong surgical cotton Industries at Shillong manufactures cotton threads. One unit of Hindustan Machine tools Ltd. at Shillong manufactures more than 3 lacs watches per year.

Table 3.7 Number of Industries working and closed in North East (31-3-1998)

States	*Industries*			*Percentage of closure*
	Working	*Closed*	*Total*	
Arunachal Pradesh	326	36	362	9.94
Assam	4430	1732	6162	28.10
Manipur	2078	169	2247	7.52
Meghalaya	587	136	723	18.81
Mizoram	917	306	1223	25.02
Nagaland	183	83	266	31.20
Tripura	809	603	1412	42.70
Total (North East)	9330	3065	12395	24.72
India	582368	301390	883758	34.10

Meghalaya has prohibited the steel industries which are disastrous to environment It is therefore that electronics, food processing, wood based industry, etc., can be established in the state. In order to develop and industrialise the state has declared Barnihat as industrial area. Apart from this, two small industrial estates are created at Shillong and

Mendipawar. Small industrial estates are, being developed at William nagar, Nangstan, Jawai and Tura. Entrepreneurship training is also provided to local youth so that they can establish their own units or go for self employment.

Table 3.8 Sick Small Scale Industries in North East (March 1997)

States	*Units with Chance of Restart*	*Units with No Chance of Restart*	*Unit with a Chance of Consider-ation*	*Total Sick Units*
Arunachal Pradesh	00	26	00	26
Assam	1100	9011	22	10133
Manipur	92	2367	248	2207
Meghalaya	20	5511	00	5531
Mizoram	24	1175	00	1199
Nagaland	01	2737	00	2738
Tripura	26	3141	04	3171
Total	1263	23968	274	25505

Industries like bakery, beverages, wood, wool (Ara machine) metal works, rice mills, floor mills, furniture manufacturing and candle stick manufacturing are working in the state. More of such small and cottage industries can still be undertaken. Cottage industries of handloom and cane and bamboo work are working in the state. According to 1990 figures the state has about 200 small scale units. There is a constant and gradual increase in this number which is providing more and more employment.

Roads and transports - Meghalaya is totally a hilly state and backward in industrialisation. About 81.9% population of the state resides in remote rural areas. As such sufficient road network is essentiality of the state so that these remote rural areas can be

Tabe;e 3.9 Length of Roads in North East (upto 31-3-1996)

States	Total Length K.M.	Tar raod K.M.	halfed K.M.	length per 100 K.M.	Length per 1000 Population	o/o of tar roads
Arunachal Pradesh	10240	3692	6548	12.2	11.48	36.05
Assam	68079	11421	52258	86.8	3.05	16.78
Manipur	10760	3595	7165	48.2	5.98	33.41
Meghalaya	8391	3946	4445	37.4	4.66	47.03
Mizoram	6910	2360	4550	32.8	9.87	34.15
Nagaland	13732	2515	11217	82.8	11.44	18.31
Tripura	14726	4577	10149	140.4	5.45	31.03
Total North East	132838	32106	100732	52.8	4.25	24.17
India	2403634	1334078	1069556	73.0	2.85	55.50

approached easily. Presently Meghalaya does not appear on the Railway map of India. No doubt the Government of India is considering to connect Guwahati with Barnihat by railway line. But it will cater to the needs of quite small area only. Because of the hilly area water transport is also not possible though the number of rivers in this state is very high. The only airport of the state is in Umrai near Shillong. The state is connected to other nearby states only by Vayudoot service. There is a regular Helicopter service between Shillong and Guwahati and Tura. Thus,, road transport is the only medium of transport in the state. Possibly the oldest road in the state connects Nartiyang and Jayantiyapur. These were the old and new capitals of Jayantiya dynasty. The construction work of this road was probably started in the 16th century and was completed in 1790 by the Jayantiya King. Another road was constructed by the Britishers connecting Therai Ghat and Mazaibajar. This is the same road by which David

Scot went to meet the revolutionary U.Tirot Singh for dialogue. The Britishers also constructed 210 km. Road between Bholagang and Guwahati

Table 3.10 Rural Electrification in North East

States	*No. of Villages c ensus 1991*	*Villages elctrification done by March 99*	*Percentage*
Arunachal	3649	2147	59
Assam	24685	19019	77
Manipur	2182	1990	91
Meghalaya	5485	2510	46
Mizoram	698	687	98
Nagaland	1216	1163	96
Tripura	855	806	94
Total	38769	28322	73

via Nangkhlao, Manflong, Cherapunji and Theriaghat.

The Britishers also constructed road connecting Shillong and Mauflong. They also constructed some more roads including 101 km. long road between Shillong and Guwahati. This road is considered to be the engineering miracle. More attention is given to the road construction work after independence. Road network of only 2785 Kms. was in existence at the time of making Meghalaya a full-fledged state. This includes a national Highway No.44 of 174 Kms. length. Road network increased to 5580 Kms. till the end of 7th Plan. Even then the road density in the state is 24.50 in 100 Sq. Kms. When the national average is 54 in 100 Sq. Kms. The only medium by which heavy goods like wood and minerals as well as potatoes, oranges and other fruits can be transported to other states is by road transport. But as this transport is very expensive it is necessary to have railway network in the state. The state as well as Central government is trying in this direction. North East Council has also sanctioned a number of road construction plans. Apart from this, ropeways are being laid down in a number of areas. A target of laying 7025 kms. of rope way is included in 8th plan. According to 1991 statistics the state owned transport plys 164 buses on 53 routes.

Electricity - Meghalaya is the only state in North East where production of electricity is much more than its requirement. Average requirement of electricity in the state is 100 megawatts, where as the production is 101 megawatts (1998-99 statistics.) Even then electric supply to remote rural areas is still a difficult problem. Dense forests and uneven valleys of the state have made the task of electric supply very difficult as it involves very heavy expenditure to lay supply lines through them.

According to 1991 census Meghalaya has total 5485 villages out of which only 2510 villages could be electrified till the end of March 1999. This means still there are 46% of villages to which electricity is a dream. Traditional sources of electricity like coal, oil and gas are used by the state for electric production. Non Traditional and rural power agency was created by Meghalaya Government in 1987. According to this agency power crisis can be solved in the state by implementing a 3 point programme as follows. 1) Electricity can be produced from wood, Gober Gas and Bio Gas. 2) Coal and Oil can be saved and preserved by using smokeless chullhas. 3) Electricity can be produced from natural resources like sun, water and wind. This agency established 40 Solar Water heater plants in 1991. In addition 408 street lights, household (200) and cookers (732) were provided by this agency.

Table 3.11 Electricity Supply Position in North East (1998-99) in Megawatts

States	*Require-ment*	*Avai-lability*	*Defici-ency*	*Percentage*
Arunachal Pradesh	44	43	-1	2.3
Assam	531	514	-17	3.2
Manipur	98	95	-3	3.1
Meghalaya	100	101	-1	1.0
Mizoram	58	55	+3	5.2
Nagaland	42	35	+7	16.7
Tripura	115	90	+25	21.7
Total North	915	862	+53	5.8
India	67905	58445	+9460	13.9

It is Thus, observed that Meghalaya produces far more electricity than required through Hydro electricity plants. Even after this there are number of areas which are unutilised as far as Hydro Electricity is concerned (See natural resources in the same chapter).

Tourism - Meghalaya the home of clouds has

ample possibilities and potential for tourism and its development. At present there are about 69 tourist places in the state. If these places are properly developed they can earn a lot for state treasury. As it is, according to 1998-99 statistics about 1 to 1½ lac Indian tourists visited the state and in addition total 1971 foreign tourists also visited the state.

Table 3.12 Number of Tourist Places and Tourists in North East (1998-99)

States	*Tourists Places*	*Indian*	*Tourists Foreign*	*Total*
Meghalaya	69	159730	1971	161701
Arunachal Pradesh	14	12222	117	12339
Assam	N.A	177514	3390	180904
Manipur	31	89664	294	89958
Mizoram	13	25231	141	25372
Nagaland	N.A	16567	86	16653
Tripura	23	170623	36	170659

There are 28 tourist attraction places in Shillong the capital city of Meghalaya. These include Birds lake, Shillong Peak, Shillong centenary monument, Polo Ground, Elephant Falls and so many waterfalls. A number of Indian Tourists visit these places. It is observed that there is no proper advertisement of these places. This and terrorist activities in the state are the reasons why tourists hesitate to visit Meghalaya.

There are other places of tourism attraction also. They are 1) Emilchang deer park. Tura peak, Dargah of Shah Kamal Baba, etc. 21 places of tourist attraction in Garo Hills areas. 2) Dwakibruggle falls etc., 28 places in Jayantiya hill area. 3) Cherapunji, Memorial of U. Tirot Singh etc. 28 such places are situated in Khasi hills area. Thus,, it can be said that Meghayala-Rich state in natural beauty of tourism attraction can earn a lot through tourism if these sources are properly exploited. This can be made possible if efforts as follows are taken 1) Proper advertisement of places of tourist attraction through Hindi and English mediums of communication. 2) Transport arrangements by State Buses for taking the tourist to other places at least twice or thrice a week as is done in Shillong on daily basis. 3) Connecting the different places by rope way.

Economic Structure of Assam

Assam, the largest State in the North-East, is an Agriculture based economy. 70% of the population of Assam is directly or indirectly connected with agriculture. Most of the agricultural activities are meant for feeding the state population. Specially zoom farming in hilly area is its example. In addition rice and fruits are also cultivated in this state. Jute and Sugarcane crop is also taken in large quantity in this state. In addition forest resources also help developing state economy.

As far as the mineral deposits are concerned the state is rich with large deposits of petroleum, natural gas, coal and limestone. Even then the state is not developed in the field of industrialisation. The state of Assam had three oil refineries. Fourth oil refinery is established in this state by the Central Government in 1999. The Central Government has given green signal to industrialists and the state to establish fertiliser plants, cement plants and a number of electricity production units, to encourage industrial development of the state. According to 1980-81 statistics, per capita income of Assam is Rs. 6663. Share of agriculture in state development is about 39% whereas about 63% population is connected with agriculture. It is, therefore, essential to develop the state economy. The state government is working on an Agriculture Plan prepared by the Assam rural

Table 3.13 Mineral Production in North East

States	Name of Mineral	1995-96		1996-97		1999-98		1998-99	
		Prod^n	Rs.	Prod^n	Rs.	Prod^n	Rs.	Prod^n	Rs.
Meghalaya	Coal	3248	1880300	3241	2019100	3234	2001500	-	-
	Limestone	440	78800	541	97400	596	71300	204	22950
Arunachal Pradesh	Petroleum	28	88732	36	114084	39	123591	76	263644
Assam	Coal	822	609[illegible]02	752	557232	662	490542	1793	1328613
	Natural Gas	1510	1661000	1698	1867800	1254	1379400	1265	1391500
	Petroleum	5043	15981267	4811	15246059	5117	16215773	5271	18285090
	Limestone	411	33637	449	41384	436	44990	509	86798
Manipur	Chromite	470	519	62	69	68	46	-	-
Tripura	Natural Gas	130	143000	154	169400	189	207900	305	335500

infrastructure and agricultural services project, with the help of World Bank, for Agricultural development of the State. This project is undertaken in 1995 for eight years. An amount of Rs. 126.6 crores is released for Agriculture, out of total Rs. 567.65 crores.

Natural Resources -Assam is the only state which has maintained its greenery. Forests in this state spread fragrance of its beauty on one side and on the other provide strength to state economy. Forests of Assam have a number of commercially valuable trees. As per available statistics Assam had 44 plywood factories, 400 ara mills (wood cutting machines) 1 match box factory and a number of units manufacturing cane goods. But because of ban on forest cutting by the Supreme Court in the total North-East area, many of the above factories are closed from Dec. 1996.

According to 1997 statistics the forests in Assam are spread on 30,000 sq. km. land and occupy about 59% of the land. Control of forest in the plains is with the State Government whereas forests in hilly areas are controlled by autonomous parishads. The State has plenty of bamboo, cooking wood and cane. The ban on forest cutting is looked after by the State Government through its forest department. But the forest mafia is illegally cutting the forest and selling them. This is also causing danger to the environment. The forest department of the state has undertaken plantation of 150 lac plants to help maintain the environment. Considerably larger part of Assam forests provide shelter to a number of wild animal races. This includes unicorn Uddaks with white wings. Golden Langoors and Chimpanzees. With a view to provide protection to these wild animal species the State Government has created five National Parks in the state. They are Kaziranga, Manas, Nameri, Dibru-

Saikhow and Orang. In addition to these the state Government has established 12 zoos. A Tiger project is being implemented in Manas National Park with a view to protect Indian Tigers.

Electricity - Assam has terrific potential for electricity production both hydro as well as thermal. Thermal electricity can be produced by using either coal or natural gas. Even after having such large

Table 3.14 Tea Garden, Area and Production in North East (1997)

States	*No. of Tea Gardens*	*Tea Gardens Area (HA)*	*Production (Tons)*
Arunachal Pradesh	22	1395	800
Assam	860	228260	4254430
Manipur	06	485	80
Meghalaya	00	00	00
Mizoram	02	-	-
Nagaland	06	280	18
Tripura	51	6010	6548

Table 3.15 No. of Industries and Workers in North East (1997-98)

States	*No of Units*	*No. of workers Working ('000)*
Meghalaya	43	7
Assam	1861	155
Manipur	77	4
Nagaland	165	5
Tripura	243	9
Total	2389	180

potential for electricity production, its development rate is very low. This is the reason why there is about 17% deficit in electricity and power according to 98-99 statistics Assam's electricity requirement is 531 megawatts as against the production of 514 megawatts (Table3.11)

An electricity plant of 572.49 m.w. production capacity is constructed in Assam. But this too is not able to satisfy the total electricity need of the State. According to 1995-96 statistics average per capita electricity consumption was 100 kwh. Rural electrification is also being done at a very slow pace.

Though the capacity of electricity production in Assam is 572.49 megawatts the plant cannot produce more than 200 megawatts. So many reasons are responsible for this. Total capacity of Namrup Thermal electric plant is 133.5 megawatts which is required to be increased. The same way total capacity of Bogaigaon thermal power plant is 240 megawatts but its condition is also like the others. Namrup thermal power plant is being modernised where under a number of generators are being provided. Nipco has constructed a power plant at Kathalguri which has started generation. Construction of 240 megawatts thermal power plant is undertaken at Amguri.

The state has tremendous potential for hydro electricity. Because of this the State Government has sanctioned a hydal power project at Karbi Langpi. But there are many obstacles in its implementation. The state Government is working on inter - state power projects and is trying to improve the power scenario. Work is undertaken for reconstruction and modernisation of number of power plants of Assam State Electricity Board. The Assam Government is seriously considering the participation of private companies in the area of electricity production. Electricity deficit of the state is being met by purchasing the power from Meghalaya. Entrepreneurs desirous of starting industries in Assam are also not taking interest for the insufficient power availability. Thus,, the State Government is putting its efforts in this direction.

Underground wealth i.e. Minerals - Assam occupies a prominent place as far as underground wealth is concerned. Assam has large deposits of petroleum, natural gas, coal and limestone. According to 1998-99 statistics total petroleum extraction was 52,71,000 metric tonnes. Oil was discovered during 1889-90 in Assam. The Assam oil company was incorporated in 1899. At present there are four oil refineries in Assam at Digboi, Noonmati (Guwahati), Boggaigaon and Noomligarh. The last one was established in 1999. Because of petroleum industry a fertiliser plant is also started at Namroop. There are large deposits of limestones in the state. 1254 million cubic metres of natural gas was extracted in Assam in 1998 along with extraction of 6,62,000 metric tonnes of coal.

Agriculture and Horticulture- About 89 % of Assam population is in rural area. Of this 69 per cent population is engaged in agriculture and allied activities. This way agriculture shares 35% of Assam economy. Rice is the main crop of Assam. According to 1995-96 statistics the state had rice crop of 33.90 lac tons. Wheat is also cultivated in the state. Production of cash crop of jute is also very important. About 8.03 lac bales of jute were produced in the state in 1996-97.

Potato, sugarcane, maize farming is also a part of Assam agriculture They are also grown on large scale. Presently 39.26 lac hectares land is under cultivation. Of this 65 % land is under rice cultivation. Apart from this, pulses and oil seeds are also grown and cultivated in the state. The state Government is paying more attention to rice production.

Assam is known for tea production along with oil production. Assam has highest number of tea gardens (860) in India. Tea is grown on 2,26,000 hectares of land. According to 1997 statistics tea production was 42,54,000 tons. Thus, it can be said that tea production has a major share in the development of Assam.

Sericulture - Sericulture includes growing of silk worms on the 'Shahtoot' trees and production of silk threads and silk cloth. People living in villages have undertaken this industry. They grow silkworms and extract silk threads from cocoons. The silk threads produced here belong to Pat, Eeri and Munga categories. In olden days every woman of this area was weaver and was weaving her own cloth. According to statistics 30% of Assam population is engaged in silk production and allied activities. Silk is produced in all the districts of Brahmaputra valley except two hilly areas. There is a very big silk market at Suab Knechi which is known as Manchester of Assam. The state government is making efforts to develop Sericulture with the help of Central Government.

Khadi and cottage industry also has a major share in strengthening Assam economy. Assamese produce their own clothes as per their needs and sell excess production in nearby markets. A number of Khadi production centres are working in the state. Belsari (Nalbari), Adabari (Kamrup) Baropujiya (Nagaon), etc., are some prominent centres. Apart from Khadi Board, the state Government provides training to the youth for production of earthern wares, as well as production of bamboo and cane goods. This is providing employment to thousands of people.

Industries : Though very rich in production of petroleum and tea, the state is still backward in the industrial area. Though absurd, it is a truth. There are four crude oil refineries at Digboi, Normati, Bogaigaon and Noomligarh. Oil India Ltd. is engaged in discovering oil deposits and extracting oil. O.N.G.C.

is also doing the same work. Whereas Assam Gas company and Gas Authority of India Ltd. are engaged in reaching natural gas to different industries.

There are three big paper mills of which two paper mills belong to Hindustan Paper Corporation in public sector. Two small units of fertiliser production are located near Guwahati. There are 44 Plywood factories in Assam which produce 60 % of total plywood production of the country. The state government has declared a new Industrial Policy in 1997. The government has given stress on providing basic facilities required for establishing new industries. The state government under its Industrial Policy implementation has opened new industrial development centres at Balipara in Shoitpur district and Matiya in Gwalpara district, whereas an export promotion industrial centre is started at North Guwahati. A software technology park is opened in Guwahati. Work on Assam Gas cracker project is in progress. It is in it's last stages. Assam Industrial Development Board is constituted in 1965 with a view to develop Industries in the State. This A.I.D.C. has provided financial assistance to more than 60 projects.

Road and Transportation : Arrangement, improvement and development of roads and transports has taken place in Assam after independence. Assam was cut from rest of the country for a pretty long time. As such difficulties were experienced specially in communication and transportation. But road transportation is now developed at fast speed. Three long bridges are constructed across Brahmaputra after independence which eased the transportation to a great extent. First bridge across Brahmaputra was opened in 1963 which connects South and North Guwahati. Another Bridge connecting Klianghar and Bhumaragudi was inaugurated in 1987. Third bridge named Nar-Narayan Setu was inaugurated in 1998. This Bridge connects Pancharatna in South and Jogithopa in North. The First Bridge Saray Ghat and the third Bridge named Nar Narayan setu are meant for Road and Rail Transport. The second is for road transport only. There are six airports in Assam. They are Borzar (Guwahati), Rorira (Jorhat), MohanBari (Dibrugad), Lilabari, (North Lakhimpur), Salonibari (Tejpur) and Kumbhigram (Silchar). Looking to the problems in Road Transport the Central Government has given concession in service charges so that air transport can be affordable to public. This concession is given to transportation for travel, to all North Eastern States. Apart from this it is made obligatory to the private companies providing air travel, to ply at least 35% flights in this region.

In totality Road transport arrangements in Assam are satisfactory. The state has a road net work of 52,158 kms. under the public works department of the state. This includes National high way of 2033 Kms. length. There are roads connecting Assam with all the North Eastern States. Easy travel is also available through the buses of Assam State Transport Corporation. In addition the state government has provided for water transportation through Ferry Boats. Water transportation for goods is also available between Guwahati and Kolkatta. Even then Assam has some areas which do not have proper transportation facilities. The state government is required to undertake a time bound programme for this.

Tourism : Assam has a special place on tourism map of North East India. Ancient Devi-Peeth - Kamakhya Temple is in Guwahati. Thousands of devotees and pilgrims from all corners of the country come here to worship Goddess Kamakhya. According to the statistics of 1998-99, total 1,78,000 tourists visited Assam and 3390 foreign tourists also visited the state. On one hand, the Kamakhya temple attracts devotees and on the other hand, the remains of Banod Madan Kamdeo temple in Tejpur also attracts the tourists. In addition ShioSagar is also a place of attraction of tourists.

Wild animals in the forests of Assam provide special attraction to the tourists. Main attraction is Unicorns which are found in Kajiranga National Park. Apart from these there are many more species of Wild Animals and birds in Kajiranga National park. Manas National Park is the home for Bengal Tigers, wild elephants, Golden Langoors, etc. Looking at the importance of tourism the state government has given industry status to Tourism. Compulsion to obtain reserved area permit is also removed to attract foreign tourists. As a result, the number of foreign tourists is considerably increased in last three years. This has provided impetus to hotel industry also. Tourist bus network in Assam is supposed to be one of the best in the country. All the tourist attractions are connected with Guwahati. The Government has also started working on a plan to have tourism fairs to attract Indian as well as foreign tourists. Tea Tourism festival is celebrated under this plan. The Government is trying to attract European Tourists by arranging such festivals as the European people have emotional relations with Assam Tea Gardens. The Government is also encouraging water sports in Brahmaputra.

Economic structure of Nagaland

Agriculture is the main source of Nagaland economy. About 70% population of Nagaland is in rural areas and depend fully on agriculture. The Naga farmers were under the impression that human sacrifice was the only way to get better crops. This their belief was afterwards converted in the tradition of human sacrifice. It is worth mentioning here that 9680 Kms. land out of the total 16,579 Sq. Kms. land (The area of Nagaland) is agricultural land and is cultivated. 52% of Nagaland area has forests.

Natural Resources **:** Nagaland obtains a major share of its revenue from the forests. Nagaland forests are divided in three categories. 1) Reserved Forests 2) Protected Forests 3) Private Forests. As a matter of fact the forests are not being scientifically exploited. Otherwise these forests would have fetched lot more revenue for the state. Even then its economic importance is great because of valuable trees like Sagon (Teak). There is a plenty of Shirish and Mahagoni trees in Nagaland forests. Cane and bamboos are also grown to a great extent in the state but on a small-scale. But there are plenty of Medicinal Plants in these forests. Forest department has created four dwelling places for wild animals. A zoo and forest training school are also established in the state.

Minerals **:** The state of Nagaland has a very limited deposits of limestone., coal, chromium, copper, slate and crude oil. Geological department is trying to discover and extract these minerals. But it could not be done now. Because of this reason the state does not have large and heavy industries.

Agriculture **:** Two types of Agricultural cultivation is undertaken in this state. 1) Zoom Farming 2) Steps Farming. Zoom farming is undertaken mainly by Sema and Lotha tribes, whereas Angami tribes use modern method of Step Farming. Step Farming is done by cutting the slopes of hills in the shape of steps. Cultivation is made on these plain steps of hills. These farms are irrigated by water channels. Water flowing down the hills is used for such irrigation.

The Government is taking all steps to stop Zoom farming. The state Government has started working on various plans and projects for betterment of agriculture. An agriculture research Centre is also established for this. Main crops in the state are Rice, Jowar, Maize and Pulses. Potatoes and Sugarcane being cash crops are grown on Large scale . The people of the state never have any dispute over the ownership of land and this is a speciality of the state. Rural social structure in the state is so designed that every member of the society gets satisfied in basic needs i.e. food, cloth, and residence. Additional labour are not easily available in the region specially during the season of cultivation as most of the people are engaged in various activities.

Industry : Nagaland does not have many industries. At present 183 small and medium industries are running in the state. On the other hand 83 industries have been closed. Thus, about 31% industries could not do well in this state. Handloom i.e. spinning and weaving is the main industry in Nagaland. Awo, Rengma and Lotha tribals produce (weave) cloth to meet their own requirements. They produce extra cloth also which they supply to other tribals and thereby earn financial profits. Most of the weaving work is performed by the women of these tribes. Preparation of articles from cane and bamboo is also another industry in the state which fetches them financial income. Naga shawls and other hand woven fabrics are in great demand in the outside markets. There is a sugar factory at Binapur with a production capacity of 1,000 tonnes per day. In addition there is another sugar factory producing Khandasari sugar which was started in 1986. Production capacity of this factory is 200 Metric Tonnes. There is one paper and pulp mill in Tuli and a ply wood factory at Tejit. A brick oven has been constructed recently in Dinapur. These projects have provided employment to the local youth. The state government is encouraging small and cottage industries. Training centres for weaving as well as Sub-Production are established at Mokokchung, Dinapur. The state government is also encouraging soap-production, candle sticks production and Apiculture. The state government has started a training centre for this. An Industrial Estate is created in Dinapur. Even then there is a limited possibility of having more industries in the state.

Road and Transportation **:** Nagaland is totally a hilly and forest land. Therefore there is dire necessity of improving roads and transportation. Nagaland has only one Narrow guage railway link connecting Dinapur to Guwahati. There was not a single good road except National highway connecting Dinapur to More. This was the condition in pre-independence period. But there is a gradual improvement in the road transport after independence. The state government is taking more interest in this field. Nagaland has 1610 km. long good roads and 5358 km. long other roads. Nagaland State Transport corporation plys its buses on 111 routes through 1207 km. long roads. North East Council has constructed roads on the border This also has helped in easing the transportation problem.

Economic Structure of Tripura

Tripura is spread over on the area of 10486 sq.km. of land. Of this only 29% land is being cultivated Thus, only 3080 sq.km. of land is under agriculture. 6293 sq.km. of land i.e. about 60% of land is covered by forests.

Natural Resources- The major portion of land in Tripura is covered by forest as mentioned above.

Naturally forest products are major source of income to the state. Very valuable trees are found in these forests They are Shaal, Garjan, Sagon, Gamar etc. Shaal trees are found mainly in Udaypur, Belonia and Sonmura, etc. Same way Sagon is found in North Tripura District. Garjan is found in North and South Tripura districts whereas Gamar trees are found all over the state. Alike other North Eastern states cane, bamboo, as well as Pineapple, Guava, Mango, Jalk Fruit (Kathal) etc. fruit trees are found in large number in the state.

Forest department of the state is paying more attention in training the people for forest conservation and educating them in the field of forest importance. The State Government is encouraging the plantation of rubber and coffee plants. Fishing industry is also a major economic source of the state.

Agriculture-As is a tradition of other tribes Tripura tribes have a tradition of Zoom Farming. But because of the efforts of the government and the spread of education such type of Zoom farming is being reduced day by day. Main crops of state are rice, cotton, pulses and tobacco, which are cultivated on large scale. Agriculture is the main occupation of the Tripura tribes. About 3/4th of Tripura population is dependent on agriculture. The Government is trying hard towards improving Agriculture yield. Jute, sugarcane and potatoes are also cultivated on a bigger scale as cash crops. Important incident in agriculture sector is more yield of wheat in the state. Wheat was grown on about 130 hectares of land in 1968-69. But now the wheat growing area is increased to two thousand hectares of land by 1975-76. Presently the wheat is grown on about 4,000 hectares of land.

Minerals : Tripura has deposits of crude oil and Natural Gas. This potential is being exploited by

O.N.G.C. by extracting crude oil and gas. Apart from oil and gas the state has the sand which is used in glass production, china clay, lignite, limestone and other building materials. These are also extracted in the State.

Industries : Prior to 1950 there were a few small, medium and large industries. According to 1991 census about 2% of the population was engaged in Cottage Industry. Geographical situation of the state is also responsible for the less number of industries in the state. No doubt the state has achieved progress in the industry manufacturing articles and other goods out of cane, and bamboos. Beauty of state handicraft has its own differentiation. That is why these Tripura articles and goods are in great demand in outside markets in the country. These goods carry their own identification. Situation in Tripura is changed to a large extent after the inhabitance of Bengaliese in the state. There is a noticeable change in the tribals of Tripura who have a great impact in this. At present about 1,11,000 looms are working in the state in the co-operative sector. There are about 150 such co-operative societies in the state.

Oldest industry in Tripura is silk production and allied activities. According to 2001 statistics about 2000 persons are engaged in silk production. Presently 30,000 kgs. of silk thread is produced from 9,200 acres of land of silk firms. In order to encourage entrepreneurship in the state, the government has developed industrial estates at Arundhati Nagar, Dhwaja, Angar, Dhukli, Kumarghat and Harmanagar. Apart from this, industrial estates are established in Udaypur (South Tripura), Kailash (North Tripura) and Agartala. These estates have units of carpet weaving, iron and steel work, footware production and hand made paper production.

The following three reasons are responsible for less number of industrial units in the state. 1) Low Quality Production. 2) Non availability of sufficient electric power 3) Transportation problem.

In order to resolve the power crisis, the government is working on Gomati Hydro Electric Project. Tea industry plays an important role in the economy of the state. There are 51 Tea gardens spread over 6010 hectares of land (1997 statistics) Tripura tea is actually of lower quality than Assam tea. The State Government is putting its efforts in this direction also.

Though Tripura has ample potential for electricity production, only 90 megawatts electricity is generated as against state requirement of 115 megawatts. Thus, there is a deficit of 21% in the area of power.

Road and Transport **:** Tripura is lacking in good roads and proper transportation facilities. There is only one good highway of 200 km. length. It joins Assam and Agartala. Even this road does not remain in good condition throughout the year. This road is, many times, damaged during rainy season because of floods and landslides. Total length of roads in Tripura was 6090 km. in 1989. Of these roads only 3700 km. long roads are good roads. Recently a meter guage railway line between Karimganj in Assam and Kumarghat in Tripura is laid down and inaugurated.There is severe necessity of a rail-link between Kumarghat and Agartala. Other prime necessity is of constructing a 200 km.Road to connect Agartala to Dharmanagar.

Tourism **:** Tripura tourism is also fetching revenue to the state. But this tourism also requires further development. At present there are 23 places of tourist attraction. As per the statistics of 1998-99 there were 1,70,000 tourists, visited Tripura of which only 36 were foreigners There are a number of places in Agartala itself which attract the tourists. These include Ujayanta palace, Kunjwam palace, Jagannath temple, Maharaja Veer Vikram college campus, Museum, Chaturadash God temple Sipahijola forest resort, Brahmakunda etc. Udaypur too has such places. Some of them are Tripursundari temple, Poonakoli Teerth, Jambui hill etc.

Economic Structure of Arunachal Pradesh

The state of Arunachal Pradesh is very rich in natural resources. 46% of its population is engaged in and dependent on Agriculture. Like in other tribes zoom farming is adopted by the Arunachal Tribes .Main crop of this state includes rice, maize, jowar, wheat and oilseeds. 51,540 sq.km. area of state is occupied by the forest (1997-statistics)

This is 61% of the total area of Arunachal pradesh .Fruits like bananas, lemons, pineapples, etc. are also cultivated in this state. Apart from agriculture, horticulture is also an occupation in Arunachal Pradesh.

The forest provides valuable wood. As a result the state had wood based industries. But many of these industries are now closed as a result of Supreme Court ban on forest cutting. The state government has started a number of training centres and camps to encourage small-scale and cottage industries. As the Arunachal Pradesh tribals weave their own clothes these tribals are being trained in this respect.

The state has sufficient potential for hydro electricity. A 750 kilowatts plant was established in 1972 at Rahu. After that two hydro electric projects of 200 Kilowatts and 100 megawatts were commissioned at Palighat and Basar respectively in 1973. Work of Hydro Electric project at Anglang Teju, Tirat -jo Twang, Virang, Siyang, etc., are undertaken by the state. Power condition in the state is quiet satisfactory. Power requirement of the state as per 1998-99 statistics is 44 megawatts whereas supply is 43 megawatts. According to 1991 census the state has 3649 villages of which electrification of 2147 villages was completed by March 1999.

Economic Structure Of Mizoram

Mizoram though very rich in natural resources is quite backward in the field of industrialisation. Eventually its economic condition is not satisfactory. Lack of transportation facilities is posing many difficulties in the way of trade and commerce.Like other North Eastern states, 80% of Mizoram population is dependent on agriculture.

Natural Resources : Mizoram is very rich in forest products. Valuable wood like shaal, bamboo, Cane are found in plenty in its forests. Forests in this state are divided in three categories. Enormous tree cutting has reduced the density of forests. Zoom farming is also an important reason for destruction of forests. Many hills have gone barren because of this. About 71.5% Mizoram area is occupied by its forest (1990- 91 statistics.)

Agriculture **:** Mizoram land has red coloured soil. This is very useful for Horticulture, and floriculture. Though 80% of population is dependent on Agriculture its per capita yield is quite less. Because of hilly area Zoom Farming is adopted by Mizoram Tribals. due to its disadvantages as well as due to educational and cultural development of this state the farmers are now shifting to Step farming. Rice, maize and, cotton are some of the main crops. Rice yield in the state is less than required as it totally depends on monsoon. As a result rice is required to be imported from nearby states. Fruits like banana pine apple, lemon, ginger, are grown on hill tops along with flowers and vegetables.

Agriculture department of the state is providing information and knowledge of modern agriculture techniques. East Iswal, West Iswal, Lungtai, Soha and Kolasai districts are declared as agriculture districts. Bulldozers alongwith labour are taken help of for removing the unevenness of the land and converting it in plains. The state had a trade of 2000 quintls of agriculture produce with Myanmar and Bangladesh.

Industries : This state is quite backward in the area of large industries. Paucity of petroleum, coal, electricity added by hilly nature of the land are some of the important reasons for lack of industrialisation in this state. Mizoram Government has developed industrial areas in Iswal, Kolasiv and Lulangal districts and encouraged the people to establish small as well as medium scale industries, in this area. According to the statistics of 1998 there is only one medium size unit in the state whereas 5531 small-scale units have gone sick. Outsiders are not showing interest in establishing industrial units in this state as there are no proper facilities of transport and communication. Innerline permit is also adding to the disinterest of outsiders. Many of the day to day needs are brought to the state from Silchar in Assam. As a result they are expensive in this state. Rural industrialisation project was started in 1963 at Iswal. Training in small and cottage industry is being imparted through this project. There is a great potential for forest produce based industries. Production of woollen carpets, baskets and furniture can be undertaken as cottage industry in this state. Like other North Eastern Tribes, women of Mize tribes weave and produce required cloth for their tribes. Thus, employment can be provided to the people through such projects.

Electricity : Electricity power requirement of this state is estimated to be 58 megawatts. But the State has availability of 55 % of requirement. First generation of electricity was made in the state in 1962 with the help of diesel generators. By 1972, 5 such diesel based power stations were established at Iswal, Lungtui, Kolasive, Saship, and Nathiyaj. At present electricity from these power stations is supplied to the entire state. Per capita electric consumption in the state is 128 kilowatts. The statistics of 1999 says that 687 villages out of total 698 villages are electrified. The state government, in order to strengthen the power position has founded a micro hydro electricity project.

The State Government, realising the importance of power, has undertaken number of projects. These include Tuipanguli Hydro Electric Project of 3 megawatts production capacity and Kantwalang Electricity project of production capacity of 3 megawatts.

Roads and Transportation : The state does not have rail link. The only medium of transportation is roads and Airways. The only national highway No.54 connects the state with rest of country. Between Silchar and Iswal this highway is of the length of 180 Kms. Because of hilly and uneventerrain the Mizos use Maruti and Gypsy type of light vehicles for human as well as goods transportation. The North -East Council is working on the project of Mizoram Border Road. According to 1996 statistics the state has roads of 8391 kms. length of which only 3946 Kms. long roads are good and 4445 kms. long roads are rough.

The Central Government has finalised a plan to connect Mizoram with other states by roads. Under this plan the following National Highways will be constructed. (1) National Highway No.44-A connecting

Tripura and Mizoram - length 328 kms. 2) National Highway No.150 connecting Manipur with Mizoram through Karimganj and 3) National Highway No.154 to connect Assam with Mizoram. The public works department has already started the work.

Tourism : Mizoram has a good potential for tourisum. But because of inner line permit the number of tourists is very less. As a result the tourism industry is facing loss. Statistics of 1998-99 states the existence of 13 places of tourism in the state but only 25,372 tourist visited Mizoram. This includes 141 foreign Tourists. A Plan is formulated by the state government to encourage tourism and attract foreign tourists. According to this a group of four or more foreign tourists can obtain inner line permit from Mizoram house at Delhi. Apart from this the department is going to start Tourism information centres at Guwahati, Kolkata and New Delhi. To facilitate tourists the department is starting tourist lodges and tourist homes at various places in the state.

Economic Structure of Manipur

Out of total area of 22327 sq.km. of Manipur only 1750 sq.km. of land is under agricultural cultivation. 15154 Sq. km i.e. 67.9% of the total area is occupied by forests. As in the other North Eastern States major part of population is engaged and dependant on agriculture and allied activities. According to certain statistics 66% of the population is directly dependant on agriculture. Apart from valuable wood i.e. forest produce, cane and bamboo trees are found in Manipur forests.

Because of hilly and forest area the state of Manipur could not be developed for a pretty long period. There are only twelve medium and large scale industries in the state (1998 statistics). But according to statistics of 1997 about 2707 small scale industries are sick.

Handloom is the biggest cottage industry in the state. Other cottage industries are apiculture and production of articles and goods from cane and bamboo and gurr and Khandasri. The state has started number of training centres in order to encourage cottage industry.

State of Manipur is very rich in minerals but these deposits are not properly exploited. Manipur is backward in the field of hydro electricity also.

Chapter 4

Impact of North East Council on Economic Development of North East

Considering the backwardness of the seven sister states of North East the parliament in 1971 passed an act known as "North Eastern Council Act -1971" and constituted a council under this Act. The council started functioning from 1972. Its Headquarters is situated at Shillong. Rajyapals and Chief Ministers of all the seven sister states are its official members.

The council secretariat is managed by the secretary. His position is equivalent to that of the secretary of Govt. of India. The council is not only advisory committee but is a funding agency also. The Central Government supplies funds under plan expenditure to enable the council for its expenditure and loans, etc. 45% of the council funds are spent on creation of transportation and communications facilities. 41% is spent on electricity and power while 10% is spent on human development and public health.

Operational Methodology of the Council

Pace of development in North Eastern states was very slow. With this point of view the council adopted the policy of coordination and adjustments amongst the seven states. Social and Economic strategies of the states are different from each other. Therefore a Regional coordination policy was formulated. This regional committee is entrusted with the following work.

(1) All the seven states will submit to the state as well as central government, the items of common interest. These are supposed to be related to interstate transportation and communication, electricity and power and flood control.

(2) To combine all the pending works in North Eastern development plans and to submit a combined plan to the Central Government for consideration as well as implement these plans.

(3) To distribute the expenditure on the projects benefiting two or more states.

(4) To watch the proper implementation of project by the states and to establish coordination between the concerned states from time to time.

(5) To pay attention to the expenditure by the states from the funds allotted to individual state for implementation of regional plans.

(6) To send proposals for survey and examining new projects and to examine the work done by the states in the field of defence and security.

Though the North East Council is mainly of an adviser type, the council is empowered to supervise the plan implementation and allotment of funds. The council has to see that the funds allotted are properly utilised. This way the North Eastern council is working as an agency providing financial assistance to the plans of the states as well as common plans. Allotment

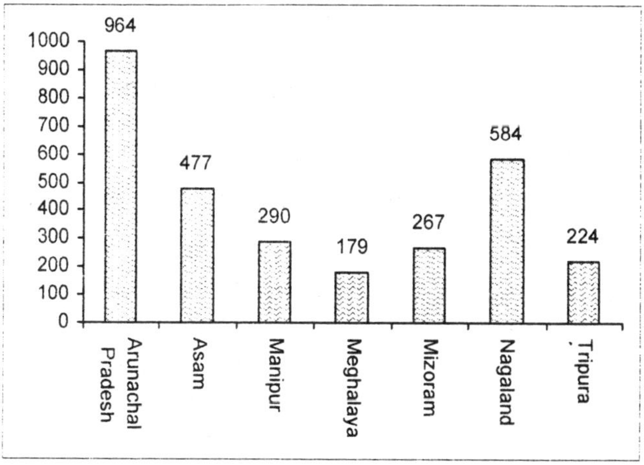

Fig. 4.1 : Chart showing Assistance given to North Eastern states by the council (1997-98)

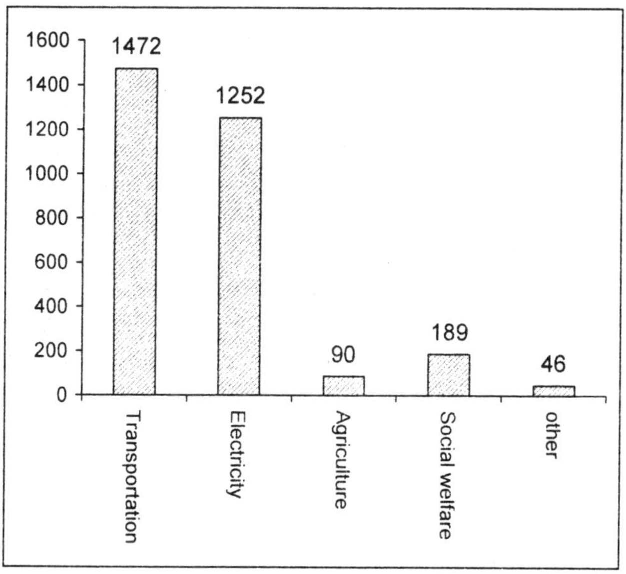

Fig. 4.2 : Experience by North East council on Various Developmental Projects (5th to 8th plan)

of funds made by the North Eastern council during

1999-2000 is given in Table 4.1.

Funds provided by North Eastern Council are mainly utilised, right from its constitution, for transportation as well as water and electricity power development. Rest of the funds are utilised for agriculture development and other social and group services.

Important Activities and Achievements of North Eastern Council

Funds of Rs 2240 crores were allocated to North Eastern Council during ninth plan. An amount of Rs 398 crores was spent in 1997-98 and Rs 425 crores was spent in 1998-99. An amount of Rs 450 crores is provided for 1999-2000. Of this an amount of Rs 215 crores is reserved for electricity and power sector, Rs 162 crores for transportation and communication. The same way an amount of Rs. 49 crores i.e. 11% is to be utilised for human development and public health. The plans of this council are implemented through the agencies of state government and public undertakings. These public undertaking are (1) Border road organisation for roads, Indian Airport Authority for development of airports, Eastern electric power corporation for ***various Developmental projects (5th to 8thplan)*** hydro electricity projects and Power Grid Corporation of India for distribution of electricity. Very few works are entrusted to private organisations by the council.

Transportation and Communication Sector

Right from its constitution in 1972, the council has completed the construction of 4800km roads and work is in progress of construction of 2 thousand 600 kilometer road. An amount of Rs 1793.46 crores has already been spent on this work. About 45% of the budgeted funds of Ninth plan have been spent on

Table 4.1 Roads and Bridges Construction Projects Undertaken by North Eastern Council (2000)

Sr. No	*Name of projects*	*Length KM*	*States*	*Cost (Rs In Cr.)*
1)	Baithalangru - Kampur-Raha	48	Assam	30.61
2)	47 Permanent Bridges	1008	Meghalaya	30.24
3)	Kohima-Bokajan	62	Nagaland	26.63
4)	Panchgram-Helakamdi	0.058 (Joint)	Assam	38.09
5)	Margerita-changlang	43	Arunachal Pradesh and Assam	23.53
6)	Jamuang-Hufen-Durlaochera	79	Mizoram and Assam	40.72
7)	Jot-Balijan-Gahigaon	35.2	Arunachal Pradesh and Assam	35.20
8)	Maharkatiya -Khoa	57	Arunachal Pradesh and Assam	33.22

road construction. The council constructed a bridge across Brahmaputra near Tejpur by spending an amount of 89 crores. This bridge was opened for public transport in 1987. This is actually the longest bridge in North East region. The council also constructed the third bridge across Brahmaputra near Jogidhopa in collaboration with ground transport and Railway Ministry. The council shared an amount of Rs. 95 crores in this work. This bridge provides Railway track and Road both. It was inaugurated in April 1998.

Water Transport : Six ships were given to Assam during sixth plan. The council and Assam government spent Rs 20 crores each to start night navigation through the Brahmaputra.

Air Transport : Air transport facilities in whole of the North Eastern region are very meagre. Of all the airports in this region only Guwahati airport has sufficient facilities to allow night landing of aeroplanes. Runways of most of the airports in this region are so short that air buses cannot land on these airports. Twelve airports in this region are earmarked for development for which the expenditure will be borne in 60:40 ratio by the council and respective states. These are Guwahati, Imphal, Deemapur, Tejpur, Jorhat, Dibrugarh, Leelabari, Silchar, Agartala, Kamalpur, Kailashahar and Shillong. Six airports at Itanagar, Pasighat, Jeero, Teju, Along, Daperijo in Arunachal Pradesh and Rupasi in Assam are planned to be constructed in ninth plan. An amount of Rs. 78.11 crores is allocated for the purpose.

Computer education : The council started encouraging computer education in the schools right from 1994-95. Required facilities are made available to 205 schools for computer education. The council provides six months computer training to the school teachers. One hundred schools are selected for computer education in 2001.

Information technology : The council in its meeting on the 14th April 2000 held at Delhi formulated a policy on information technology. The council desires to take help of Information technology for development (social as well as economical) of North eastern region. The council is preparing a blue-print for this. This includes development of existing polytechnics and engineering colleges for the purpose. The council is providing facilities to these institutions to increase their potential. There is a proposal to establish Information Technology Parks in the capitals of all North Eastern states.

Sattelite facilities at Shillong : The council has established a Long Sensing Satellite centre at Shillong to supervise and examine the development activities undertaken in the North East Region. This technique helps in making surveys and examining the possibilities of proposed roads and their designs .The council has established North East Space Application Centre at Barapani near Shillong with the collaborations of Space Research Development Department.

Industries and Minerals : The council has planned to encourage and develop the industries based on the tissues of Pineapple, Banana and Bamboo by providing help to them. Apart form this the council has a plan to establish a tea processing unit for small tea producers by providing financial help to them. The council has proposed to spend Rs 112 lac on the common project of agriculture. The council has made budgetary provision to encourage latex and rubber based industries in Tripura. It has made a budgetary provision of Rs 100 lac to encourage handloom industry by small entrepreneurs. All these provisions are made in Ninth plan.

Fisheries and AnimalHusbandry Development : The council has given financial help to a common fisheries project between Mizoram, Manipur and Meghalaya. The same way the council extended help of Rs 5.9 lacs to Assam Agriculture University at Raha to enable it to make available good quality seeds for agriculture during 1998-99. Financial assistance to voluntary as well as cooperative organisations is also given for Animal Development, by the council.

Agriculture and Horticulture Sector : The council provided financial assistance for purchasing trucks and other transportation vehicles, to cooperative societies in order to facilitate transportation of agriculture produce to remote areas. The council is providing funds for construction of warehouses in rural areas for agriculture produce. According to council sources the council has allotted an amount of Rs. 6 crores, 42 lacs, 72 thousand and 590 to 68 registered cooperative societies in the region.

Electricity and Power Generation **:** The council is providing more attention to Hydro electricity, Irrigation and flood control. Surveys including feasibility survey for 22 projects have already been completed by March 1999. These projects include 19 hydro-electricity projects, two irrigation projects and one multi object project. Some hydro-electricity projects e.g. Kopali have already been completed. Some big electricity projects e.g. River Ranga and Dayang have been undertaken with the cooperation of Nipco. The council has given proposal for 14 projects during Ninth plan. These projects include four hydro electricity projects, three irrigation projects and one flood control project.

Public Health Sector **:** No significant work could be undertaken in sixth plan in this sector. But financial assistance was given to Guwahati Medical College and Dr. B. Vora Cancer Institute during eighth plan. It is proposed to undertake 12 projects in this sector during ninth plan. These projects are

(1) To start a Medical college at Imphal.

(2) To start a regional Paramedical and Nursing training institute at Iswal.

(3) To start a regional LGB institute of Mental Health at Tejpur.

(4) To assist the construction of 'Pay cabins at three medical colleges in Assam.

(5) To start a centre for diagnosis of epidemics, at Dibrugarh Medical College.

(6) To start a centre for diagnosis and treatment of Tuberculosis and other chest diseases in Dibrugarh Medical College.

(7) To provide special financial assistance to Homoeopathy Medical College at Jorhat.
(8) To provide assistance to Royal Medical College at Guwahati.
(9) To give assistance in renovation of Civil Hospital at Shillong.
(10) To strengthen the Ramkrishna Mission Hospital at Itanagar.
(11) To Provide financial assistance to K.L.P. Sinod Hospital at Shillong.
(12) To give financial assistance to Shankardeo Eye Hospital at Shillong.

The council has constructed a Hostel with 100 rooms for the students of North Eastern region coming to Delhi for education. It has undertaken the task of establishing an Inter-state Bus Terminus at Deemapur in Nagaland. The Council also under took the responsibility to start Regional Institute of Medical Sciences at Imphal for the benefit of the people of North Eastern region. It has proposed to provide 100 seats for MBBS and 19 seats for Postgraduate students along with an attached hospital with 881 beds. The council has allotted finance to extend scholarships to the students studying for professional courses. This scheme is expected to benefit three thousand students. The council has also taken steps towards Youth Welfare and Development of sports in this region. Under this, assistance is given to a number of clubs and voluntary organisations.

When Protector becomes Destroyer

As a matter of fact North Eastern Council has turned into an elephant who has two types of teeth; (1) Show Teeth (Ivory)and (2) Original Teeth. The funds allocated and provided by the Central Government for development of North East are not being spent properly. Only 40 to 45% of the funds are actually spent on development work. According to the secretary of the council who enjoys the status of the secretary to Govt. of India, a considerable portion of the funds provided by the Central Government goes in the hands of corrupt people. Another considerable big amount is spent on the employees and maintenance of the headquarters situated at Shillong. Most of the employees including officers are more interested in their own development rather than the development of the region. Some voluntary organisation go to the extent saying that the North Eastern council is a white elephant which is more known for misuse of the funds allocated for development of the region. It has become a daily routine of the officers to put obstacles and adopt red tapism while passing the projects But the secretary of the council has some other say. According to him the North Eastern Council is not totally under him as the Rajyapals and Chief Ministers of the states are its members. As such the projects submitted by them are undertaken by the council. Secondly this council does not distribute the funds directly, as such accusation of corruption can not be verified. Any way whatsoever is the case regarding the role of and corruption therein, reorganisation of the council is very badly needed.

Chapter 5

Background of Terrorism in North East

It is very difficult to mention a definite date of insurgency of terrorism in North East. But according to recent history the start of terrorism in this region can be dated back to 1826 when the then British Government occupied Assam under the agreement of Yandabu. The complete region was divided between various tribes and groups. The Britishers started development activities in this region. In 1940 Christian missionaries arrived in this region. They started sowing seeds of awakening in these tribes. A large convention of Assam-Kachhari youth was organised on the 12th August 1927 at Titabar in Assam. The Kachari youth voiced their discontent towards the Hindus who were said to be treating them as untouchable and a resolution stating that they, the Kacharis, have differences in the political, social, and religious systems of Hindus.

Simon Commission arrived in India in 1928. All the people in India showed them black flags but some tribes in Assam welcomed the commission and they were with the commission. This was simply the spark of discontent in these tribes. The Nagas in Naga hills also started showing their discontent during nearly the same period. The Nagas put forth their demand to protect their culture before the Simon Commission. As a matter of fact, Khasi and Jayantiya Hill Council, Mizo Hill Council, Garo Hill Council and Mikir and North Kachhar Council were in existence. But the Nagas were not prepared to accept this. It is said that insurgency of discontent started then only. The Britishers kept the Naga demand pending for 16 years. At the end they constituted Naga Hill District Council in 1945.

First meeting of the council was held at 'Vokha' in 1946. A resolution was passed to change the name of this council as Naga National Council. In the beginning the aim of this council was to protect and maintain the social entity and self respect of Nagas. But afterwards a resolution was passed to keep Naga Hill area in Assam itself but as autonomous unit. But within a period of one year India got independence in 1947 and the Nagas made a demand to the council government for declaring their area as a Soverign Republic country. This was denied by the central Government. After this the Governor of Assam Sir Akbar Haidari went to Kohima to have talks with Naga National Council leaders. This resulted in a Nine Point agreement which was duly signed by the Naga leader and by the government through the governor of Assam. It was specially stated in the agreement that the governor of Assam will reconsider the agreement as the agent of Govt. of India and consult the Naga representatives regarding the continuance of the agreement. Explaining the provisions of the agreement it was clearly told to the Naga representatives that the Nagas can be given more autonomy but within the jurisdiction of constitution of India.

During nearly the same period Japa Angmi Fizo was elected the chairman of Naga National Council. The N.N.C collected General public opinion in favour of severing the existence of Nagas from India. The Nagas denied payment of tax to government and voted for independent Nagaland. The Nagas boycotted the Zilla Parishad elections along with general elections in 1952. The Nagas declared on 22nd March 1956 that they are Sovereign Democratic Government. According to this declaration they announced a 100 member parliament with a ministerial cabinet of 15 members. This democratic government announced the appointments of Governors, Ambassadors, district collectors etc., 'Honge Ribon' a resident of Naga village on Burma border, was made the first Prime Minister.

By 1956 the Nagas organised a troop of five thousand trained Gorillas. An era of violence, ransom and killing was started in 1956. Three Nagas filed their papers as candidates for the assembly in 1957. They were elected unopposed. But 'Satsuo Angami' one of these three was murdered by terrorists. Propaganda chief of N.N.C, Shri T. Shekhar was also murdered in 1956. These murders removed the false attraction towards so called struggle for independence from the minds of Nagas. But the approach of the Central government and reserve forces was very calm. The Nagas, in general, got disturbed by the killing of their leaders and started to criticise the violence openly. A soft group of Nagas started their efforts for peace talks. Naga peace committee was formed in 1956. The then prime minister Jawaharlal Nehru promised that Nagas can be given more autonomy in Indian Republic provided the Naga Youth resign from the way of violence. In 1957 the Naga Church Council's 500 members appealed to the Naga Christians to bring peace to the area. A convention of Nagas was organised during third week of August 1957 at Kohima. This was attended by 1765 representatives. These include a number of Naga ultras who attended the convention in disguise.

Table 5.1 Start of Militancy/Terrorism in North East

State	*Year*
Nagaland	1947
Manipur	1960
Assam	1979
Tripura	1960
Mizoram	there is no militancy now
Meghalaya	1990
Arunachal Pradesh	1988 (on very small scale)

After this the N.N.C deputation met the Rajyapal of Assam and Prime Minister Nehru at Shillong and Delhi respectively. A proposal of talk was accepted by both the sides. With a view to have further talks all the political prisoners were released. Six thousand underground Naga ultras also came out after this and participated in peace talks. The process went on. A deputation of representatives of all Naga tribes called upon Prime Minister Jawaharlal Nehru and handed over a reminder to him. The reminder was first given thought and consideration by the Foreign Minister and then by Nehru. Jawaharlal Nehru after giving full thought and after consultation of the said reminder, declared in parliament that a new state consisting of Naga Hill and Twansang Mountain area is being created and accepted, in the name of Nagaland. Nagaland was finally declared fullfledged Indian state No. 16 in 1963. i.e. three years after the declaration in parliament.

According to one historic proof, the then Assam Governor had prepared a plan, 'crown colony' which is known as 'Coup Land plan'. He, in this plan, had recommended to British Government to separate the eastern region in south of Brahmaputra from rest of the country and to rule it by the British Government directly from England. The plan was sent to Viceroy of India and the British Government in England. By this time a large number from Naga tribes was converted to Christianity by the missionaries. Robert Reed the then governor was dreaming of this on the basis of mass conversion of Nagas. But during the meantime India became independent and Reed's dream could not come in reality. In 1947 when India gained independence the converted Nagas came together and started a revolution demanding 'Nagaland' for Christians. When the Indian Govt. came to know that this revolution is directly and indirectly encouraged by some missionaries, the Govt of India expelled a number of missionaries from India. In spite of this the revolt continued under the leadership to Japu Angami Fijo. A storm of separation and revolt continued upto 1957 under his leadership. But in 1957. Fijo fled from India and took shelter in London where he died in nineties. Even after his death the fire of sovereign Nagaland was still burning. The wonderful fact regarding Fijo is that he fought for India's independence from Azad Hind Sena as a corporal and was also made a war prisoner. But, it can not be guessed how and why his views were changed after release from prison.

Fijo's Nagaland National Council became inactive with the death of Fijo. But after that, another separatist organisation 'National Socialist Council' came into existence. But this too was divided in two parts in 1988. One part is working in Nagaland under the leadership of T H Moiwa and the other in Mynmar border area of Nagaland whose leader is Khaplang.

Inspired by the Nagaland people, other tribes also adopted separatism and revolted for independent state. There was a revolt in Mizoram in the end of sixth decade under the leadership of Laldenga. This revolt continued for 25 years. At the end Laldenga realised that independence can not be obtained by violence and /or armed revolution. As a result Shri Laldenga started working towards peaceful and respectable settlement with the Central Government by leaving violence and armed revolution. Finally there was an agreement between the then Prime minister Rajiv Gandhi and Laldenga in 1986 and full-fledged state of Mizoram came in existence. Elections were held in a short period in Mizoram in which Shri Laldenga was elected and became Chief Minister of Mizoram in a democratic way. Even after Laldenga' joining the National mainstream, a number of ultra organisations came up in Mizoram. Hamar people convention (H.P.C) is one of the major organisations.

In Manipur also there were a number of separatist movements. A separatist organisation Revolutionary Government of Manipur, came up in 1965, Shri Samarendra Singh was its leader. This organisation was broken in 1980. But another organisation People's Liberation Army was formed under the leadership of Vishweshwar Singh. This was near about a terrorist organisation. This organisation of P.L.A., was also broken in two factions in 1980 and a faction under the leadership of R. K. Tulchandra Singh was known as Revolutionary Party of Kanglipal (Prepak). This organisation was under the influence of separatism and regionalism. But this organisation was scattered after the death of R. K. Tulchandra Singh.

Tripura National Volunteers (T.N.V.) was active in Tripura in the seventies. After the surrender of

Shri Vijay Harbhal of T.N.V. in 1988, the T.N.V. became dead organisation but a new organisation Tripura National Liberation Front came in existence after T.N.V.

Meghalaya too had a new organisation during the first half of eighties. The name of this underground organisation was Meghalaya United Liberation Army. But this organisation lost its existence in a short period.

If we look at the above incidence it can well be said that terrorism and separatism was started in Nagaland in North Eastern region. As far as Nagaland is concerned, the era of terrorism in Nagaland started immediately after India's independence (table 5.1). Terrorism started in Manipur in 1950 but was on a very small scale. The terrorist activities assumed seriousness by 1960. There was no terrorism in Assam right upto 1979. A movement to expel foreign infiltrators from Assam was started in 1979. ULFA a terrorist organisation rose from this movement and the situation started taking serious turn. Terrorist activities were started by Bodo tribes on the pretext of so called negligence towards their area.

In 1960 there was a large-scale infiltration of Bengalis in Tripura. This posed a threat to the original inhabitants that they would assume minority status in the state. This gave rise to terrorism in Tripura. Terrorism in Meghalaya and Arunachal Pradesh is quite recent. An incidence of terrorism came to light in 1988 in Arunachal Pradesh. As a matter of fact this state does not have much more terrorism but according to fresh information coming from Arunachal Pradesh that youth from some tribes in plains as well as hills of Arunachal Pradesh are forcing the businessmen to leave their area and supporting terrorism. Mizoram had severe terrorism activities during Laldenga's movement. Govt. documents now say that there are no such terrorist activities in Mizoram now. But the fact is something else. Now also some organisations are recovering ransom from the businessman and ordering them to leave Mizoram. As a matter of fact Mizoram markets were remaining open upto 8 to 9 p.m before 1980. But today all the shops are closed and traffic in Mizoram halts by evening. The question that if there is no terrorism, why the people in Mizoram do not want to stay outside their homes after evening, comes up. But the people here have a very innocent answer to this. They say that they are habituated to be at home before the evening because of terrorist movement which was a serious threat to them. The same habit is continued.

Chapter 6

Militant-Organisations in North East and Their Modus Operandi

As per official figures there are only two dozen militant organisations which are active in North East. But actually about sixty smaller and bigger such organisations are (as per unofficial figures) operating to achieve their objects. Main object of these organisations is to terrorise and then kill the businessmen, outsiders etc. if they do not bow down to their wishes. These organisations are exploiting the geographical situation of this region combined by very inefficient administration. These organisations do not have any ideology. On the other hand, they are working to achieve their silly motives.

Highest number of militant organisations of this region are operating in Manipur and Assam. Overall there are equal number of communal and militant organisations. These militant organisations started enrolling the local youth with them. They started using them to recover various taxes from the local people. In a short period these organisations started various taxes under various names like -ULFA tax, SULFA Tax, FREEDOM Tax, and PROTECTION tax, etc. They recover these taxes from one and all including rich, poor, urban and rural dwellers, employees, businessman, tea gardeners, farmers and even workers. Some people started paying such taxes at their own and some out of sheer fear. They brought the tea gardens of North East region under their purview. There are about 70 such tea gardens in this region. Then started the era of abduction, murders and recovery of heavy ransom. This is still continued on a smaller or larger scale.

These militants, terrorists recover tax from all the trucks coming to and going from Assam. They charge tax on goods under transportation like building wood, coal, crude oil, and goods of daily needs. Such incidents of loot and ransom take place at many places by joining hands with local officers. There are always clashes between Naga Terrorists and Kookie terrorists on the problem of recovering tax from the local markets as well as on More-Imphal highway. A transport company was plying a passenger bus between Silchar (Assam) and Imphal. The owner of the transport company was killed by the terrorists only because he refused to pay tax to them. As a result transportation through this highway is totally stopped. People avoid travelling during night through this road and prefer to travel only in day time. Century old Naga - Kookie clashes have restarted. The terrorists in Nagaland put obstacles on the road to stop the passenger vehicles passing through the road. They make the travelling passengers to alight from the vehicle and loot everything from them. Such incidences are a regular feature in this area. These terrorists collected crores of rupees in this way during last some years. Many political leaders from this area have deposited heavy amounts in Bhutan, Bangladesh, Pakistan and Metropolitan cities of India also. They have invested this and other accumulated amount in property business.

Declaration of 'Bandhs' (closure), Bomb blasts in railway, buses and even in markets are costing the lives of many innocent persons in this area. And this is a regular feature.

Birth of ULFA

This organisation came into existence in the beginning of Assam movement (1979-85). It was formed with the main object of driving away the infiltrators who came form Bangladesh to Assam. But many more objects were included in its objective clause during the movement. These objects were connected to the things which were hurting the Assamese for a long period. These were unemployment in youth, neglect of Assam by Central Govt. Protection and preservation of Assamese culture etc. Because of inclusion for these things the ULFA could gather massive public support.

Primarily this movement was being organised and run by ASU Assam Students Union and AGSP-Assam Gan Sangram Parishad on the democratic and non-violence principles. But youth were not satisfied by the way of conducting the movement. They had revolutionary thinking. These youth wanted to undertake armed struggle. This group of youth therefore, formed a new organisation ULFA on the Seventh April 1979.

In the beginning the entry of members was being made through founder members of ASU and Assam Communal Youth Students Parishad. These members took active participation in Assam movement. Some of the chief members were Suren Dihingiya and Bheemkant Badgodai. But afterwards they went

Important Militant Organisations in North East.

ASSAM

Banned

1. United Liberation Frant of Assam (Alfa)
2. National Democratic Front of Bodoland (N.D.F.B)

Un-Banned

1. Bodoland Liberation Tigers (B.L.T)
2. Muslim Liberation Tigers of Assam (M.U.L.T.A.)
3. Rabha National Security Force (R.N.S.F.)
4. Bodoland Tigers Force (B.L.T.F)
5. Carbi National Volentier (K.N.V.)
6. United People's Democratic Solidarity (U.P.D.S.)
7. Carbi Volentier Force (K.V.F.)
8. Kamtapur Liberation Organisation (K.L.O)
9. Coach Rajbanshi Security Force (K.R.S.F.)
10. Dimacha Halonga Dalonga (D.H.D.)

MANIPUR

Un-Banned

1. Peoples Liberation Army (P.L.A)
2. United National Liberation Front (U.N.L.F.)
3. Peoples Revolutionary Party of Kanglipal (Pripak)
4. Kanglipal Communist Party (K.C.P.)
5. Kangli Yalol Kamba Lup (K.Y.K.L.)
6. Manipur peoples Liberation Frant (M.P.L.F)
7. Revolutionary Peoples Front (R.P.F.)

NAGALAND

Banned

1. National Socialist Council of Nagaland (Isak-Muiva)
2. National Socialist Council of Nagaland (Khaplang)

Un-Banned

1. Naga-National Council (Adino)/ Naga Federal Government
2. Naga-National Council (Khodao)
3. Palang United Liberation Front (P.U.L.F.)

TRIPURA

Banned

1. All Tripura Tiger Force (ATTF)
2. National Liberation Front of Tripura (N.L.F.T)

ARUNACHAL PRADESH

Un-banned

1. United Liberation Voluntiers of Arunachal Pradesh (U.L.V.A.P.)
2. United Pupils Voluntiers of Arunachal Pradesh (U.P.V.A.P.)
3. United Liberation Movement of Arunachal Pradesh (U.L.M.A.P.)

MEGHALAYA

Banned

1. Hinyatrep National Liberation Council (H.N.L.C.)
2. Achik National Voluntiers Council (A.N.V.C.)

Un-banned

1. Hinyatrep Achik Liberation Council (H..A.L.C.)
2. Achik Liberation Matgirk Army (A.L.M.A)

MIZORAM

Un-baned

1. Our Peoples Convention (H.P.C.)

underground and Paresh alias Pawan Barua, Arvind Rai Khowa, Anup Chetia (real name Golap Barua) Pradeep alias Jagannath Gogai, Naren Doka alias Hirakjyoti Mahant and Siddharth Fukan alias Sunil Nath captured the organisation.

ULFA has two units : (1) Political unit (2) Armed Volunteers unit. Arvind Rai Khowa is the chairman of the political unit and Paresh Barua is the chairman of other unit. Political activities and social work were with the Political unit. The second unit was collecting money by spreading terrorism and threatening as well the operation of plans. ULFA on one side collected money and on the other side undertook the social movement e.g. banning liquor sale, locating and causing arrest of the corrupt officers, or punishing them, announcing social boycott and other social punishments to those who used to misbehave with the girls. Because of these activities, the ULFA could create a very respectable and high image in the minds of Assamese people. They started naming them 'Angels'.

Beginning of Terrorist Activities **:** State Bank of India branch at Nampur (upper Assam) was robbed of Rs. 5.20 lacs in December 1982. This incidence was quoted to be one of the common robberies. But actually this was the beginning of terrorist activities of ULFA performed to finance armed struggle. Shortly after this i.e. in February 1983, elections were held

Table 6.1 Details of Terrorists Activities in North East (upto 31-12-2001)

States	*Total Incidence*	*Terrorists Killed*	*Terrorists Arrested*	*Protection Force Killed*	*Arms loot*	*Arms Recov-ered*	*Terrorists Surren-eted*	*Gen. Public killed*
Assam	458	282	173	80	42	285	304	248
Nagaland	128	65	80	01	-	96	59	16
Manipur	265	170	577	26	16	74	07	65
Tripura	370	30	547	36	23	95	373	237
Meghalaya	70	07	47	15	17	18	48	29
Mizoram	01	-	01	-	-	-	-	-
Arunachal Pradesh	46	20	31	18	13	22	06	05

in Assam. A number of ULFA members and sympathisers of ULFA were killed during these elections. Naturally these elections were termed as Bloody Elections'.

Considering the non-fruitfulness of Assam movement, ULFA members arrived at the decision of the final conflict. Finance was required to undertake armed struggle and also army training. For this the

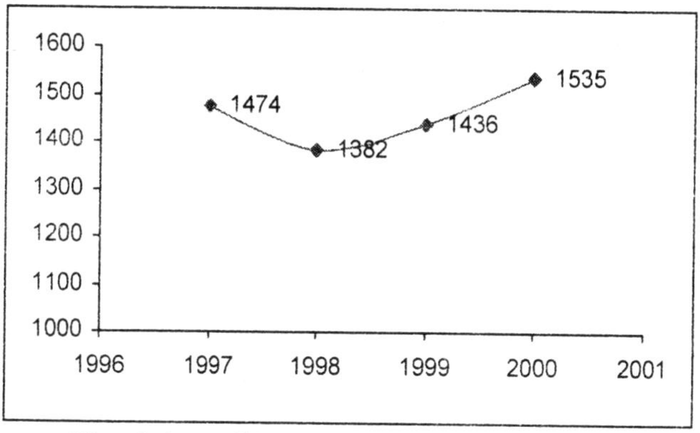

Fig. 6.1 : Militants Arrested in Assam.

Table 6.2 Number at Abductions and Killings in Assam

Year	*Abduction*	*Killing/ Murders*
1997	113	247
1998	148	392
1999	123	179
2000	111	254

ULFA members looted Rs 8 lacs from Silpubhari UKO Bank at Guwahati. About two hundred to three hundred ULFA members were sent to Myanmer for army training. An agreement between the revolutionaries and Central Government was entered into on the 15th August 1985. Then the organisation became nearly inactive. But by passage of time, interest of revolutionary members in Assam Gan

Parishad started breaking and their faith in AGP shaking. Next in this series of incidences was that these members had a meeting on the 6th of March 1987. It was decided in this meeting that those who were responsible for 'Bloody Elections of 83' should he punished. These members undertook the programmes of social and cultural development and improvement, side by side. These programmes were undertaken under the banner of so called Assam Communal Development Parishad. The ULFA claims 7th April 1979 as the date of its establishment but according to secret government information ULFA was legally constituted in October 1981. First five members of this organisations became its office bearers. They were (1) Buddheshwar Gogai (chairman) (2) Suren Dihingiya (vice chiarman) (3) Sommeshwar Gogai (advisor) (4) Bhimkant Burgohia (ambassedor) and (5) Pradip Gogoi (member). A draft constitution was also approved for the organisation on the same day. Bhupen Budhagohai, Bhadreshwar Gogai, Paresh Barua, Golap Barua, Chakra Gohai, Navneong, Kiran Barua, Davitra Gogai, Rajiv Rajkuwar and a number of other militant members from Dibrugarh and undivided Shivsagar districts joined ULFA as founder members.

As per Government statement first group of ULFA was sent to Myanmar for army training during July and August 1983 which returned in January 1984. While returning they brought with them China made M-20 pistol, Self loading Rifle and a sub machine gun along with other weapons. After this a number of trainees went to Myanmar and received weapon training. Bomb blast, Guerilla warfare and violence and as well as training of spreading terrorism. As per an official report about 300 ULFA members had their training at N.S.C.N. camps located in Chola area of Myanmar.

Declared Objectives of ULFA :- As per the constitution of ULFA its main object is to free Assam from India and implementation of Scientific Socialism in Assam added by paving way for revolutionary development of Assamese community.

Following objects are mentioned in the constitution of ULFA

(1) To make Assam a sovereign nation by way of armed revolution.

(2) To protect the interests of people from neighbouring states of Nagaland, Manipur, Mizoram, Meghalaya, Aruanachal Pradesh and Tripura along with that of Assam.

(3) To have total control of the state on all revenue sources of Assam such as Crude oil, Natural Gas, Forestry, etc.

(4) To gain public support against exploitation by India as well as non Indians.

(5) To stand against any kind of suppression of Assamese people.

(6) To oppose the powers aiming at specific and/ or common interest of the people

(7) To Consult those who believe in the objects of ULFA and gain their political support.

Organisational Rules : ULFA has two types of memberships.

(1) Local (2) Central. Local members are entrusted with the work of wall-painting, distribution of propaganda literature, communication and making lodging arrangement for central members when they happen to come to their place. These members are also organisers of local people for convincing them to join ULFA.

Central members have organised action squads. These members generally remain underground. Local member are also divided in various units. Each unit is entrusted with specific job. Generally such jobs are kept secret and not made known even to other units.

Code of Conduct for ULFA Members

Do's and Don'ts for ULFA activists **:-** The central underground wing of ULFA had framed the rules for Do and Don't for ULFA activists. This wing includes United Liberation Front of Assam and joint squad established for Assam freedom.

What to be seized and what not to be seized?

(1) Scooter, Motorcycle, Bicycle should not be forcibly acquired. If need there be such vehicles can be demanded by request and returned after the work is completed but this too can be done by obtaining prior permission of the District Parishad.

(2) Car and any such four wheeler should not be acquired without the prior permission of Dist. Commander. That too can be done in case of dire necessity.

(3) Every activist must travel either by bus or by bicycle. The activist may use car or motor only if badly needed.

Laws and Punishments

(1) Any common person from general public shall not be either publicly punished or executed unless Dist. Committee gives green signal.

(2) Dist. Parishads will convict a person only on submission of undoubted and sufficient proof.

(3) If any one criticises the organisation with noble intentions his criticism is welcome and if found concrete, his suggestion will be implemented.

Employment and Education

(1) ULFA activists shall create atmosphere for education

(2)) Any student connected with ULFA shall not resort to copying or any unfair means during the examination. He shall neither encourage such things.

(3) Bad system of Ragging of new students shall be totally stopped.

(4) Libraries will be established, conventions and Symposiums will be organised. Books depicting revolts will be read.

(5) Habit of merry making and unfruitful or unnecessary talks, specially at road side tea stalls and such other places will have to be stopped.

(6) Every ULFA activist must learn some handicraft so that he can earn his own bread.

Culture and Conduct

(1) Pay respect to elderly people

(2) Stop Goondaism

(3) Be polite and conservative in expenditure

Religion, Language and Culture

(1) Give respect to other religion, language and culture.

(2) Be connected with some social organisation.

Warning

One who does not follow the above conduct rules should be prepared to pay the cost.

Beginning of Exploitation of Businessmen and Tea Gardens

Construction of road, stopping sex traffic, banning consumption of liquor, etc., were some of the social works undertaken by the ULFA. Because of this ULFA started gaining sympathy and support from the people. Requirement of finance for this was started to be met by this militant organisation by exploiting the businessmen and Tea gardens. This was the beginning.

The ULFA demanded a large amount from Girdharilal Hartalka, the ex-chairman of Kamrup chamber of commerce in October 1988. He was murdered on the 15th October 1988 as he refused to pay the ransom. This murder spread a wave of terror in the business community. This fear reached the high tide when on 20th January 1990, Shankarlal Birmiwal, the chairman of Kamroop Chamber of Commerce was also killed by the ULFA. Late Birmiwal had made a 'Call of Bandh' in protest of ransom recovered by the ULFA activists, though the ULFA had warned him not to do so.

Again Shri Surendra Pal, chairman of Assam Frontier and brother of industrialist Swaraj Pal was murdered in Tensukhiya on 9th April 1990 in broad day light. This spread terror in the region where the ULFA had more impact i.e. Dibrugarh, Shiosagar, Mhedaji, Lakhimpur, Shonitpur, Mangade, Nagaon, Guwahati etc. As a result a number of businessmen and industrialists from the area started closing their establishments and leaving Assam.

On the other side AGP (Assam Gan Parishad) government in Assam was not getting success in stopping the ULFA activities. Eventually the AGP government was being accused of encouraging the ULFA. Meanwhile huge amounts of ransom were being collected from the businessmen added by murders of political leaders. ULFA was bent upon finishing the Congress leaders and their supporters. By now about eight Congress leaders were killed.

The ULFA activists and supporters had good approaches in Administration as well as police force. Naturally the police department was also not daring to do anything against them. This caused demoralisation of police force.

Meanwhile on 15th July 1990 the ULFA activists abducted Shri H. L. K Das, Managing Director of Guwahati refinery alongwith his son and driver. They put forth the demand of release of three of their personnel for safe release of Shri Das and others. The demand was accepted and an agreement was made. As a result three hard-core ULFA activists including Hirakjyoti Mahant were released on the 29th July 1990. But the same day Shri Daulat Singh Nege the S.P. of Dibrugarh was killed by throwing a bomb at him. This murder, further, demoralised the police.

During the days of such violence the ULFA started increasing its strength by enrolling new members. This is evident from the fruitless efforts of Assam Government to stop this militancy and the parallel government of ULFA was doing well in the state. The people of Assam also regarded ULFA as a seat of Justice. The situation went to the extent that the then Chief Minister Shri Prafulla Kumar Mohant started finding Robinhood face in ULFA.

Propaganda Secretary of ULFA Siddharth Fukan called a number of Press Conferences during 1989 to 1991. He put forth the principle of Sovereign Socialist Assam. The reason quoted by him was Assam was not a part of India in 1826 when Yandabu agreement was signed between British and Burma and therefore ULFA adopted armed struggle for the fulfilment of the demand. As a matter of fact the Assamese people were divided on this issue.

Operation 'Bajrang' against ULFA :- Considering the increasing terrorism and Government (Assam) inefficiency in curbing it, the central government dissolved the state government and implemented 'President Rule' in Assam. The same time the government banned the ULFA. This was on the 28th November 1990. The government simultaneously started "Operation Bajrang" against ULFA.

This operation went on from 2nd November 90

up to 19th April 1991. But it also could not be quite successful. This is evident from the fact that no top ULFA leaders could be caught but the army destroyed almost all camps of ULFA and also their communication network. About 3000 activists were also arrested. But the army could not trace out ULFA top leaders. Eventually the Operation Bajrang was stopped and the army was sent back to their Headquarters.

Meanwhile the ULFA declared cease-fire unilaterally and allowed the elections to pass out peacefully in May 91. Congress (I) was elected to power in this election. But on 30th June 1991 when Shri Saikia alongwith 36 member cabinet took oath, the ULFA abducted fourteen officers. These officers included Personnel department secretary Shri. S.K. Tiwari, Supply Superintendent Ranjit Das, Deputy general Manager of Oil and Natural Gas Commission of Jorhat Shri Narendra Sharma, Chief Geologist Bholanath Jayaswal, Deputy Manager of Stores and Marketing Shri Shiosunder Gupta, Superintending Engineer C. R Mohanti, ONGC Engineer Keshao Pal, T S Raju, B.P. Shrivastava, Russian Engineer Grishchiko Sargsai.

Demand for release of arrested supporters

ULFA demanded the release of all its members and supporters who were arrested during the Operation Bajrang. Primarily Shri Saikia responded to the demand and agreed to release those, against whom no special chargesheet was filed. But the ULFA took it as Government's weakness and started putting forth many demands. Meanwhile the ULFA executed T. S. Raju and V. P. Shrivastava. These killings added fuel to the fire and the situation took a serious turn. As a result the army was called on 14th September at midnight and another 'Operation Rhino' was started. The army was made known about the Assamese culture and other connected things with a view to avoid the recurrence of mistakes of Operation Bajrang. Thereby expected results started coming.

ULFA secretary general Golap Barua alias Anup Chetai was arrested at Calcutta along with his wife Joly Barua and two other ULFA leaders. Immediately after this arrest important information and clues started pouring in and strong ULFA activitsts were rounded up. Deputy Commander of ULFA Jyoti Mahant was killed in clash at Guwahati. Other leaders including propaganda Chief Siddharth Fukan were also arrested. ULFA Chief Rai Khowa and commander-in-chief Paresh Barua could not be rounded up.

***Cease fire Declaration*:** Operation Rhino destroyed the ULFA to greatest extent. As a result the ULFA declared unilateral sease fire on 17th December 1991. The ULFA declared its acceptance of constitution of India and their preparedness for peaceful talks. Considering the change in the approach of ULFA and to bring normalcy in the situation for talks, top leaders Golap Barua, SIddharth Fukam and some other leaders were released from the jail. According to the report of Home Ministry of Govt. of India (2000) top and active leaders of ULFA are Arvind Rajkhowa (chairman), Paresh Barua (Commander in chief), Sash Choudhary (Foreign secretary) Raju Barua (commander of operation wing) Asanta Bagh Fukan and Pranati Deka (both high profile leaders). The report further states that the impact of ULFA is in Nalwali, Nagaoan, Jorhat, Dibrugarh, Rangia, Tinsukhiya and Guwahati in the state. The ULFA has relations with I.S.I., LTTE, People Liberation Army, Bodo Liberation Tigers force etc., They have their camps at Jaflang in Bangladesh alongwith Moulawi Bajar, Marshala, Sukmi, Koypani and Orang in Butan.

If the situation is looked at and considered as a third party one can quote that the following reasons are responsible for the spread of ULFA activities in Assam.

(i)Free transportation of militants-terrorists along with arms and ammunition because of open boundaries.

(ii)Inefficient and corrupt administration.

(iii)Demoralised police force for some reason or the other.

(iv)Infiltration of ULFA supporters in administration and police force and

(v) all type of cooperation by Pakistan supported I.S.I.

Demand of Separate Bodoland - Terrorism and Terrorist activities

Of the various tribes in Assam, Bodo tribes formed a major part. Their population is about 42.96 lacs. As per the history Bodos came to Assam during 5th century and stayed in Brahmaputra valley. They came from Central Asia.

During 15th century Ahoms came from eastern part. They attacked Brahmaputra valley and established their control. They drove away the Bodo tribes to the plains. Clashes and small battles between the Bodos and Ahoms continued for about 300 years. Finally the Bodos inhabited themselves in Northern plains of Brahmaputra valley. Area of Kokarazadi and Ubalzudi has about 90% population belonging to Bodo tribes. While Bodos, in smaller and larger number are living in Rengia, North Lakhimpur, Sadia, Barpeta, Darang, Nalwadi also.

Bodo Tribes are known for their different language, culture and clothing. Rest of India was ignorant about the Bodo tribes till 1985-86. But when they started their movement for Separate State on the lines of Assam movement that is in 1985-86 they came in contact with rest of India. This made the people to take interest in Bodos.

Old demand of Bodoland **:-** It is not the fact that the Bodos started demanding Bodoland only in the eighties. But their demand is quite old. For the first time in 1927 they demanded separate Bodoland from the then British government. The Kachhari (Bodo) youth had organised a convention in those days when Simon Commission was in India. They passed a resolution in that convention and submitted their demand for separate identification of Bodo tribes and for forming separate Kachhari regiment.

The tribals living in hilly areas of North East persuaded their demand after India's independence. As a result the states of Nagaland and Mizoram were formed during 1962 to 72. In the same way new states of Meghalaya and Arunachal Pradesh were also formed But the tribes in the plains lagged behind among which Bodo tribes the are main.

Main problem of Economic Backwardness

Social and economic backwardness is the main problem of Bodo tribals. According to official information 70% of the Bodo population is land-less though 90% of the population is fully dependant on agriculture. Land of this area is under the control of outsiders for a pretty long period. The AGP government of Assam did also accept that about 2.5 Lac acres of the land is in possession and control of outsiders. The central government interfered in the Bodo clash and called for tri-party talks in 1989. But these talks could not produce any result. The same way Janta Dal government at centre also had a number of meetings with concerned parties but with no result.

The Bodo tribal wanted to protect their identity,

self respect and for this they pay more stress on the demand of separate state for them. They formed a student organisation 'Akhil Bodo Student Union' (ABSU) and a political party Assam Maidan Janjatiya Parishad (PTCA) in 1967. Shortly after its formation the PTCA was divided but the demand for separate Bodo Movement continued.

The seriousness of Bodo movement can be known from the fact that this movement was carried on, on the lines of the movement of AASU and AGSP which was carried on during 1979 to 1985.

According to the Assam agreement of 1985 the youth leaders came in power. But within a year after assuming power these leaders had to face a number of difficulties. The plan to eradicate foreigners from Assam was still under preparation and the Bodo movement flared up. This was the reason why the Chief Minister Prafulla Kumar Mahanto had to call the army to curb the serious, violent and attacking Bodo Movement in 1989.

During this movement the Bodo youth resorted to burning houses. The situation took a serious turn when these youth started attacking the protection forces and started seizing arms from them. Non Assamese started fleeing from Bodo area. The movement became still dangerous when they started aiming at government employees. Routine life was totally disturbed because of 'Bandh' calls. Bomb blasts in trains, on railway track and other places enlightened the terror and seriousness of the movement

Strategies behind the Curtain of Movement

The Bodo activists put 92 demands before the government. Main demands of these were -

1) To create an independent state of Bodo land on the North of Brahmputra.

2) To create an autonomous district for tribal area on the south of Brahmaputra.

3) To include Bodo Kachharis of Karbo Anglang in the Sixth schedule of the Constitution

4) To provide maximum reservations to Bodos.

5) To include Bodo language in eighth- schedule of the constitution.

The then Chief Minister Prafulla Kumar Mohanto and Home Minister Bhrugul Kumar Fukan told that almost all demands related to social and economic development can be accepted, but Assam shall not be further divided. Thus, the government denied the creation of Bodoland. Shri Mahanto and Shri Fukan convened a meeting of Bodo leaders. But alike other meetings this meeting also could not produce any result.

On the other side of this movement, a stage was being created to formulate political strategies under the disguise of this movement. The AGP which was in power blamed the Congress to encouraging the Bodo terrorist and activities. The then social welfare minister Sushri Rekharani Das accused the Central Minister of states Shri Mohan Das that he had a secret agreement with the ABSU leaders. Meanwhile many Bodo leaders started saying that this problem can be resolved only by armed revolution. The same time Shri K N. Hazari of ABSU formed armed 'Bodo Security Force' to save the Bodo tribal from the dual policy of Assam leaders and AGP. A camp for training Bodo Youth was established in dense forest of Bhutan along with a underground gun factory.

Sensing the seriousness of this movement and violent determination of the Bodo leaders the Mahanto Government took initiative and requested them to have a meeting on the 28th February 1989. But the Bodo leaders were prepared for the talks only if their demand for separate Bodoland was to be considered. Naturally the talks failed. Then the home minister of Assam Bhrugu Kumar Fukan wrote a strong letter to the central government alleging the central government for having direct hand in the Bodo movement.

After blaming the central government the AGP government in Assam started strict action against the ABSU militants. As a result many of its top leaders fled away to Meghalaya, West Bengal and Myanmar. As per Shri Fukan, demand for separate state is irrelevant as Kokrazad which was supposed to be Bodo majority district had only 27% population belonging to Bodo tribes.

The Bodos accused the government for police atrocities on them. Some incidences of burning their houses as well as rape also come to light. On the other side, Bodos started feeling danger to their language and culture by way of imposing Assamese language on them. While Shri Fukan said that all the residents of Brahmaputra valley are outsiders and there are no tribes (Adivasis). As such every one living in Assam is Assamee. As the suppression of Bodo movement by AGP government started increasing, the Bodos were becoming more violent and started accusing the AGP that it is a party of some special class of Hindus.

After the death of ABSU chairman Upendranath Brahma, it was felt that the Bodo movement was going to go direction-less. But in a very short period Shri Vishwamutiari was made chairman. He continued the movement and always maintained pressure on state as well as Central Government. As a result after tri-party talks the central government appointed a committee under the chairmanship of Shri Bhupendra Singh to find a permanent solution. The committee had three members (19th September 1990).

Proposal for Greater Autonomy **:-** The expert committee was asked to submit its report by 31st October 1991. But because of the delay in Census operations the committee could not submit the report in time. Again the ninth tri-party talks took place on the 7th January 1992. But no unanimous decision could be made.

Other Militant Organisation in BODO area

(a) ***National Democratic Front of Bodoland*** **:-** This terrorist organisation formed in nineties is active and engaged in efforts of severing the Bodo area from the country. The government of India declared this organisation as illegal and banned it. They were engaged in collecting ransom and appointing unemployed Bodo youth in its private army. In the beginning this organisation was working under the name of Bodo Security Force (BSF) and this organisation was working for abducting the businessmen, government employees and the common people as well, for getting ransom. The organisation had its units at every village and district places. This organisation killed 171 persons during the period from 23rd November 1998 to 30th June 2001. They established their camps in the border area of the country and the NDFB was operating from these camps. NDFB had also joined hands with ULFA and NSCN for separating Bodoland from India.

(b) ***Bodo Liberation Tigers*** **:-** Though independent and different from other organisations BLT was engaged in killing, abduction, looting, etc., under the pretext of separate Bodoland. The government of India has banned this organisation also. It is said that BLT killed about 15 Bhutani citizens in December 2000 by joining hands with NDFB.

(c) ***Bodoland Tigers Force*** **:-** This (BTF) organisation is also active in this region, operating on the lines of BLT and NDFB for the same object.

Karbo Anglang Movement and Terrorism

Apart from Bodo and ULFA, Assam has one more problem that is troubling Assam and it is the demand for separate state of Karbo Anglang. Various tribes in Assam are struggling for their social, cultural, economic and political rights as they are ruled by non-tribal upper class Assamese groups for a long period and are not satisfied by that rule.

Karbo tribes from the hilly district of Anglang are struggling for autonomous state for the last 15 years. The basis on which the demand for Karbo Anglang state has come up is not new. It has its roots in the Assam Reorganisation Act of 1969. The Assam leaders while passing the above Act promised the Mikir and North Kachhar hill tribes that they may be given autonomy if they are not included in Meghalaya, though this area is joined with Garo, Khasi and Jayantiya hills. An option was also given under which they were allowed to be part of Meghalaya. Two autonomous Zilla Parishads were established in this area under the same arrangement. A provision was also made in para 244(a) of Indian constitution that an autonomous state will be given whenever the people of these districts desire so. The ASDC had taken this base for its demand for autonomous state.

People demanding autonomous state say that Assam government did not pay proper attention to the development of their area even after the creation of new states from Assam. According to them, though there is autonomic administration in District Parishads, these DPs do not possess proper authority in that their budget is prepared by the Assam government, they do not have right to create jobs as well as make appointments. The District Parishads do not have any authority in the development plans also. That is why there is growing dissatisfaction in the people.

The ASDC is in power for so many years in the region. Even then it is running the movement . This may be the lone sample wherein a ruling party is conducting movement. The ASDC leaders always supported thc Assam movement. The Assam movement was stopped after the settlement of the issues by the Rajiv Gandhi government at centre on 15th August 1985. The ASDC still has occupied the office at Difu in the District Parishad and has not called off its movement. Following are the militant organisations of Karbo Angland

(1) Karbo Volunteers Froce (KVF)

(2) Karbo National Volunteers (KNV) and

(3) United People Democratic Solidarity (UPDS) : The only aim of these organisations is to press for their demand for separate state, through violence and terrorist activities. They adopt the way of abduction, ransom and even killing of non-Karbo people. Another organisation was formed in March 1999 in the name of UPDS. This organisation absorbed two other terrorists organisations Karbo National Volunteers (KNV) (2) Karbo Peoples Front with them. But they were divided in two groups in 2001 at the time of peace talks. (1) Group Supporting talks and (2) Group Opposing talks.

This organisation is flaring the emotions of Karbo tribes against non Karbo people, specially Biharis. The UPDS made ghastly attack ont he Bihari labour. Kiti Rongkar is the chairman and Horen Singh is the supreme commander of this organisation. Both were arrested on the 22nd October 1999. As such this organisation is now doing its activities under its Lieutnent Secretary Lin Timung.

Other Militant Organisations of Assam and Their Area of Activities

(a) Kamtapur Liberation organisation (KLO) and

(b) Koch Rajwanshi Security Force (KRSF); (c) Rabha National Security Force (RNSF) (d) Dimacha Halong Daogo (DHD) and (e) Muslim Liberation Tigers of Assam (MULTA). KLO and KRSF are doing their activities and demanding a separate state of Kamtapur which includes Western Assam and Northern part of West Bengal. As a matter of fact a number of militants from these organisations have surrendered. Since then their activities are as good as stopped. It is also said that these organisations had established contacts with ULFA and Bodo. It is mentionable that the Koch Rajwanshi people are the residents of Kooch Bihar, Jalpaigudi, Darjeeling of North West Bengal and Ghubaddi, Bongaigaon, Gwalpara, Kokdazar and nearby area of Western Assam. Their aim was to secure the right of plebiscite for the people of Kamtapur area. This has a specific reason also, which was the illegal infiltration of Bangladeshis in large number and illegal occupation of lands by them. This caused danger to self respect and culture of Koch Rajwanshi people. The Koch Rajwanshi people ruled West Bengal and a large part of Western Assam in 15th Century.

Terrorism and Militant Organisations in Meghalaya

Terrorism in Meghalaya started in early eighties after the start of ULFA activities in peaceful Assam. Though Meghalaya has joint border with Assam and Bangladesh the terrorists did not have their eyes on this peaceful valley of Meghalaya. Frequent infiltration by Bangladesh army jawans and engaging themselves in violence is still going on. But the ULFA terrorists used to cross Meghalaya border after preforming any terrorists activities in Assam. As a result Local Khasi and Garo youth also engaged themselves in collecting ransom and started exploiting regionalism. These youth were specially troubling the businessmen who came from outside, Nepalese and Bengalese etc. Terrorists activities started in Meghalaya on the second August 1990 when the local youth accepted and adopted regionalism. It actually started when some youth of Federation of Khasi Jayantiya and Garo people (FKJGP) came to Bada Bazar area of Shillong and started demanding documents of trading licence and other connected things. They not only terrorised the businessmen but misbehaved with them also. As a result the businessmen kept the market closed for three days. This founded a deep crack between these two groups.

The same time the FKJGP started convincing the adivasi-tribes of this area that if all the non tribals and businessmen go out of the region, they will have full control on the Bada Bazar which may lead to decreasing unemployment and thereby improving the social and economic conditions of Adivasis tribals. Closure of market posed many difficulties before the people in general, But the FKJGP took its benefit in an other way. It encouraged the Khasi youth to start movement against trading community. The FKJGP put five shops of Bengalese on fire.

Now the media also started publishing the statements of terrorists in a respectful manner. Leaders of local students union published their statements in newspapers for giving ultimatum to the outsiders to leave Meghalaya. It seemed that there was no government administration and the area was ruled by these terrorist organisations. According to unofficial figures there are 200 to 300 hard-core terrorists in the state. Rise of HNLC is required to be viewed by peeping in past. The Khasi Students Union (KSU) had put two demands before the Meghalaya government headed, that time, by Captain Sangma. It is said that the government did not accept any of the demands. As a result a group of KSU formed this new organisation HNLC.

This organisation was divided in two parts during nineties. (1) HNLC and (2) ANVC. But the Meghalaya government did not pay any attention to this division. The same way majority of the people also did not take notice of it. Till this time the organisations were regarded as revolutionaries. But these organisations started giving their orders to the people Abduction, ransom and killings became day -to-day activities of them. According to general public corruption, unemployment and decreasing confidence in political leaders are some of the reasons why these organisations could continue. As a matter of fact the State Government had recommended to the Central Government to ban these organisations. At present there are four separatist organisations which are not banned.

(a) Hinutrape Achik Liberation Council (HALC) : This organisation is more active in Garo and Khasi area. The regionalism has reached to such a height that it enjoys public support to a great extent. But for outsiders this organisation is like a villain. Every now and then collecting money from businessmen, bank robberies, declaration of Bandh, burning of shops and establishment are their activities. This organisation came into existence in 1989-90 and started demanding separate Garo Khasi Land. It has its connections with NSCN, ULFA etc.

(b) *Hinutrape National Liberation council (HNLC)* : This organisation is also separatist organisation and is much active in Khasi area. It operates on the lines of HALC. It was formed in 1991.

(c) *Achik Liberation Matgrik Army (ALMA)* : This organisation is also known for its violence and terrorist activities. It was formed in 1995. It demands separate Garoland. Its activities are in Garo area.

(d) ***Achik National Volunteers Council (ANVC)*** : This organisation too is demanding separate Garoland and operates on the lines of above mentioned organisations. Its chief is Shamark.

These organisations believe that their areas can not be developed till the business and trade in this area is in the hands of outsiders.

Terrorist Organisations in Tripura

Terrorism is in existence in this state more specifically for the last 20 years. Actually militancy in this state started right back in 1960, when Bengalese came to this area in a very large number. Entry of Bengalese in this area posed a danger of going in minority by the original residents. They started revolting in a violent way. Tripura National volunteers- a terrorist organisation was founded in the seventies. Shri Vijay Hankhal was leading the organisation. But he produced himself before the administration in 1988. As a result the TNV became dead. Following militants organisations are at present operating in Tripura.

(a) ***National Liberation Front of Tripura (NLFT)*** : This organisation was founded in December 1989 with an aim to separate Tripura from India and to declare it as a Christian Nation. It is said that the Church provided all sort of legal as well as illegal helping hand to this organisation. It established its training camps at Rija, Risalong, Myani reserve forest, Japai and Chatgoan hilly areas. Because of its anti-national activities the Govt. of India, declared it as illegal organisation and banned it in 1997. With a view to save themselves this organisation established its camps in Bangladesh. According to report of the state government, camps of NLFT were working on Bangladesh border. About 200 persons were undergoing training in these camps (Report of May 2000)

(b) ***All Tripura Tigers Force (ATTF)*** : This organisation, too, is a separatist organisation and dreams of freeing Tripura by terrorist activities. It also operates on the lines of other such organisations. As a matter of fact its activities were decreased during 2001.

Terrorist Organisations of Manipur

Many separatist organisations were active in this state from time to time. Revolutionary Government of Manipur was founded in 1965. This was a separatist organisation. Its command was in the hands of Samarendra Singh. But this organisation was scattered in 1980.

Struggle for supremacy between the Kooki and Naga tribes is a common thing in this state. They had a number of armed battles between them right from independence of India which cost many lives from both the sides. There are many militant organisations in the state. But now only six such organisations are active, even though they are banned.

(a) ***Peoples Liberation Army (PLA)*** : This organisation was formed in 1980 under the leadership of Vishweshwar Singh. Another organisation Peoples Revoluntery Party of Kanglipal (PREPAK) was also formed in 1980. This organisation engaged itself in collecting big amounts from traders, banks, money lenders, contractors, government officials and other wealthy people. With a view to gain public support in its activities it started Anti drug movement. It warned the people that they could be executed if they consume drugs. This created a wave of sympathy for this organisation and public in general started praising these activists. This organisation had its camps at Chhottodhamai, Nayapattan, Longla, Ramnager, Ambur Khana, Adampur and Sonarpa Tea Estate in Moulavi Bazar region of Bangladesh.

This organisation killed the principal of a Catholic school only because he was found to be engaged in drug trade and other vices in early nineties. But PLA afterwards changed its procedure. Now they started sending demand notes, to traders, contractors, Govt. officers asking them to pay certain amount within a given period. The then Chief Minister late Ranvirsingh did also accept that the government officials had also received such notes

(b) ***Peoples Revolutionary Party of Kangliwal (PREPAK)*** : This organisation was formed by division of PLA in 1980. It was led by K Tulchandra Singh. This organisation was full of regionali and separatist feelings. But it could not continue after the death of K. Tulchandra Singh.

(c) ***United National Liberation Front (UNLF)*** : This organisation was operating on the lines of PLA.

(d) Kangalipak Communist Party (KCP)

(e) Kangli Iole Kanva Loop (KIKL)

(f) Manipur Peoples Liberation front (MPLF). are other such organisations.

Terrorism and Terrorist Organisations in Arunachal Pradesh

Being the border state of Assam and Nagaland added by impact of Christian missionaries from Nagaland as well as ULFA and other terrorist organisations, Arunachal Pradesh is also succumbing to terrorism as its border line youth are cultivating the regionalism and separatism feelings. Even then militancy in this area is in primary state. There was no militancy in this area prior to 1980 and the area was considered to be peaceful valley of Arunachal Pradesh.

Presently main activity of the militants here is to collect money from the traders, government employees coming from outside. Following are main militant organisations which are not banned.

(a) United Liberation Volunteers of Arunachal Pradesh (ULVAP)

(b) United Peoples Volunteers of Arunachal Pradesh (UPVAP)

(c) United Liberation Movement of Arunachal Pradesh (ULMAP)

Militancy and Militant Organisation Mizoram

Tribals of this area revolted against Government of India for an independent sovereign country for them. This was in sixties. The revolt took place under the leadership of Laldenga and was continued for 25 years. Finally they had to bow down and arrive at a respectable agreement. Final draft of agreement between Laldenga and the then Prime Minister Rajiv Gandhi was signed in 1986 which is known as Mizo agreement. As a result separate state of Mizoram was created legally and Laldenga became the first Chief Minister.

As per the state government, Mizoram, at present, does not have any militant activity. Stray incidences of group clashes in the state are due to the communal strains. But the fact is something else. There are a number of organisations coming up like mushrooms. Their activities are similar to militant activities.

Mizoram has a Tribal organisation of Hamars. It is known as Hamar people convention (HPC). This organisation collects money forcibly for the upliftment of their tribes. At times it resorts to violent activities also.

Militancy and Militant Organisations in Nagaland

Of all the North Eastern states Nagaland has worst militancy. Militancy or terrorism always has its impact in some form or the other right from the independence of India. The converted Nagas to Chritianity, joined together in 1947 and demanded a Christian Nagaland Nation. The government of India, that time, received information that some foreign missionaries working in Nagaland were behind this movement. As a result these missionaries were expelled from India.

Another movement for a sovereign Nagaland Nation came up in 1955 and movement for that was started under the leadership of Japu Angami Fijo. Thus, Nagaland was stormed with the wave of separatism and for that revolt. Japu Angami Fijo ran away from Nagaland to London in 1957 where he died on 23rd May 1991. Even after the death of Angami the fire of sovereign Nagaland which was lighted by him is still burning in Nagaland. Although the Naga Rashtriya Parishad founded by Angami Fijo is now totally dead and Thus, inactive. But then a number of separatist organisations came up. Of these Nationalist Socialist Council of Nagaland (NSCN) rose up as the most active organisation. This organisation, too, was divided into two groups in 1988. One part is active in Nagaland under the leadership of T. H. Muwaiwa. The other part is active in the Burma border area under the leadership of Khaplang. The government of India declared both these organisations as anti-national and put a ban on them..

Though terrorism existed always in Nagaland on a smaller or bigger extent, it had assumed a serious turn in nineties. As a result it has become very difficult for non-Nagas to live in this state. It is a noticeable thing that Marwaseis, Assamese, Bengalese, Biharis, and Udia community people are living in the area of Dimapur, Mom Twensang and other remote areas of Nagland. They belong to trade, Govt. or private employment and labour class. Non Nagas are called here as 'People from Plains'. There is no law and order existing in this area. Every now and then the terrorists organisations warn them to leave Nagaland immediately. These non-Naga people are now losing their belief in the government promises. Government employees are forced to pay tax to these organisations. If some one hesitates, he is terrorised and made to pay tax. Eventually many outsiders have sent back their families.

Dimapur is the only business centre in Nagaland. The law and order situation here was quite satisfactory but during the period prior to 1977. But the revolt and violence erupted in 1977 frightened the non-Nagas, to such an extent that there remained no courage in them to resist the Nagas i.e. the original residents of Nagaland. The politicians having regionalism added fuel to the situation and strengthened the division between Nagas and people from plains. Now the situation is that the militants enter anybody's house, ransack it and loot any amount available. The frightened dwellers can not resist them. Many business establishments are now closed as a result of such terrorists activities. Many of the traders have already left Nagaland. The Rajyapal of Nagaland Shri Omprakash Sharma, while inaugurating the 9th session of assembly said that the people in Nagaland are now fed up with terrorism and they want to lead a peaceful life. That is why they have declared a number of places as peace zones. All this clearly shows that the people here want peace. He further said that the rate of killings and violence is quite low during the last three years when cease-fire was declared by NSCN and the central government.

The Rajyapal further stressed that the law and order situation was gradually improving. He told that there were on an average 17 murders per month prior to the cease-fire. There were killings during the first month after the cease-fire. As a matter of fact these murders were made out of gang wars. During the three years of cease-fire there were only 85 murders in the state whereas during the three years prior to cease-fire the number was 282.

The Chief Minister of Nagaland Shri Loramthanga mediated between the central government and the NSCN during the talks held at Bangkok on 8-9 November 2000. He had already submitted his report to the central government.

At present the following militant organisations are operating in the state.

(a) National Socialist Council of Nagaland (Ishak Muaiwa) : This organisation was founded in 1988 under the leadership of T. H. Muaiwa. Afterwards Ishak also played an important role in this organisation. Actually this organisation is working for separate Nagaland nation and its leaders control and run the organisation from foreign countries. This organisation has a good hold on the Naga tribes of this state. Its training camps are operating at Salopi and Chhakheng situated in Chitgoan hills of Bangaladesh and hills of Myanmar.

This organisation receives massive aid from foreign agencies. In addition its activists are to collect money from local traders, Govt. employees, etc., by threatening them.

(b) National Socialist Council of Nagaland (Khaplang) : The second division of NACN is led by Khaplang. Its pressure area is border areas of Myanmar. This is also at separatist organisation and operates on the lines of the other group led by Muaiwa. Its victims are the transporters and contractors.

(c) Naga National Council (Adino)/Naga Federal government

(d) Naga National Council (Khodao)

(e) Pangal United Front (PUF)

Chapter 7

Terrorism-Separatism Role of Christian Missionaries and I.S.I.

As a matter of fact people belonging to all races, religions and creeds live in North Eastern states. But Mizoram, Nagaland and Meghalaya have maximum Christians. Percentage of Christian population as per 1991 census is 87.47 in Nagaland, 85.73 in Mizoram and 64.58 in Meghalaya (see table 7.1). According to 1991 census the population of Christians in India is 1.88 crores which is 2.3% of total population. Of the Christian population 44% stay in North Eastern states of India.

History tells that Christian population in these states was very less during the pre-independence period, more specifically before the Britishers entered this area through Burma. Maximum population was belonging to Hindus. Christian missionaries followed the Britishers to this area. The inhabitants of this area were very backward and were leading their lives in poverty. These missionaries took advantages of this. They showed colourful dreams of better standards of life, and so on. They started health and education services for them and distributed money also on the pretext of help. Thus, this allurement was encashed by the missionaries who started converting them to Christianity. Mizoram, Nagaland and Meghalaya had greatest impact of conversion. As a result more than 80% of the population became Christian. The missionaries tried to spread their philosophy to Manipur and Tripura also. But the Hindu culture in these areas has deep bonds with Indian and Hindu culture. Naturally their efforts could not be fruifful to that extent. Christian population in Arunachal Pradesh was 10% in 1981. It increased to 17.5% by 1991.

Table 7.1 Christian Population in North East

States	*Percentage (1991)*
Meghalaya	64.58
Tripura	18.00
Mizoram	85.73
Nagaland	87.47
Manipur	34.11
Arunachal Pradesh	17.5

Programme of conversion of simple, poor, Scheduled Castes and Tribes was on its rise till the eighties. According to Christian historian Shri F. S. Dawn, the percentage of Christian population was increased by 64 % during 20 years from 1951 to 1971. This overall percentage was 171 in all North Eastern states (Nagaland 215.6% and Tripura 298%) According to him there were only 50,000 churches in India at the time of independence. The number is increased to 3,69,0681 by 1971. There are about 45 thousand churches only in North East region. If we believe in the statement made by Hindu Manch, it comes to light that an organisation named Operation Mission has published a book '*Operation World*' which has a mention of conversion and its strategy in India. This mention of conversion in India starts from page 273 of this book. A map of India is printed and published in this book on page 273. This map shows that Arunachal Pradesh is not the part of India. Total conversion of Arunachal Pradesh population to Christianity by 2000 is aimed at in this book. Accordingly it has come to light that the Christian population in this state has increased to 10% by 1981 from 0.8% in 1971. It is further stated on page 477 of the book *Operation Mission* that the church at Imphal, the capital city of Manipur has yearly budget of Rs 20 Lacs for converting 100 persons. This church has aimed at 100 such churches during coming 10 years.

According to Hindu Manch, Churches receive huge financial aid from foreign countries. This amount comes to India in the names of various non government organisations. From here it is transferred to missionaries for using it towards conversion. Indian Home Minister Shri Lal Krishna Advani had made a statement in 1998 wherefrom it is evident that 70% of such financial aid reached the missionaries. According to statistics of Home Ministry an amount of Rs 19.80 crores comes to India of which an amount of about 14 crores is shared by these missionaries. According to the ministry, the countries which sent such aid are America, Switzerland, Britain, Germany and Italy. According to an estimate 70% of foreign grants go to these Christian missionaries.

Table 7.2 Details of Money Received by Churchesin India from Foreign Countries

Year	*Total Aid (Cr. Rs.)*	*Share of Northeast (Cr.Rs.)*
1970	120	84
1979	300	210
1985	600	420
1998	700*	490

* Rs. 1980 as per home Ministry

Note :- Milk powder, clothing and medicines are given separately.

As a matter of fact the movements of Laldenga in Mizoram and of Fijo in Nagaland could be run on the basis of such aid received from foreign countries. It is a common theme in these Christian majority states, that is to threaten, abduct and kill the non-Christian and specially Hindu traders and collect ransom from them. The situation that all the shops and establishments are closed by 6 p.m. daily is self evident in this regard. Local government as well as the police find themselves disabled in this regard. If any one refuses to pay money to the youth coming in groups, its results are terrific. News items published in the newspapers are the eyewitness of the situation.

Role of Church in Spreading Terrorism

The education and culture which is being preached in the children and youth in Christian majority states is in no way connected to Indian culture. The things and subject matter included in the school and college syllabus in these states are such that all the castes, tribes, etc., can not get acquainted with Indian culture and thereby restrict the youth in these states from joining mainstream of India. These states are producing the population which feels happy in degrading and dishonouring the rest of India. They think themselves belonging to western culture specially the churches.

The North eastern states where terrorism is on large scale are the states of Nagaland, Tripura, Mizoram and Meghalaya i.e. the Christian majority states. Missionaries from other religions than Christian are not allowed to work in these states. There are a number of terrorist organizations which always aim at non-Christians. They abduct them and also kill them. Most important things in these states is that the total politics here has great influence and impact of churches.

Following paragraphs give the state-wise analysis of direct and/or indirect support of churches to terrorism.

Mizoram

Out of the total population of 8,91,058 of Mizoram 7,63,940 are Christians. (percentage being 85.73) Following are some examples showing how the non Christians in this state are troubled by atrocities.

Example 1: Riyang tribes in Mizoram originally belong to Hindu religion. Their population is about 70,000. Christian militants drove them away from Mizoram in September-October 1997. As a result they were required to take shelter in refugee camps in Kanchanpur division of Tripura. The reason quoted for this expulsion was communal. Whereas the fact is that the Christian in majority could not tolerate them in the state. The Human rights organisation visited these camps in October 1999 and the Mizoram government assured the Central Government that it will call back these Riyand tribes to the state. But even today the situation is not normalised.

Example 2 : During the Mizo movement of eighties the Christian terrorists put on fire the Radhakrishan temple situated in the centre of Iswal and completely destroyed it. It was rebuilt by the army.

Example 3 : About a thousand terrorists belonging to Christian community entered the Assam border near Helakandi. They were armed with rockets. They spread terrible violence there in that they destroyed by putting ablaze 171 houses, 2 temples and 2 schools. Important things in this was that all these belonged to Hindu community whereas the

Christian families in that area did not suffer any loss rather they were deliberatedy saved. The same way some youth activists of young Mizo Association distributed pamphlets to the residents of village Gutguti in Adachandi District and ordered them to evacuate the area by the 15th April 1998. These pamphlets were in Mizo Language.

Example 4 : Mizo Jarai Pal and Young Mizo Association etc.- the youth organisations totally destroyed four Chakma villages on 1st February 1998. Chakma families were forced to take shelter in forest.

Example 5 : There were about more than 500 shops run by non-Christians in Iswal only till the seventies. But today there are only 50 such shops. Others have left Mizoram because of threatening, ransom, abduction and killing by the Christian terrorist.

Meghalaya

Meghalaya has 14,89,259 Christians out of its total population of 23,06,069 and 69 i.e. 64.58% (census 2001)

Example 1: Nepali Hindus who were the residents of Meghalaya for so many generations were expelled from the state by burning their houses and looting everything they had. This was during nineties.

Example 2 : There are about one thousand smaller or bigger shops run by the traders from Rajasthan for generations, in Bada Bazar area of capital city of Shillong. Two to three generations of these traders were born and brought up in Shillong. Some of the traders have already left Meghalaya for the same reasons of terrorists activities of ransom, etc. But some are still there. But they do not go to shops in person and run their shops through servants.

Example 3 : There were about 5 clashes between the traders and terrorists in nineties. Shops were burnt and destroyed. The police even after lodging complaints could not take any action against these terrorists. There is a shop in Bada Bazar the owner of which comes to Shillong at the most twice or thrice in a year.

Nagaland

Population belonging to Christianity in this state is 17,39,459 which forms 87.47% of total population of 19,88,636 of Nagaland. Christian terrorism is quite higher than is estimated in this state.

Example 1: A media group which was publishing an English newspaper from Guwahati was forced to stop its publication only because it was hampering the interest of smaller newspaper owners of the state. The media group was threatened for dire consequences if the publication was not stopped and this was done by Christian terrorist in the Nineties.

Example 2 : A so-called Christian terrorist organisation (NYLF) sent a threatening letter to some of government officers regarding financial irregularities and asked them to leave Nagaland. Shri S.C. Das registrar of PWD was one of them. He afterwards publicly apologised. This is the case in 1990.

Example 3 : Shri Joshi the Dean of agriculture college was shot dead on the 19th February 1990 for his so-called involvement in activities against Nagas.

Example 4 : A secret deduction of 25% of salary paid to employees who have come from outside is made once in a year so that sufficient amount can be made available to so called terrorist organisations for running their activities. It is told that these terrorists, therefore, do not trouble such employees and keep their mouth shut.

Example 5 : The Christian terrorists go on creating violence in nearby areas of the birth place of great freedom fighter Rani Gaidulu, only because 80 to 90 % people of this area have not accepted Christianity.

Example 6 **:** There are two groups of National Socialist Council of Nagaland (NSCN). Chiefs of both the groups belong to Christian community. They receive money from the organisation of missionaries 'World council of churches'. This separatist organisation getting financial help from missionaries and arms from China has its offices at New York, Genewa, and Hague.

Tripura

The number of Christians in this state is less in comparison with other North Eastern states. There are only 18% Christians in this state (census 1991). Even then there is a great influence of these Christians on the tribals and terrorists and separatist organisations. These missionaries provide them money and weapons both. So many incidences of this have come to light. National Liberalisation Front was established in Tripura in 1989. Its main aim was to defect Tripura from India and make it a sovereign nation. These missionaries have a tremendous frightening impact on tribes in remote areas that none dares to oppose them. Otherwise such persons are troubled and terrorised.

Example 1 **:** Worshipping and praying Hindu deities in the Christian majority areas of Tripura is prohibited., About 35 members of tribes were killed during 1995 to 2000 as they were found to break the above prohibition order. A Hindu Saint Swami Sakshi Kali who was known for his services to Hindus was killed in August 2000.

Example 2 **:** The terrorists killed the Hindu priest of Jayantiya tribes in December 2000.

Example 3 **:** The National Liberation Front declared in December 2000 that all the Non Christian prayers and worships shall be stopped. After a few days of this declaration two Hindu temples and one Buddha temple were destroyed completely by the terrorists. These terrorists have threatened the Riyang tribes, that if they worship Hindu gods or keep their pictures in their houses, they will have to suffer serious consequences.

Example 4 **:** Four workers of Rashtriya Swayam Sevak Sangh were abducted from Shishu Siksha Niketan at the village of Kanchanchhara in subdivision of Langtararveli of Tripura on the 6 th August 1999. This was done by the terrorist organisation which is sponsored by the Baptist church. They demanded a ransom of Rs two crores and closure of Semi army force Tripura Rifles .' All the four were hacked to death after many atrocities made on them, These workers were (1) Shri Shyamal kantisen Gupta (60) (2) Subhankar Chakrawasti (39) (3) Devendra Nath De (51) and (4) Sudhanay Das (51).

Manipur

Most of the Manipuris are followers of Hindu Vaishnav cult. This is the reason why Christianity could not have much impact on them. But some such incidences have come to light, that can be the signs of more disturbances. Objectionable leaflets were also distributed in the valley of Imphal. This can be taken as clear indication of future.

Arunachal pradesh

According to the 2001 census the percentage of Christians in remote as well as plains areas of Arunachal Pradesh is increased to 19. So many churches are also established in this area. Solid proof of conversion also could be had from this area. It is said that the Christian terrorists have their involvement in recent disturbances that took place in Arunachal pradesh.

The above noted are such facts that cannot be kept unnoticed or side tracked. It is necessary for the unity of the nation that people are allowed to follow the religion of their choice. They may be allowed to adopt any method of worship and prayer. But they should tie themselves in one thread of unity and solidarity of the nation. I could notice clear distance between the original population and those who have come from outside in the North Eastern states specially Mizoram, Meghalaya and Nagaland. One feels to be a guest in one's own country. The people, even the guests coming from outside are so much frightened that no one dares to come out on road after evening. This atmosphere of fear lasts the whole night.

Whenever there is an incidence of clash it is termed as communal and is for establishing supremacy over the other community. In fact these clashes are never communal clashes but are the incidences of atrocities and violence against the minority Hindu tribes and castes by the majority Christian groups. But all these incidences are either not recorded or not paid any heed to them. This is because the police force is fully dominated by local Christians. Cases are not filed as the minority people are afraid of speaking anything against them. Even the people coming from outside prefer to keep mum to the extent that they do not disclose the things to their own people.

Role of I.S.I

Involvement of Pakistan sponsored Inter Services Intelligence in the spread of terrorism and Separatism in North East can not be denied. This organisation ISI is always waiting for chance when it can supply money as well as arms and ammunition to its own Network and important terrorist organisations of North East so that it can create disturbances in this area. It does not get directly involved in North East specially Assam but indirectly helps the ULFA and Bodo terrorists. Police has collected solid proofs for this. According to army sources the ISI provided training to the terrorists along with teaching qualities of hard core terrorists. Pakistan visit of commander-in-chief Paresh Barua of ULFA is solid proof for this. The ISI trained the ULFA terrorists in Guerilla warfare and rocket launching. Pakistan has also arranged a passport for Barua for his visit to Singapur. In return the Jamaat-e-Islami terrorists are allowed to enter the areas of Silhat and Kachhar. It is also reported that the arms and ammunition brought form Myanmar and Thailand are collected and stored in the Masjids and Madarsas at Silhat-and Koka Bazar.

Some wireless communications between ULFA and ISI were captured by Indian Army. In this communication it was heard that ISI was supplying the information of movement of Army to ULFA. There were proofs of involvement of ULFA and ISI in bomb blast made in a train carrying Indian Army Jawans at the time of Kargil war. The strategy behind this was to restrict or obstruct the army Jawans arrival at Kargil so that Indian Army would not get help and eventually Pakistan may win.

Bangladesh and Myanmar can also not be Ignored

The North East region is surrounded by Bangladesh, Myanmar and Bhutan on all sides except on west that too a smaller part. It is very convenient for the terrorists to run to these countries after performing a terrorist activity. This has become more easy because the borders are open. More than 20 training camps of ULFA only are there in the Saflang and Moulawi Bazar areas of Bangladesh. The ULFA leaders Anup Chetia and Arvind Rai Khowa always took help from hard-core Islami people. The same way number of training camps of ULFA and NSCN are being run in Myanmar also. The ULFA and NSCN (K) have formed a terrorist organisation named Indo Burmese Revolutionary Front in order to perform terrorist activities in North East. It is noticeable that Kochin Independent Army (KIA) also provides help to the terrorist organisations in North East. There are proofs about the fact that the KIA has made some land available to these organisations for running their training camps. Though India has friendly relations with Bhutan, its border areas are used by the terrorists organisations to run their training camps, specially ULFA, National Democratic Front of Bodoland, Bodo Liberation Tigers Force. These areas are Marshala, Salim Sukami, Koipani and Orangep. According to a report the ULFA has about 20 such camps and the Bodo terrorists have 4 camps in this area of Deothang and Koipani. Although the Bhutan government has given an ultimatum to these organisations to vacate the areas, even then the camps are still there.

Chapter 8

Terrorism and Initiative by Central Government

All the seven North Eastern states are inhabited by a number of tribes. Naturally they are different from each other. Even if you go form one market to the other you will experience the difference in language, its dialect, style of living, religion as well as nature of the people, whom you come across. The way of thinking, culture, etc., are totally different between the people in plains and people in hills or valleys. Caste feeling is very high in these tribes though they apparently look calm and quiet. Feeling of regionalism in these people is so deeply rooted in their minds that one cannot show them down by argument. This very feeling makes them strong and here starts the terrorism. Primarily smaller organisations on local level cultivate these feelings. These organisations start collecting money from local people, traders, industrialists and owners of tea gardens for maintaining their cultural entity and save it from others. The youth who generally manage the activities of such organisations start exploiting the fear which they have earlier planted, either by printing receipts for so called taxes or even oral threatening. After a short while the politicians, for there own benefit, start giving protection to the activities of such organisations. Added to this is the open border with neighbouring countries which ultimately become their hiding dens. They come in contact with the ISI and Jamat-e-Islami terrorists including those of Myanmar from the open borders. These terrorists sell them the dreams of independent existence inducing them to adopt terrorism. Local police, many times, gives a deaf ear to these youth thinking that they belong to their villages and known to their families. Secondly, they the police, in their inner mind feel that these youth are working for maintaining their own communal entity and therefore why restrict them. Action is taken in solitary cases. In other cases people do not want to purchase danger by filing any report, nor the people talk about these activities. This gives impetus to terrorist activities which in turn assume dangerous nature.

Communal tensions rise because of the activities of underground terrorist organisations and atmosphere of disturbance and tension is created in these areas. The areas which are prone to such atmosphere are Assam, Manipur, Nagaland, Tripura, Meghalaya and Arunachal Pradesh. Links between various terrorist organisations, fleeing beyond the open borders, hammering the local tribes for the demand of plebiscite, troubling the outsiders and making them to leave the places and using the local media for propaganda that their areas are always neglected and gaining the international sympathy are some of the characters of these organisations.

Nature of terrorism in this area is quite complex. The process of changing the tribals to modernity and main culture has also created the atmosphere of instability in these tribes. Pakistan agency ISI as well

Table 8.1 Details of grant amount Paid to North Eastern states for satisfying their needs of security (Amount paid by 31-12-99) (Rs. in Lacs)

States	*Establishing Police station*		*Police Quarters*	*Police Training*	*Commu-nication*
Arunachal Pradesh	Allotted	32	537.5	10.96	163.75
	I.M.E.C.	32	537.5	10.95	
	Paid	14.4	241.87	4.92	
Assam	Alloted	68	8291.25	179.81	374.5
	I.M.E.C.	68	8290.75	179.81	
	Paid	61.2	7461.67	161.83	
Manipur	Alloted	28	1382.5	26.46	124.25
	I.M.E.C.	28	1382.5	26.46	
	Paid	21	725.81	19.84	
Meghalaya	Alloted	08	22.14		107.5
	I.M.E.C.	08	22.14		
	Paid	7.2	19.93		
Mizoram	Alloted	12	282.5	11.89	56.75
	I.M.E.C.	282.45	11.89		
	Paid	10.8	254.21	10.7	
Nagaland	Alloted	28	1606.25	31.72	122.25
	I.M.E.C.	1605.5	31.37		
	Paid	4.2	1300	31	
Tripura	Alloted	08	818.75	30.63	62.25
	I.M.E.C.	08	818.75	30.63	
	Paid	08	364.44	22.97	

Note : (1) Under Central plan 'POLNET'

(2) IMEC - Inter Ministerial Empowered Committee

(3) The table shows amount under 10th Plan

as some outside forces add fuel to it. Free going out and coming in from the open borders and arms ammunition brought in through these borders and infiltration on large scale make the situation more complicated. Non availability of jobs to educated youth in this area is also one of the reasons of terrorist activities. Such educated youth are attracted to terrorism because of unemployment.

According to the report of Home Ministry of Govt. of India, situation in the states of Assam, Nagaland, Manipur and Tripura is so much disturbed that undertaking of work of development has become very difficult in these states. Killing, abduction and ransom have assumed the nature of cottage industry in these states. In a nutshell it means that these activities are aimed at earning easy money through illegal ways. They have nothing to do with any philosophy or ideology.

Initiative by Central Government

The Central Government became more active in nineties to meet the serious situation in this area and for its development. As a matter of fact, Northeast council was founded in 1972 for the purpose. Development works were started and completed actually after Assam and Mizo movements. But its pace was slow. These works caught speed only in the nineties. An eye on Central Government efforts:-

(1) ***Ban on main terrorist organisations*** : The Central Government passed an act "Illegal activities (Restriction) Act 1976". The Central Government banned a number of terrorist organisations. These include two main organisations United Liberation Front of Assam (ULFA) and National Democratic Front of Bodoland (NDFB). Other six organisations which came up as mushrooms are also banned. They are Peoples Liberation Army, UNLF, Peoples Revolutionary Party of Kanglipak (PREPAK), Kanglipak Communist Party (KCP) Kangliyole Kanwagroup (KYKL) and Manipur Peoples Liberation Front (MPLF).

National Socialist Council of Nagaland (Insaf Moiwa) (NSCN-I) and National Socialist Council of Nagaland - Khaplang (NSCN-K) who were desirous of

Independent Nagaland nation right from India's independence were also banned. The same way All Tripura Tigers Force (ATTF) and National Liberation Front of Tripura both from Tripura were also banned. Since, according to government, the terrorist activities in Arunachal Pradesh, Mizoram and Meghalaya are not much, no organisation in these states is at present banned.

Table 8.2 Details of Amount Paid Towards Reimbursement of Expenditure on Security (Rs in Crores)

States	*1997-98*	*1998-99*	*1999-2000*	*Total*
Assam	131.91	78.86	48.07	258.84
Nagaland	-	35.61	13.23	48.48
Manipur	-	19.43	3.74	23.17
Tripura	-	28.55	17.53	46.08
Total	131.91	162.85	82.57	376.93

(2) ***To Declare Disturbed Area*** **:** The following areas are declared to be disturbed and sensitive by the government of India because these areas are prone to terrorism. This was done under Armed forces (Special powers) Act 1958 (amended in 1972)

The areas are :

(a) Total area of Manipur, Nagaland and Assam

(b) Districts of Tirap and Changlang in Arunachal Pradesh

(c) 20 Km areas of neighbouring states along the Assam borders

Tripura government has also declared total area coming under 22 police stations and partial areas under 5 other police stations, as disturbed areas.

(3) ***Deputing Protection Forces*** **:** The Central Government has deputed 'Central Para Military Force' (CAMF) in the areas influenced by terrorism, for the help of Civil Government. The Central Government is

Table 8.3 Central Assistance in Plan Expenditure of North East States

States	Plan Expenditure			Central Assistance			Per Capital Plan Expenditure		
	1997-98	1998-99	1999-2000	1997-98	1998-99	1999-2000	1997-98	1998-99	1999-2000
Arunachal Pradesh	600.00	625.00	665.00	478.10 (80)	534.82 (86)	574.17 (86)	5941	6033	
Assam	1510.28	1650	1750	1308.77 (87)	1443.13 (87)	1616.11 (87)	579	621	
Manipur	410	425	475	386.81 (94)	456.27 (107)	506.08 (106)	1925	1949	
Meghalaya	382	400	465	327.31 (86)	376.31 (94)	421.77 (91)	1860	3841	
Mizoram	290	333	360	309.08 (107)	335 (101)	384.67 (107)	3452	3841	
Nagaland	291	300	315	350.72 (120)	347.40 (116)	396 (125)	1970	1967	
Tripura	439.91	400	475	417 (95)	589.75 (136)	506.08 (106)	1378	1346	

Note : 1) Figures in bracket show percentage of Central assistance

2) All figures except per capita expenditure are (crore)

charging 10% of the expenditure for this as levy from Assam Government. But other six states are exempted from this levy due to limited resources of these states. Looking to the increasing terrorism even after deputing the protection forces and demand from the state government, the centre was not in a position to fulfil the demands. The Central Government prepared a plan to form India Reserve Battalion with the view to reduce the burden of the protection on forces and to strengthen the states to create their 'Armed Police Battalions' with the condition that it will be managed by the states. The Central Government paid 50% of the expenditure of formation and maintenance of this force as grant to the states and 50% was paid as an interest free loan to the states. The Central Government advised the states that all directions given by it must be followed in its structure, to provide the force with arms and equipment and transportation. The government included the defence expenditure on the North Eastern states, under the head of expenditure of their armed police force.

The Central Government has already permitted to create 13 such IRBs in North Eastern area. State-wise battalions are as follows : Assam-4, Manipur, Arunachal Pradesh and Tripura - 2 each, Meghalaya, Mizoram and Nagaland- 1 each. Apart from this Manipur, Mizoram and Tripura are allowed to have one more battalion.

Tenth Finance commission of India has allowed the allocation of Rs 144.3 crores for police quarters, Police training, Police communication, Creation of police posts, Repairing and reconstructing the jails and development of fire fighting machinery in the North Eastern states (see Table 8.1).

(4) *Peace Talks* : The Central Government is firm on the principle that violence of any type for any reason shall not be tolerated. The government believes in resolving the problems and thereby bringing peace, stability and development. Under the principle the government has kept its doors open to all militant groups. But no terrorist organisation showed any response to the talks under the framework provided by the government. Talks with only one organisation of Nagaland - National Socialist Council of Nagaland (Ishak - Muwaia) are in progress. As a part the government has agreed to a cease-fire with this organisation. Conditions of cease fire are as follows - 1. Cease fire will be applicable to the total population and not the terrorists only 2. NSCN (IM) will not give shelter or provide protection to any other terrorist group or organisation 3. The NSCN will not attack any thing which will cause death of any one, injury to any one and damage to property. 4. The terrorist group will not jam the traffic and will not bring any obstacle in any financial and/or developmental work 5. Identity cards will be provided to the workers of NSCN (IM) and they will not move in uniform and with any type of weapons from town to town and in the town. 6. The central force will not cross the specified area of the terrorist groups. 7. Protection force will not be deputed within 2 kilometres from NSCN camps 8. But patrolling can be allowed within one kilometre area of these camps by informing the camp in-charge of the specific camp. 9. Implementation of these conditions will be observed by NSCN; NGO and Central Government.

(5) *Reimbursement of expenditure on Defence* : All the north eastern states are facing the terrorism for last so many years. Naturally they are required to spend a lot on maintaining peace and civil defence. This, in turn, badly affects their exchequer and the developmental works are thereby affected. These states, therefore, approached the Central Government for reimbursement of extra expenditure on civil defence. The Central Government considering their demand chalked out a plan for this. According to this plan the Central Government included the following capital and semi capital expenses in civil defence expenditure. They are - purchase of new vehicles and to convert existing vehicles to bullet proof vehicles, purchase of automatic and semi automatic weapons, purchase of bullet proof jackets, purchase of modern communication equipment, (mobile etc.), Bomb destroyer apparatus, Purchase of apparatus that gives pre information of bomb blast, purchase of computers etc.

Apart from the above the following revenue expenses are also included in this head: Expenditure on jails; Expenditure for training the policemen and jail workers in facing the terrorists kept in police custodies; Expenditure of India Reserve Battalion; Expenditure of deputing army men and other civil defence men by the state government; Expenditure on compensation to affected persons and their families because of terrorist activities; Expenditure in sending the arrested terrorists to Jails outside the state; Expenditure on air travel of persons being brought to the state on special occasions.

(6) *Modernisation of Police Force* : Condition of the police force in North Eastern states is pitiable.

The State governments do not have sufficient funds to improve it. The terrorist organisations have plenty of modern arms and weapons better than those with police force.

Looking to this the Central Government is implementing a plan of providing 100% grant of the expenditure on modernisation of police force in North East as a special case. This plan includes provision for arms and ammunition, equipment, vehicles, communication equipment etc. An amount of Rs 35.63 crores was given to these states for the above purpose

Table 8.4 Details of construction of Roads Bridges and Fencing along Bangladesh Border (1999) (amount in Lac rupee)

State	Head	Amount Physical	Allotted Financial Rs.	Returns Physical	Returns Financial Rs.
Assam	Road (KM)	186.32	4546	119.95	8164.94
	Bridges (meters)	4683.00	5486	3871.11	
	Fencing (Km)	152.31	2173	139.46	1713.65
	Total	1220.5		9878.59	
Meghalaya	Road	211.29	4323	211.29	5566.42
	Bridges (meters)	1479.73	1475	1359.73	
	Fencing (Km)	1198.06	2840	198.00	2838.50
	Total	8638		8404.92	
West Bengal	Road (KM)	1770	37900	1425.50	39298.63
	Bridges (meters)	12562	14069	12384.00	
	Fencing	507	8366	482.44	8499.55
	Total	60335		47798.18	
Tripura	Road	545.37	14877	423.65	12647.05
	Bridges (meters)	1914.23	2757	1324.27	
	Security		360		42.59
	Total	17994		12689.94	
Mizoram	Road	153.4	3727	105.78	4076.13
	Bridges (meters)	1078.64	1533	772.04	
	Total	5260		4076.13	
Grand Total					
	Road (KM)	2866.38	65373	2286.17	69753.17
	Bridges (meters)	21717.6	25320	19711.75	
	Fencing	857.37	13379	819.96	13051.7
	Security		360		42.59
	Total	104432		82847.46	

during 1997-98. The same way an amount of Rs 12.48 crores was paid in 1998-99, Rs 65 crores in 1999-2000 and Rs 86.86 crores in the period from 2000 to 2002.

(7) *Surrender of Terrorists and their Rehabilitation Policy* : The Central Government prepared and started implementing a plan of 100% grant on surrender and rehabilitation of terrorists. Misled youth and defamed terrorists caught in the net of armed forces are encouraged to surrender. But they are required to promise that they would not participate any more in terrorist activities.

Only the armed terrorists were allowed to surrender under this plan. The plan was primarily implemented for a year. A social organisation was permitted to run a rehabilitation camp with the help of armed forces. Professional training of their liking or interest was provided to these terrorists. A stipend of Rs 2000 p.m. (max) was also paid for a year. Assistance in getting employment opportunities to them was also provided. Petty criminal cases filed against them were withdrawn. But this plan did not come encouraging in these states.

(8) *Construction of Border Roads and Fencing along the border* : Work of construction of road and fencing along the Bangladesh border joined with Assam, Meghalaya, Tripura and Mizoram was started by Central Government in 1987. This is a part of Assam agreement and aimed at restricting the entry of Bangladesh infiltrations in Indian states. Its progress and expenditure incurred on this is shown in table no 8.4 (upto November 1999). A high level committee under the chairmanship of central home department secretary is appointed to see the progress of this project. Primarily it was decided to complete this project by March 2001. This committee again made a provision of Rs 1334 crores for completing the remaining construction of 797 kilometre long road and fencing along 2429.5 km long border. It is expected that this work will be completed by December 2007.

(9) *Strategic intiative with bordering nations* : The central government received a report that the terrorist organisations of North East - NSCN, ULFA, NDFB, Maitei terrorist organisations of Manipur, ATTF and NLFT are in contact with neighbouring nations i.e. Myanmar, Bangladesh and Bhutan. On this the Central Government took an initiative to establish strategic relations with these countries. The Central Home Secretary visited Bangladesh. The secretary put the subject of Defence before that government. A joint action committee was formed after this. This committee met at Dhaka and New Delhi for mutual interests and Defence problems. As a part of line of action in this direction the Home secretary again visited Dhaka on 21st to 23rd November 1998 and discussed the problems of Defence, illegal infiltration and border crossing by criminals and terrorists.

The same way the Government of India entered into an agreement with Myanmar for peace and Defence in the border areas. There were a number of meetings at National and state levels. The Myanmar government talked about providing help on some defence problems. Myanmar provided help in controlling the terrorist activities in North East. A request was also made to the Government of Thailand as there were reports that these terrorist organisations of North east procure arms, ammunition illegally from Thailand. The Central Government brought the matter of training camps of Bodo terrorists and their hiding dens in Bhutan to the notice of Bhutan Government as reported to Govt. of India. Keeping in view all these protections on the borders,

The Bangladesh Home minister also visited New Delhi on the 22nd December 1999. Then also the matters relating to mutual interest and defence were discussed.

But what are the facts ?

The Central Government makes high claims of restricting the terrorism in North East. But a question still arises; whether the situation in these states is coming to normalcy or not. On the other hand the situation in North East is like a patient whose disease has increased by administering medicines. The feeling of separatism and terrorism is so deep rooted that it is not being destroyed. As a matter of fact various packages in defence head are declared from time to time for these states of North East India.

It is a fact that the complete North East region is surrounded by other nations - Bangladesh, Myanmar, Bhutan and to some extent China and as such these states have great strategic importance and the problems of these sensitive states are more complicated than other states of India. The Central Government is allotting new projects and finance for these states without charging any interest. Even then the situation in these states is worsening than improving.

If one visits Assam, Nagaland, Manipur and Tripura one can experience the horrifying situation prevailing in these states. Horrible scene of Bangladesh infiltrators can be seen in a large number in the areas of Assam which has a joint border with Bangladesh. Open border and moral support of local people in Muslim minority areas are reasons that are encouraging this infiltration in huge number. Actually Assam movement was run to restrict the entry of Bangladesh infiltrators in Assam. But this movement is seen to be ineffective rather damaging in this area.

According to the 2001 census the proportion of increase in population in the border area is very high. No officer has any appropriate answer to this. On the other side the political leaders in this area are more interested in their vote bank than the country. Names of illegal infiltrators are entered in the ration cards and thereby legality of their existence in this area is being bestowed upon them. After implementation of Assam agreement only 694 persons are declared as illegal infiltrators, and 6273 are declared to be foreigners. But only 187 persons could be sent back. This may either be taken as the inefficiency of the state government or can be attributed to the vote politics. As such it will not be exaggeration that the truthfulness of Assam movement has become questionable or doubtful. What else can be the reason of Bangladeshi majority in these five border districts and only 187 persons could be sent back.

As a matter of fact every caste or tribe has its own militant organisation. Some are small and some are large. But the number of tribes in this area is very high. Naturally the number of such organisations is also high. Atmosphere in this area is so frightening that if any of these organisations gives call for Bandh through newspapers, whole market remains closed and day to day activities come to a stand still. As the local police is unable to take action against them their courage is further increased. With the result they start going to the extent of collecting ransom, abduction and even murders. As a matter of fact, main object of such Bandhs is not in National interest but they are aimed at proving themselves to be stronger. They do not have any object or intention of development of their castes and or tribes to which they belong. They do not have anything to do with any ideology or philosophy. Actually Mizo movement and Assam movement had certain ideology. But now forming an organisation and engaging in militancy has become a fashion in this region.

Some terrorists who had surrendered earlier think and behave in a way that they have received a licence from the government to perform criminal activities. They have adopted a profession of collecting money from the contractors for allotting them contract, or getting the allotment of contract in their own name by threatening them on the basis of their past. The sufferers also keep their mouth shut for reason of safety.

State governments of North East states and the Central Government are jointly spending an amount of Rs. 1.5 thousand crores on internal security. But expected results are not coming forth for various reasons. The main reason for this is non coordination between the police forces of the states. Naturally the activists flee beyond the border and hide in neighbouring state after performing terrorist act. Secondly the terrorists have modern weapons like automatic guns and other equipment where- as the police force does not.

If one talks about surrender by terrorists, it is seen that total 2,932 terrorists that too only from Assam have surrendered to government during the period from 1998 to 2000. As per government figures an amount of Rs 6 to 7 lacks per surrendered terrorist have been spent on effecting surrender and rehabilitation.

Table 8.5 Number of Terrorists Who Surrendered During 1998 to 2000

	1998	*1999*	*2000*	*Total*
ULFA	227	552	1625	2404
NDFB	37	49	128	214
Others	06	75	233	314
Total	270	676	1986	2932

If we consider the persons speaking Hindi or who have come from outside to the region, we get astonished to note that about two thousand persons were killed, 546 persons were abducted and a ransom of Rs 350 crores was collected during eleven years from 1990 to 2000. Apart from this two thousand 115 members of 300 families left this region leaving their establishments only because of the fear of ransom.

Chapter 9

Terrorism and Initiative by the State Governments

Bringing peace to the region and developmental works have posed a challenge before the State Government of Northeastern states because of the continuance and impact of terrorists in these states. Whenever the news of terrorism activities in these states reaches the other part of the country, people there start thinking that the state governments are not taking any remedial measures against this terrorism and simply look towards the centre for curbing such terrorists. Because of the terrorists activities development of these states has assumed the nature of scaling the Everest. The State Governments have from time to time taken the initiative towards this. This includes encouraging the terrorists to surrender as well as making available opportunities of employment. Actually political awakening and will power for curbing the terrorism in these state has arisen from 2000. As a result the Chief Ministers of all the seven states have now decided to work jointly for this. As the first step all these Chief Ministers have come together and formed a stage "North Eastern Chief Ministers Forum (Manch)", so as to enable them to fight against the terrorism and disturbing activities of Pakistan sponsored ISI.

This formation of 'Chief Minister Manch' has assumed importance because in the past, the terrorism was getting political protection. Such blames of protecting the terrorists were being levelled on the then Chief Ministers. Not only this, but many times they were proved. Governor General V. K. Nair had reported to the Central Government that the Chief Minister Rishang Kishing of Manipur was protecting the terrorists in that state. But the then P. V. Narsimha Rao Government at Centre gave a deaf year ear to it. On the other hand, the governor was removed. The Congress Chief Minister Shri Hiteshwar Sakiya was also accused of giving protection to ULFA by his own party assembly members in writing. The Chief Minister of Tripura was also accused for this. The Prafulla Kumar Mahanto government in Assam was dissolved for the same reason. The Chief Minister P.K. Mahanto placed on assembly table a white paper on the activities of ISI in the state and started action against the terrorism in the state. He did this very courageously even at the cost of his vote bank.

Important and interesting thing in this movement against the terrorism is that all the political parties and groups have come out of the sphere of their political ideology with the object to curb terrorism. Assam has a joint government under the leadership of Assam Gan Parishad. Leftists also have joined this movement. The Bhartiya Janta Party has an important partnership in joint government in Meghalaya. This united front includes local groups

Table 9.1 State- wise Revenue Receipts

(in crores Rs.)

States	*93-94*	*94-95*	*95-96*	*96-97*	*97-98*	*98-99*	*99-2000*
Meghalaya	661.17	579.36	783.24	856.90	859.76	1080.65	1282.73
Assam	3481.60	5317.39	4580.30	4234.30	4985.90	5267.96	7108.64
Manipur	740.22	645.67	766.75	1095.80	1024.31	1055.25	1212.76
Nagaland	937.35	799.83	955.25	1016.72	1128.66	1430.68	1292.81
Tripura	774.67	888.99	1041.08	1155.18	1265.41	1560.08	1671.33
Total India	34186.82	166021.55	180433.50	195727.32	230237.68	262841.13	303178.12

Table 9.2 State wise revenue payment

(Rs in Crores)

States	*93-94*	*94-95*	*95-96*	*96-97*	*97-98*	*98-99*	*99-2000*
Meghalaya	681.48	587.04	778.44	785.44	850.71	1007.51	1431.70
Assam	3620.02	3997.75	4390.40	4266.74	5022.10	5204.32	7943.14
Manipur	637.24	674.97	810.64	1013.79	1132.97	1115.86	1224.50
Nagaland	961.62	906.01	1039.96	1095.75	1230.31	1490.51	1285.97
Tripura	784.69	880.21	989.54	1178.80	1350.22	1530.73	1831.46
Total India	134648.55	161353.79	177583.77	202768.77	228134.78	260360.86	311286.25

Table 9.3 States Total and per capita expenditure on Health by states

States	1980-81	1985-86	1986-87	1987-88	1988-89	1989-90
Arunachal Pradesh	--	--	19	25	26	26
Assam	40 (22)	71 (32)	100 (44)	167 (71)	179 (75)	172 (70)
Manipur	14 (98)	12 (75)	35 (219)	30 (176)	35 (205)	37 (219)
Meghalaya	16 (120)	15 (100)	27 (169)	32 (200)	38 (236)	47 (277)
Mizoram	-- --	09 (150)	03 (50)	29 (483)	29 (416)	30 (434)
Nagaland	16 (197)	32 (355)	39 (453)	49 (490)	49 (447)	68 (574)
Tripura	06 (31)	13 (57)	23 (96)	20 (121)	35 (140)	40 (161)

i) This expenditure includes Medical, Family planning, public health and electric supply.
ii) Figures in bracket showing per capita expenditure
iii) Rupees in Crores

also. Arunachal Pradesh and Nagaland have Congress Governments. Tripura has leftist government whereas Manipur and Mizoram are ruled by Local (group) party governments. But all these Chief Ministers have unanimously demanded that the terrorism in North East be declared as national problem.

The process of forming the North East chief Minister Forum is as follows.

Table 9.4 No of Population-wise Doctors in North East

States	No of Doctors In Govt. Medical Agencies	Population per doctor	As on the date
Arunachal Pradesh	233	13536	31-12-90
Assam	2660	18750	31-12-91
Manipur	684	12675	31-12-91
Meghalaya	322	15357	31-12-90
Mizoram	146	15000	31-12-91
Nagaland	202	15401	31-12-91
Tripura	673	13822	31-12-90

There was a change of Government in Meghalaya and Shri E. K. Mawlong became Chief Minister. He, immediately after assuming the power, went to meet Chief Minister Prafullakumar Mahanto on the 15th March 2000. There he proposed to resolve the problem of terrorism jointly by all the North Eastern states. Next step was a convention of all North East Chief Ministers held at Shillong on the 12th May 2000 under the chairmanship of P. K. Mahanto. The North East Chief Ministers Forum, was declared to be formed in this convention only. Next meeting of this Forum was convened at Arunachal Bhavan in New Delhi under the chairmanship of Mukut Maree on the 21st May 2000. Accordingly a call was given for Peace Rallies to be taken out on block as well as district levels in all the North East on 8th June 2000. All the Chief Ministers submitted a joint memorandum to Prime Minister Shri Atal Bihari Bajpai. This memorandum of 13 Pages was submitted on the 21st June 2000. Following three important demands along-with others were put forth through this memorandum.

(1) The militancy is on rise in all the North Eastern states and all the militant or terrorists groups have relations with each other. Their object is to get separated from India. Enemy countries are helping them. As such Central Government should declare this as a 'National Problem'. Additional protection force be deployed in these states. International Border be sealed to stop the cross border terrorism. Joint and coordinated steps may please be taken for this and the neighbouring countries be pressurised to destroy the terrorists camps in their areas.

(2) The Central Government should bear all the expenditure to modernise the police force in these states. A plan in this respect be undertaken at the

Table 9.5 No of Hospitals and Beds therein in North East

States	*Hospitals*	*Rural Area*		*Urban area*		*Total*
		Beds	*Hospitals*	*Beds*	*Hospitals*	*Beds*
Arunachal Pradesh (1-1-92)	251	1654	11	822	262	2476
Assam (1-1-91)	151	3949	117	8712	268	12661
Manipur (1-1-96)	27	862	05	752	32	1614
Meghalaya (1-1-93)	00	00	09	1867	09	1867
Mizoram (1-1-96)	06	196	11	1108	17	1304
Nagaland (1-1-92)	21	257	10	793	31	1050
Tripura	13	365	13	1445	26	1310
Total India	4621	122453	10416	501366	15097	623819

earliest. The same way the Central Government should bear all the expenditure of 'India Reserve Battalion' which is created and placed in North Eastern states.

(3) Infiltration of people from other countries in this part has assumed a dangerous shape. If proper action is not taken to stop this, there would be regular clashes which might have bad effect on the centre also.

Apart from infiltrated Bangladesh Nationals, a number of Nepali nationals are residing in this region. This has adverse social and economic pressure on the local inhabitants. As such the Central Government should undertake a detailed identity card project for this area. These cards should be distributed in this area. Other steps should also be taken to curb the infiltration and expelling them. A uniform law for identifying the foreign nationals and expelling them should be passed and implemented. The fencing along India Bangaladesh border be completed at the earliest.

Along-with the above demands the forum submitted the following proposals and demands before the Prime Minister and Finance Minister and mentioned the financial difficulties experienced by them in increasing the pace of developmental works in the states.

These Demands Were

(1) To start 'Border Hot', which was stopped during 1965 Bharat Pakistan war and start the 'Steal Well Road' between India and Myanmar.

(2) To reorganise the North East Council

(3) To give leniency in 'Forest Cutting Order' of Supreme Court.

(4) To reserve a quota in all the three wings of forces, for the youth of this region.

(5) Rail, Road and Air services in this area be modernised. All the states be joined with 50 seater Air services.

(6) To have talks with Bangladesh for awarding transit permission through Bangladesh.

All these demands are not new. But their submission by all the Chief Ministers jointly is the indication of their strong will to develop their region at fast pace and joining the main stream. Situation in Manipur and Tripura is worst. Terrorism is on increase in these states and it has become impossible to curb or even decrease it as the administration as well as police force seem to have joined hands with these groups secretly. State Director General of police S. L. Jugeshwar Singh is accused of having secret relations with the terrorist organisations and the Central Government has recommended his removal. Even then he is still on the post. The terrorist groups had maximum protection in Tripura.

Chapter 10

Contribution of Outsiders in the Development of North East

Total population of North Eastern states has 9 to 10 per cent of people who have come from Bihar, Uttar Pradesh, Rajasthan, Punjab, Haryana, Gujarat, etc. Maximum number out of these have settled in Assam. The so-called outsiders are those who have come to this area since quite a number of years in search of livelihood or for business. These people have settled in this area. They adjusted themselves with the original residents of this area and have made themselves as part of Northeast. Along with this, people have been coming to this area in the recent past also. These outsiders can be divided in three categories (1) Labour class working in tea gardens (2) Business community engaged in trade and industry and (3) Officers and Employees of government as well as private establishments.

About 40 lakh labour is working in the tea gardens of Assam only, of which 70% belong to Bihari community. About 20 lakh labour speaking Hindi are also working in other establishments. Majority of these labours also belong originally to Bihar and Uttar Pradesh. Assam population is 2.3 crores. It can be well understood that a sufficiently large part of this population is of Bihari and Uttar Pradeshis, Majority of this population belong to labour community working in tea gardens and other establishments. Some are rickshaw pullers, some run small tea or pan shops. The Bihari and Uttar Pradesh labour started coming to this area during the Second World War. Apart from the labour, some Biharis have adopted teaching profession and are teachers in schools or colleges. Some have entered in other professions. The Biharis are not grouped at any place but are spread all over in Assam. These Biharis belong mainly to the Districts of Muzaffarpur, Vaishali, Doghar, Chhapra, Samastipur, Darbhanga, Katihar, Purniya, Arariya, Kishanganj, etc., of Bihar.

A group from Rajasthan, Gujarat and Haryana also came to this region during the same period. These groups came here with a different object of establishing business and trade and spread over the complete area of Northeast. Marwadi community from the West Bengal came first to this region. Afterwards this community from Rajasthan, Haryana, Punjab, Uttar Pradesh, Delhi, etc., came to this area in sufficiently large number. These people belonging to remote western districts of India came to a small city Sadia in remote eastern part of India and proved their supremacy in trade and business. Presently this community is spread in Dibrugarh, Kamrup, Barpeta, and Kokrazar, etc., districts of Assam. The forefathers of the present people belonging to this community gave a new shape and boundaries to the trade here, on the basis of their efficiency and hard work. Agrawal family of Tinsukhia (1842-1919) contributed a lot to the development of Assamee language and culture.

Shri Harivilas Agrawal and his son Chandrakumar Agrawal have helped to a large extent in developing Assamee culture during second half of 19th century and first half of 20th century, respectively. Shri Jyotiprasad Agrawal (1903-51) belonging to the same family has acquired a good position in Assamee community. He was a great Assam poet, musician, film maker and a freedom fighter. The credentials of first Assamee film also go to Jyotiprasad Agrawal. Name of the film was Jayamati. He founded a new era in the area of theatre by playing a drama 'Sonitkumari' in 1925.

Shri Nawarun Verma who has come from Bihar translated the *Assamiya Ramayana* by Madhao Kandali in Hindi. He as well transcripted the *Assamiya Shankardeo Keertan Ghosha* from Assami script to Deonagari script and made commendable efforts to reach Assami Literature to Hindi area. Late Shri Chhaganlal Jani prepared the Hindi Assami dictionary. The same way Dr. Deoraj translated many Manipuri short stories and Lokkathas (folktales) in Hindi. Shri K. L. Agrawal started a Hindi daily Purwanchal Prahari in 1989 and thereby started to voice the sentiments of Hindi people along-with spreading the North East culture. A journalist Ravikant Rai is publishing monthly magazine with the object to publish Northeast literature through the Magazine *'Ulupi'*. This is an effort to establish an image of Linguistic, Cultural Unity and Coordination. Apart from this the Hindi teachers who have come here because of their literary ability became the mouthpiece of Northeast culture and literature.

Largest business community in Assam had established their concerns in the important cities of Guwahati and Shillong. Gradually they extended their area to Manipur's capital Imphal, Dimapur in

Nagaland, Tripura Capital Agartala, Mizoram capital Aizawal, Arunachal Pradesh capital Itanagar, etc., by starting their establishments and by starting Industries they brought people from outside i.e. Bihar, UttarPradesh, etc., and employed them in their concerns. Local people were also given employment. But the fact is that the local people are not skilled or efficient enough to compete with the persons who come form outside These industrialists say that local people are not that capable enough for hard work, as are the people from Bihar, etc.

Contribution of these outsiders in beautifying and developing these cities, whether it is Tinsukhia or Guwahati, Shillong, or Imphal, can not be neglected. Tinsukhia is another big city of Assam after Guwahati. It is regarded as biggest city of Upper Assam. This city which is in neighbourhood of Arunachal Pradesh and Nagaland is surrounded by a number of tea gardens. The tea traders and professionals played an important role in making Tinsukhia flourish. Labour for tea gardens were brought from Bihar and Uttar Pradesh. Naturally markets were created to meet their needs. Number of tea gardens went on increasing and thereby the number of labour also increased and there was a natural increase in their needs and subsequently expansion of markets. Gradually Tinsukhia assumed the status of business centre. Then came labour and ministerial staff. Along with them came rickshaw pullers, petty shopkeepers, coolies, trucks' etc., and a large number of other professionals followed them. As a result trade and commerce in Tinsukhia is on the shoulders of about 80 thousand Hindi language persons. Naturally the government derives benefit from them.

As per shri G. L. Agrawal, the managing director

of G. L. Publication, the propaganda that the outsiders squeeze the local residents has no truth in it. On the other hand it is the fact that these outsiders have done a large number of important works that helped the development. The question of squeezing does not arise at all. Actually the fault lies with the State Governments, as they did not implement the development work with proper speed. They were very slow in economic as well as social development. They could not create employment opportunities. Above all they used the discontent in the people for their political benefit and self. Every thing was all well till the eighties. But since then the local leadership started awakening regionalism in the minds of original residents, for their own political benefits. This resulted in fall of calamities on the so-called outsiders who were dwelling in this region for years together. The ULFA murdered Shri Surendra Pal, chairman of Frontier Tea Company in 1990. He was then on a short visit of tea gardens. During the same period, the then President of Chamber of Commerce Shri Shankar Bimriwal was killed only because he called Bandh to protest against the ransom, abductions and killings by the terrorists. These incidents created a fear in the minds of these outsiders. During the same period the local youth belonging to terrorist camp burnt the houses and shops of outsiders in Shillong. As a result, trade and industry in whole region including Assam started closure. The situation today is that the entrepreneurs start getting threatening letters from the militants and students organisations giving threats for employing local youth only. The situation took a serious turn in 2000 when all the Hindi language people came on the hot-list of these organisations. They started killing these people. In a period of 2 months about 200 Bihari labour and others were killed.

According to 1981 census the percentage of the outsiders is 6.453 of the total population of Mizoram. These include Nepalese, Bengalese, Assamese, Biharis, Punjabis and South Indians. All these people belong to government employees, labour, Assam Rifles, CRPF and traders and contractors.

Contribution of Nepalese, Sikhs, Bengalise, and South Indians towards development of Northeast can not be forgotten.

Chapter 11

Causes and Diagnosis of Terrorism and Separatism

Separatism and terrorism in the North Eastern States was studied by a number of persons from various angles. Some studied the problem from historical background and some studied the same from the angle of economic backwardness. Some placed the blame on geographical situation as well as history along-with economic backwardness.

Some tried to resolve this problem by social analysis. Whereas some have blamed Tropical or Regional Political mentality for the problem of separatism and terrorism in North East. The outsiders (Originally belonging to other states but living in this area for generations) and the infiltrators from Bangladesh and other countries are nowadays, being blamed for the problem. The regional parties hold the Central Government responsible whereas the Central Government holds the inefficient, careless and lethargic governments in these states, as responsible for rise and increase of terrorism for separatism. During this cat and mouse game, actual sufferers are the people in general.

We are going to discuss and analyse the reasons responsible for the terrorism and separatism in this region, which could not yet be curbed. These reasons can be enlisted as follows :

1) Historic conditions
2) Geographical situation
3) Regionalism
4) Social and Communal reasons
5) Division of states
6) Army Action
7) Problem of infiltration
8) Economic condition and unemployment
9) Political motives
10) Cultural situation
11) Weak, inefficient, careless law and order situation
12) Mutual understanding between politicians and terrorists
13) Role of Central Government
14) Foreign Protection.
15) Administration and corruption
16) Colonial history writing and misunderstandings
17) Role of Christian-Missionaries and I.S.I.
18) Inner line permit
19) Combination of Student Organisations and Militants
20) Role of media

(1) *Historic conditions / Reasons* : The British are responsible for the Separatism mentality and for that the terrorism in the people of North-East India. It is the fact that only the British had sewn the seeds of separatism in this area. But they are not the only people responsible for today's terrorist activities in this region. Though painful but it is a fact that we are, mainly, responsible for the present nature and fury of terrorism and not the British.

It is a fact that some of the then British officers mainly Prof. Koopland and Hattam and Mills had prepared a plan and submitted it to the British Government recommending therein, to separate this mountainous area along India Burma border and present Arunachal Pradesh, from India. This they did just before India got independence. But it was their bad luck and India got independence early, making Koopland Plan unsuccessful. This does not mean that the British did not have their contribution in the North East terrorism. Help provided to Fijo and Laldenga by the British is known to all and cannot be hidden. Added to this are the activities of British journalists Donald Mize and Gaibin Wang. These two journalists met the underground Naga activists in 1959-60 with the help of British Tea Garden owners and published articles in British media which were pro Naga activists and gave undue publicity to them. Today also a number of European human rights forums provide their stage to the separatist organisations in North East. It is every now and then discussed that the then British joint commissioner had active contribution in forming the Naga Club and Naga National Council as well as in drafting the memorandum that was submitted to 'Simon Commission'.

It is also a fact that the British separated the people in plains and mountains from each other by implementing inner line Regulation in 1874. The British analysed the history of North East from the view point of colonialism-defined the history, society and culture. Even after the impact of this the Naga National Council had expressed its desire to remain as a district of Assam and thereby to remain as a part of India. This was conveyed to the Govt. of India through an application. The Mizo Union did also express its desire to remain in India. Actually this was the largest and strongest organisation of Nagas. All the tribes in the then Assam except the Nagas were happy over the provisions of India's Constitution (VI Schedule) which promised to provide internal autonomy to Zilla Parishads. The act of Assam Government of tabling a bill making Assamiya as official language of Assam provided an opportunity to Khasi, Jayantiya, Garo and Mizo tribes to demand a separate state. Karbi dunaza Kachhari tribes opted to remain with Assam. The latest band of separatism was voiced, just prior to independence by the Naga National Council when 'Fijo' became its leader.

(2) *Geographical Situation* :-Entire North East Indian region is situated around and within the Brahmaputra river valley and number of mountains. That is the reason why there were less than limited means of conveyance up to 1970. Naturally this region was nearly cut from rest of India. This psychological pain troubled the people of this area. Geographical atmosphere was the greatest obstacle in the process of constructing roads and laying Rail-lines. This area had very limited air services also. But now this distance is being decreased. Railway lines are being laid and roads along border are also being constructed. Even then there are so many other places which are still out of reach.

Looking at the situation it is felt that the government should take immediate steps for increasing the pace of development and should have a time bound programme for this. Responsibility for proper implementation of the plans should be given to local tribes and political groups by placing confidence in them. Actually it is seen that bridges, etc., are constructed but they are blasted by the terrorist groups. These terrorist groups feel it is advantageor to them if this region remains cut off from rest of India.

The geographical structure of this area is such

that it is very easy for the infiltrators to enter this region. A town 'Daki' in Meghalaya is surrounded on three sides by Bangladesh. This is the town via which the coal is exported to Bangladesh. Though there is a border post, it is a very easy and simple access to Meghalaya. The same way it is very easy to cross over to Myanmar from More border post in Manipur. According to Border Security force and custom officers such infiltration is very easy. Guns like A.K.47 are manufactured and made available there for Rs. 10 thousand only which are smuggled into this area and sold at very high price making this as a business.

Up to date and modern arms and weapons are sold in Bangkok market. The smugglers have undertaken the business of purchasing them there and after smuggling in, sell them for a price of rupees counted in lakh to the people in border areas. As a result of easy access, terrorist training camps are run in Bangladesh and Myanmar for the youth of this area. The same way the Bodo youth cross over to Bhutan, undergo terrorist training in the camps run there and return to Bodo area.

Chinese and Korean goods are smuggled in India through More in Manipur. These goods are sold at a very low price. Imphal market has plenty of foreign goods available at low prices. Eventually the handloom and Handicraft industry in this area is losing its existence.

(3) *Regional Mentality* : Every community is always proud of its culture. It loves its motherland. This feeling is now converted into mentality. It is further increased by the spread of education in this area. That is why every tribal group has formed its so-called organization. These organizations always encash this feeling for the benefit of a few people. It is a fact that when the regional ambitions do not find place in central stream, or when the central authorities neglect the regional ambitions, these people start shouting separatist slogans to obtain its shelter and here starts the terrorism.

Almost all the terrorist organisations always use so-called injustice to them, as their weapon. This is because they can derive their own benefits by fuelling this regional mentality.

It is the responsibility of the State Government to ensure that there is no differentiation between groups. Secondly the governments should ensure that no group carries such impression. Not only this it should be seen that their freedom is not jeopardised or their cultural identity is not being demolished. The fact is that unluckily it has happened and regional separatism is fuelled

(4) *Social and Communal Reasons* : Social structure of North-East is many-fold. Complexity of Geographical structure and backwardness in the means of conveyance have kept this area away from rest of India. As a result blind beliefs, traditionalism, group killings and backwardness have shadowed everything in this region. It is well known that the social, economic and cultural activities mainly depend upon the social structure of that region, the race to which the concerned society belongs. Their social qualities, ambitions, communal and respect identity, awakening, faith, their natural relations, religion and religious beliefs, traditions, languages, linguistic culture, public beliefs and literature of any region always have a great and deep impact on the social, economic and cultural activities of that region. If we study the social and cultural activities of North-East, we come to the conclusion that there are many specialities which do not have any similarity with the original stream of the country.

Almost five crores population of North-East consists of Aryans, Dravids, Mangol tribes and subtribes and Moth & Khwameth people belonging to Austrian race. Their communal multiplicities are the base of activities of these communities and thereby communal identity of there communal groups is always maintained.

Comparatively smaller and backward, minority communities and tribes are living in this area which has a majority of educated, developed and impressive Aryas. These smaller tribes and communities always wanted to protect themselves from the impact of Aryas. This has created strong will in them for the purpose.

(5) *Division of States* : In early post independence period the complete North-East region was known as Assam and was ruled by Assam Government. But the erstwhile state of Assam was divided in seven states for protection of the culture, and nature of the original tribes and because of political pressure. Hence it is evident that wherever and whenever the tribal started and continued the movement for the purpose of separation from Assam, the Central Government yielded to these terror and furious movements and divided the State of Assam in present States. Assam being the border state, division of this state in smaller states was thought to be strategically necessary. But this division had adverse effect and eventually any smaller or bigger tribe rises and undertakes the movement for more autonomy and/ or separate state. The state of Meghalaya with the population of about eighteen lakh was formed with a so called point of view of protecting the religion, culture and traditions of Khasi, Garo and Jayantiya tribes. Now the Garo community having population of 8 lakh only are demanding the division of Meghalaya.

The Bodo's in Assam are not satisfied with more autonomy and pressing for separate state of Bodoland. The Kookies in Manipur are demanding Kookie land. The same way the Bengalis and Santhals are demanding the division of Tripura in two States. If these incidents are looked at in totality one can unhesitatingly say that the division of Assam in seven States is also responsible for the terrorism and separatism in this area. This situation demands immediate and stern steps to be taken by the Central Government. As well as steps towards economic development of this area should be given top priority.

(6) *Army Action* : The Central Government had to send army very frequently to North-East specially on the request of the concerned State Governments with a view to curb the terrorism as the State police could not stand to the occasion efficiently. The army which is to be used against the cross border enemy was required to be used against our own people. Atrocities of Central Protection Forces during Assam movement is the fresh example of this. This ultimately gave rise to discontent against the Central Government in the minds of local people.

The army Jawans used their guns against the innocent and peace loving people just like butchers. Eventually New Delhi should stop talking about army action to curb the terrorism and should come forward to accept that the centres role in North East in post independence period is one of the original reasons of this terrorism.

(7) *Problem of Infiltration* : The problem of infiltration in North-East India is very serious and dangerous. This region is surrounded by four nations. Of these Bangladesh is posing a threat and causing danger by infiltration from that country. 1980 movement in Assam was based mainly on the point of

Bangladesh infiltration. About 70 per cent of North-East border is open which has made infiltration very easy. 443 km long border of Meghalaya is joined with Bangladesh through which infiltration is rampant. These Bangladesh infiltrators cross the border via Selsela, Jigjak and Dalu common development Board in Western Garo mountains, Myashinram in Eastern Khasi mountains as well as Ramikor in western Khasi mountain district. Similarly Meghalaya, Kachhar district of Assam is also suffering from infiltration. These Bangladesh infiltrators are located in Karimganj and Helakanti areas also. But unluckily this problem is becoming more and more dangerous because of protection of local leaders and public representatives to these people. The problem of Chakma refugees is pending as it was, for a long time in Tripura. This creates feelings of separatism and terrorism in local people. According to the report of Lt. Gen. (Retd) S.K. Sinha, the Rajyapal of Assam, cent-percent infiltrators coming from Bangladesh are Muslims. Census figures also show the same thing. This is clear from the Table 11.1. Due to Pakistani atrocities in Bangladesh during the decade of 1951 to 1961, the Assam Hindu population was increased by 37.17% and the Muslim population by 30.99%. This is because of Bangladesh infiltration. It is clear from this that the Bangladesh is trying successfully to convert the border districts into Muslim majority districts. The districts of Ghubadi, Khanpada, Barpeta and Hailakandi are already turned into Muslim majority districts (census 1991). Further by 1998 the districts of Nagao and Kaimganj have majority of Muslim population. Moregaon district is proceeding fast towards this. This rise in population has its direct impact on voter lists. The local political leaders encourage infiltration for guaranteed Muslim vote bank. There is a 30% increase in number of voters in 17 assembly constituencies and 20% increase in voters in 40 constituencies during only three years from 1994 to 1997. It seems impossible to stop such a legal crossing of border unless the political parties change their mentality. Assam has a common border of 262 km including 92 km by river, with Bangladesh. The proposal to put barbed wire fencing along this border is mooted a number of times. It is also a fact that Bangladesh has common border not only with Assam but with other states also. These states are also used to reach Assam. Unlucky situation is that the security workers, themselves, allow such infiltration by corrupt practices. Secondly, the ISI is providing training of cutting such fencing wires.

Table 11.1 Rise in Population Because of Infiltration in Assam (%)

Year	*Infiltrators*	
	Hindus	*Muslims*
1951-1961	37.71	38.35
1961-1971	37.17	30.99
1971-1991	41.89	77.42

A number of agencies are engaged in curbing the infiltration. But the results are not encouraging. Result of Assam agreement is before us. It is, therefore, necessary to issue identity cards to the population living in border areas and security arrangements along the border should be tightened.

(8) ***Economic Reasons and Unemployment:*** Complete North-East region though very rich in economic resources is quite backward economically. About 45 per cent of the population lives in poverty, cottage and small industrialists do not get proper returns. In most of the cases the middlemen swallow a major part of the earnings. A number of economic packages are being given but their benefits do not reach the needy for whom such packages are meant. Eventually the development becomes meaningless. The CAG report of government of India also says that the funds provided to these states under plan expenditure head are not properly utilized as well as in stipulated period. As a result such funds become stale and are lapsed. Ex Prime Minister H.D. Devegowda had constituted 'Shukla Commission' and Vipparai Committee for looking into the development process of this area and declared an economic package of Rs. 6,100 crores. The Gujarat government declared a package of Rs. 7200 crores and Prime Minister Atal Behari Bajpai declared a package of Rs. 25,000 crores in 2000. As it is, these North-East states get 90 per cent as grant and 10 per cent as loan from central pool. According to one understanding the Central Government spent Rs. 30,000 crores for the development of Nagaland having population of 12 lakhs, during last 25 years. But the corruption in this area is so rampant that even 15 per cent of these funds could not reach the grass root level.

It is not the case that the Central Government hesitates to allot funds as developmental help. But the 'CAG' report of 1999-2000, very clearly, states that there were much irregularities in utilisation of these funds because of absence of proper plan and programmes which is the result of mismanagement. The ultimate result of this is that the youth of this area feel that the Central Government gives them step-motherly treatment. Eventually they resort to weapons and terrorism takes birth here.

The intellectuals have their own opinions. They say that the Central Government never thought that it owns the people of this area. An English newspaper Sentimental says with example that the Central Government is interested in getting and carrying raw material from this area. The general public has to go for movement for getting any things. Two bridges across Brahmaputra are constructed but this too required a movement. Establishment of an oil refinery was and is the essentiality of this area. Against this a toy refinery of 0.85 million tons is established here and the main plant was transferred to Barouni in Bihar. The same way the head offices of tea gardens are situated outside the state. Apart from this, tea, crude oil, valuable wood and so many other items are taken away from the state but the state did not get proper returns from this. Eventually there is an increase in unemployment. The state did not have proper industrialisation on a large scale. Whatsoever industries are established here, they belong to outsiders. This gave impetus to terrorism.

(9) *Political Motives* : Politics in this area is also one of the important reasons of terrorism and separatism. All the political parties, small or big, with an object of winning elections, have always encouraged and fuelled the regionalism and encashed this feeling at the time of elections. Political situation in this area is also abnormal. Meghalaya and Manipur are experiencing political instability to such an extent that it is very difficult to know as to when government will fall and which government will come in power.

All the North-East states are engulfed in terrorism and its fury for the last three decades. The leadership of all the political parties in India can be said to be the father of this situation. Indian freedom struggle ended with an unnatural division of India. Today's Arunachal Pradesh was known as NEFA at the time of independence. Tripura and Manipur were princely States and Nagaland was a part of Assam. But the terrorism started along with the independence. Naga leader Fijo took refuge in Britain and started the movement of separate Nagaland and was managing it from there, that too with the foreign help. He continued to add fuel to the division movement. After sometime the Central Government entered into an agreement with the Naga leader and a state of Nagaland was created in the sixties. Meghalaya, too, was given the status of Indian state in seventies with a view to calm down the tensions in the Adivasis. Prior to this Shillong was the capital of Assam. During the Pre-independence period the city of Shillong was having great importance as the Governor of Assam stayed in Shillong and administered the whole North-East area. It was also an educational centre of North-East. The whole North-East area gathered a new face in the nature of seven states which were created by bowing down to the pressures and on the pretext of protecting the original tribal, their culture, traditions etc. Whenever any original tribe (Adivasi Community) created pressure by way of terrorism in this area. The Central Government created a new state for them. Lastly the Central Government bowed down before the terrorist movement under the leadership of Laldenga and a new state of Mizoram was created. Even after creation of these many states by yielding to the pressures, a number of movements are still run.

(10) *Cultural Situation* : There is a cultural multiplicity throughout North-East area. This culture separates one community from the other. Even after such a cultural multiplicity in this area, regionalism is deep rooted in their hearts. That is why these people feel that their dances, music, sports, drawing and painting, handicraft, dramatics, etc., are not given proper attention by rest of India and a step-motherly treatment is being given to them. This creates a feeling of separatism in them. But the fact is that the Central Government has established Television and Radio stations in this area for maintaining the cultural multiplicity and spread of their culture. The Doordarshan operates a 24 hours channel for the North-East where-from glimpses of North-East culture and arts are telecast.

(11) *Weak, inefficient, careless law and order situation and police* : The North-East states lack in tight Police administration. The police is not efficient enough to create mutual beliefs between the original residents and outsiders. Severe inequality is seen while recording any FIR in the police stations. Eventually recording FIR against the terrorists is stopped. The traders started feeling that it is beneficial for them to continue their trade in these states by satisfying the terrorists.

Table 11.2 Police Force and Crimes in North East

States	*No of Police-man (1996)*	*Murders (1998-99)*	*Other Cognisable Offences (1998-99)*
Meghalaya	7594	139	1829
Arunachal Pradesh	4132	(97-98) 76	(97-98)1848
Assam	48658	(97) 1452	(97) 36562
Manipur	10745	192	2867
Mizoram	5977	37	1780
Nagaland	16997	(97-98) 200	(97-98) 673
Tripura	12800	(96) 228	(96) 3360

The situation is still worse regarding filing a report against terrorist. If anyone dares to file a report, the terrorists immediately know this. The security of the reporter and his family is endangered as a consequence. It is not a secret that the police and the terrorists recovering illegal money have mutual understanding. It is said that the terrorists recovered more than Rs. four crores of ransom. It was recovered by the terrorists from Jayantiya mountains in Meghalaya. The same way the Garo terrorists recovered about Rs. two crores. This was during 2001. As a result the traders belonging to outside are closing their establishments and are leaving Shillong.

The Assam government feels that the Bodo terrorists might have recovered Rs. 75 crores as ransom in 2001. The surprising fact is that the sufferers do not dare to file a report with police because they very well know that the local police is unable to provide them any sort of security. The same is the case in Shillong also. Here also no one dares to file any such report with the police though ransom recovery and abduction is very common. The police and officers are in knowledge about the ransom recovery and abduction but there is no written report with them regarding such incidents. North-East terrorism is no more a politically aimed activity but has become a profession of recovering *goonda (rangdari)* i.e. terror tax. It has become easy for these terrorist groups to confront with the semi army forces (Ardha Sainik Bal), as they can secure modern and up-to-date weapons by this money. About 44,000 security men, including police, army, security forces are posted in the state of Manipur having total population of only 18 lakhs. Even then such a small state can not be controlled and terrorism be curbed. According to the government of Assam about 2000 persons were killed and 84 persons abducted by the terrorists during 2000-2001. This terrorism has destroyed the assets of crores of rupees by way of bomb blasts, etc., along with 39 rape cases.

Table 11.3 Projects of Modernisation of Police Force in Northeast (2000-2001)

States	Financial contribution	
	By state (in crores)	By Central (in crores)
Arunachal Pradesh	2.30	72.02
Assam	73.15	36.575
Manipur	8.20	4.10
Meghalaya	3.08	1.54
Mizoram	9.91	4.955
Nagaland	5.68	2.84
Tripura	12.79	6.395
Total	115.11	128.245

Table 11.4 Security Structure in Northeast (2000)

States	No of Police Stations	Civil Police men	Armed Police men	Total	Indian Security Force
Arunachal Pradesh	66	2987	2913	5900	2
Assam	240	22977	30946	53923	5
Manipur	57	4743	9241	13984	3
Meghalaya	26	5955	2626	8581	2
Mizoram	31	2948	3852	6800	2
Nagaland	45	7367	9020	16387	2
Tripura	44	7786	4596	12382	4

On the other hand if any honest police officer arrests a terrorist, he is shot dead. The then S.P. of Dibrugarh was killed after the release of three ULFA activists in 1990. The same way, Shri Ravikant Singh, S.P. of Tinsukhiya was shot dead along with four persons in 1996. This has spread a wave of demoralisation in police force, which is still on an increase. Eventually the police stood in dilemma and started avoiding direct action against the terrorist. According to some statistics about 600 policemen were killed during the last one decade. The fact that some policemen had direct relations with the terrorists which cost the lives of some police officers, has come to light.

As a matter of fact the Central Government has taken a number of steps to modernise the police force and its administration in 2000-2001. It has also provided funds as contribution towards this project of modernisation.

(12) *Mutual understanding between Politicians and Terrorists* : The role of political parties in flourishing of terrorism cannot be treated as negligible. On the other hand their role is as important as that of others. The secret agency have collected proofs of involvement of political parties in terrorism. The secret agencies also have proofs of shelter being provided to these terrorists by politicians and thereby increasing their morale. Rise of ULFA in Assam and simultaneously killings of a number of Congress workers is, in itself, a proof that Assam Gan Parishad had its deep relations with ULFA. Many times AGP and ULFA are supposed to be two sides of a coin. The same is the case with other local political parties. These parties do not support these organisations openly. But at the same time they avoid talking about them. Help taken by these political parties from terrorists organisations at the time of elections is not a secret fact.

National Liberation front of Tripura which is involved in terrorist activities has direct support of Indigenous Peoples front of Tripura. Whereas All Tripura Tigers Force (ATTF) is open supporter of CPI(M). Both these terrorist organisations regularly undertake terrorist acts in various places of Tripura.

Though the state government has declared some areas as 'Disturbed and Sensitive Areas' and deputed a large number of security forces therein, there is no decrease in violence in these areas. Even after proper coordination between Assam Rifles, BSF, CRPF, TSR and Police Force the violent activities could not be controlled. It is, no doubt, a serious matter.

The areas with majority tribal inhabitants are still not developed. Eventually the Adivasi youth adopt the way of terrorism right from childhood.

It is observed that the terrorists frighten and threaten various political parties and collect money as well, from them, in Manipur. It is a fact that the chief minister of Manipur Shri Radhavinod Koijam expelled six of his cabinet colleagues from his cabinet for their relations with terrorist organisations underground. His action was based on the report of justice (retd.) Shri S.K. Hom Choudhary. It is therefore needed that these political parties should sever their relations with terrorist organisations, that too at their own.

(13) *Role of Central Government* : As a matter of fact the Central Government has taken and is taking lots of initiatives to stop terrorism. But it seems that they are not sufficient (see chapter 'role of central Govt. and terrorism). Banning any organisation adversely glamorises it. These organisations start and continue their activities under new banner. Ignoring the seriousness of the problems as well as old ways of gaining power by using wrong methods, and Indian colonialism, unconstitutional methods have sparked the terrorism in the forties which is now converted itself in dangerous fire flames. As a matter of fact the complete North East region remained neglected up to the nineties. This gave birth to anger and hatred towards Delhi, in the minds of North East population.

Very short-sighted decision of Central Government taken in 2001 regarding Manipur has been the reason for wide spread violence. This gave a serious blow to the centres initiative to resolve the problems of North East. As a result, Assam and comparatively peaceful Arunachal Pradesh got disturbed. This can be taken as short-sightedness of the Home Ministry. The Central Government thought that the cease-fire in Naga majority areas would be welcome by the complete North East region. But the brains engaged in resolving the problems could not understand that such an initiative may hurt the tribal who are determined to protect their communal entity and pride.

The Central Government did not take public representatives of this area in confidence while extending the cease-fire areas to other states. This is an example of centres short-sightedness. The centre may quote that all the chief ministers of North Eastern states had agreed to the extension. But the centre could not foresee that taking such a decision, without understanding fully, the structure of North East might hurt the sentiments of these people and in turn may prove to be damaging the very purpose. Had various communal organisations, student leaders, etc., been taken into confidence, there would not have been such a fury of violence in Manipur.

It is the astonishing fact that the chief ministers of North East states are not true representatives of the communal groups and therefore their decision may not satisfy them. The governments in Meghalaya and Manipur go on changing frequently because of the tribal politics. The law and order situation here has reached such a state that some communal organisation or student organisation issues orders to the non tribal, on almost every day. Forcible recovery and collection of money from outsiders specifically traders is a regular activity. But the local administration and police remain silent observers. Thus, they run their own parallel governments.

Even then it is a hard truth that whenever any communal organisation wants to go ahead in politics, it uses the weapon of opposing any move or initiative taken by Central Government. These organisations adopt means to infuriate communal feelings. As a matter of fact Manipur incident is quite different and indicates long standing effects.

It is far more important problem of bringing peace to Nagaland than terrorism in Assam and other North East states. The strongest terrorist organisation of Nagaland is Nationalist Socialist Council of Nagaland (Isak and Muwaia faction). Therefore, neglecting the role NSC in the process of bringing peace in Nagaland may pose a greater problem and obstacle in the process. That is why the Central Government is compelled to accept many of their demands. They demanded to extend the boundaries of seize fire before starting peace talks. The centre yielded to this demand also, that too without understanding or forecasting as to how this extension would affect other states. The Nagas also live in the districts of Ukhrul, Tamenlang, Sanapati, and Chandel of Manipur, another five districts Golaghat, Jorhat, Shiosagar, Karbi Agland and North Kachhar (some part) in Assam as well as two more districts -Tirap and Changlang.

Extending the cease-fire area to Assam, Manipur and Arunachal Pradesh caused tension in the people of these places. They did not like it. These people feel that this is step towards yielding to the long standing demand of NSCN about a greater Nagaland and thereby these areas might be joined with Nagaland. As a matter of fact the centre is calling it as misunderstanding. The people of North East do feel that the centre had promised such things in past. But afterwards changed the borders of states. The people here are awakened and do not want to get fooled by the statements of Central Government. Eventually there was a revolt in all three states of Manipur, Arunachal Pradesh and Assam. If the demand of greater Nagaland is accepted the state which will have to suffer a lot is Manipur. Presently the area of this state is 22327 sq. km of this the above quoted districts of Manipur have occupied the area of 15519 sq. km. Naturally the Manipurians will not allow this division, signs of which are apparent.

No doubt the centre reversed the decision of extending the cease-fire area. But this has given a chance to terrorist organisations to talk about it alongwith other things. The largest terrorist organisation of Manipur-United Nationalist Liberation Front (UNLF) feels that extension of cease-fire area to three states is not going to help in resolving the Naga problems as well as any satisfactory outcome is not expected from this. The UNLF further feels that the centre wants to encourage the communal clashes so that they cannot be united. The ULFA, also, has said that they would not tolerate any distracting and disturbance with Assam borders.

Thus, a question arises. Whether the centre was not knowing the feelings of the people of North East or took this decision purposely? Softening and curing the wounded feelings of these people will now consume additional time and the Naga organisation also got an opportunity to remain stern on their stand. As per Naga revolutionary Muwaia, who is presently in Bangkok, 'cease-fire' is 'cease-fire' and it does not have any relations with the area. But the same time he does not deny the demand of 'Greater Nagaland'.

He further says that the Naga brotherhood in other states wants to join their brothers and there is nothing uncommon in this.

In totality it can be said that the soft and sober methods through which the centre is trying to resolve the problems of North East may prove to be self destructive, the signs of which are apparent.

(14) *Foreign Protection* : Terrorism in North East India has a considerable protection from other countries. Myanmar has dictator rule and that government feels that the Government of India is helping the democratic movement in their country. Burma (Myanmar) was geographically part of India till 1931. The British government separated it from India. There was democratically elected prime minister in 1952. The then Government of India sacrificed one district from Manipur with a view to have good friendly relations with Myanmar.

This was done on the request of the then Myanmar government. But now the same district has become the training centre for training people to undertake activities against India. Even after dictatorship in Myanmar the government of India is trying to establish better relations with Myanmar and for that it is not supporting the democratic movement. Same way it is doing a foolish act of continuing indirect support to terrorism there. Bangladesh has hatred for India. The terrorism under government protection and help in Bangladesh is beyond one's understanding. Indian border with this country is open. Government of India has curbed the infiltration from the Indian borders in Punjab, Rajasthan and Gujarat by putting barbed wire fencing and flood lights across the border. The same arrangement is a serious need of North East as well as rest of India.

There are internal as well as external reasons

of terrorism in North East. This region is connected with rest of India across a narrow land near Siligudi. Otherwise the complete region is surrounded on all sides by foreign countries. This situation helped in easing the inflow of outside help to the violence of separatist elements. These elements were getting help from China for some days. The help from Pakistan is continuously coming except for some period after the creation of Bangladesh. The ISI from Pakistan is providing help to a number of terrorist organisations. Apart from this help the Indian terrorist organisations have their training camps in Myanmar and Bangladesh. The training camps of Bodo and other terrorist organisations are run even in southern part of Bhutan for last some years. Because of the geographical situation added by foreign help from China, Pakistan, etc., the separatist organisations undertaking terrorism are becoming stronger day by day. But the real reason for the strength of these organisations is our internal weakness. Demoralisation and bad inefficient administration, lack of political foresight as well as colonial way of thinking by the government are also responsible for this problem. As it is whole country is suffering from moral weaknesses and inefficient and bad administration. But the North Eastern states come under the category of privileged states.

The terrorism in North East had China's strong support right from 1950 & 1960. Firstly the Nagas sought help from China. After that the Mizo revolutionaries and afterwards Maitei revolutionaries of Manipur established political relations with China. Accordingly they received both money and weapons from that country. China provided training to 17 P.L.A. militants in Lhasa. Two Mizo groups went to China in 1988. But afterwards they developed some ideological differences with China. Actually China wanted that these people should adopt the path shown by Mao-Tse-Tsung. But Naga and Mizos had strong impact of Christian ideology. Eventually they did not agree to China's proposal of adopting 'Mao-way'. These people went afterwards to such an extent that the paper pages from Mao's 'Red Book' were used by them as toilet papers. Later on Rajiv Gandhi visited China in 1989 and there was improvement in bi-lateral relations with China. As a result China stopped taking interest in the ideology of terrorism in this area.

(15) *Administration and Corruption* : Though the total population of North East India is only 4 per centof the total population of India, the centre allots 20 per cent of the total funds meant for all the states, to this area. 90 per cent of such amount is given as grant and 10 per cent as loan whereas this percentage for rest of the states in 30 and 70 respectively. If the total amount paid to Nagaland during 1999-2000 (Rs. 1,211 Crores) is divided among Naga families, each family would get Rs. 4169 per month. Such is the huge financial help from centre. The same is the state of affairs with other North Eastern states. But the development is far below expectation. This deficiency in such development work is attributed to the centre by corrupt administration. Lack of development is also one of the reasons of terrorism.

In spite of maximum per capita expenditure the public could neither get the benefits of development nor could they enjoy security. The state machinery swallows all. About a thousand crore rupees are recovered by the underground and criminal organisations. The state government is unable to stop it. Corruption has become rampant and the administration totally dilapidated. The problems become more complex with Central Governments attitude of providing funds but ignoring the situation. The state of immorality cannot be allowed to continue any longer. Our irresponsible political behaviour and lack of foresight have contributed a lot to the complexity of problems.

(16) *Colonial history writing and Misunderstandings* : Indian historians are blindly adopting and accepting the history written by the British. Today the situation is such that if any one puts forth his discoveries and analysis in a new method which is other than the old and traditional and founded by British, he has to face public criticism. His discoveries and inferences are not accepted. This has caused the brainwash of our people who have undergone English education. Their brains have gone colonial. The situation is more harsh in North East. Racial definitions of the societies clashes between mainstream and people cut from main stream were imagined by the British with not any good intentions. As a matter of fact both these assumptions are wrong. Though the Kirats belong to Mangol race the *Mahabharata* regarded them as 'Kshatriyas' and upper caste. As per Mahabharata 'Uliupi' is Naga Princess as well as from 'Aryans'. The British historian Gate ill-defined the word 'Asur' and the word 'Di' from Bodo which means water. Gate adopted this and thereby gave undesirable turn to the history of Assam. He conveniently forgot that 'Asur' was not 'Anarya'. On the other hand-Asur-Vrutta was Brahmin and a learned saint of Vedas. Synonym of bodo word 'Di' in Sanskrit is 'Toy' i.e. water.

The British had planned to keep North East area cut from India. Accordingly, though not as planned they separated the people in planes from the people in mountains. As a matter of fact there was no such separatist mentality in these people. The same way neither the North East and rest of India remained separate nor the people in planes and people in hills.

This area was never under Muslim rule except for short period that too a part of it. This area was always with rest of India even from *Ramayana* and *Mahabharata* era. Assam was under 'Gupta' rule also. Assam kings had their extended territories even up to Orissa and Chattisgarh for about 400 years. One or two Assam rulers/kings performed 'Ashwamedh Yagya'. Assam was connected not only to rest of India but with East, Central and South East Asia by roads. These facts do not prove that separatism is inherent in these people. Even after existence of all these facts, impact of colonial history is so deep that Indian historian S.K.Varpuyari also was impressed by it and talked about splendid isolation. It is essential to mention here that common people in Northeast do not have separatist mentality. But because of terrorism and other things they do not publicly criticise separatism and terrorism.

The British started tea gardening in Assam about ten years before the Second World War. People in rest of India even did not know 'what tea was?' But later on tea became most popular. Naturally the British started expanding the tea gardens. They needed labour to work in these gardens. As such their agents used to visit Bihar and its village. They started attracting the labour by offering them attractive wages, which was about 8 to 10 times higher than what they were getting in Bihar as well as Kolkata. Physical environment of Assam at that time was not good. Most of the labour started suffering from Malaria, Indigestion and Typhoid. Means of conveyance were not easy. Eventually the labour from Bihar was unable to return to their native places. Many of them used to marry the girls from Assam and get established there. It is because of this that the people in Bihar and east Uttar Pradesh started assuming that the girls in Assam knew black magic and they learnt it from Kamara Kamakhya (Kamakhya shrine in Kamrup district) and thereby they turned the Biharis into goats, and so on. Today also there are a number villages, the residents of which feel that the Assam girls have transformed many youth from their villages to goats. They further believed that these girls were such experts in black magic that they could turn a man into a goat and a goat into man at their sweet will. This assumption prevailed there for about 12 years. But the fact was that the Biharis were forced to live in Assam for want of conveyance to return. Naturally they married girls from Assam and permanently stayed there and forgot their native places. If at any time any of their relations came to Assam in their search these Biharis started not to recognise or not to own them. Naturally such persons used to get annoyed by this. Therefore on returning to their places used to tell that the Assam girl had transformed them to goat. Such assumptions prohibited people from outside to go and visit North East area.

(17) *Role of Christian Missionaries and I.S.I* : Role of Christian Missionaries and I.S.I of Pakistan in encouraging and supporting separatism and terrorism in North East can not be ignored. About 44 per cent of total Christian population of India is in the North Eastern states and Nagaland and Mizoram have majority population of Christians. As a matter of fact developmental work done by the missionaries in this area is also commendable. But it is also the fact that there are some such missionaries and Churches whose attitude and behaviour as well as role is not only suspicious but also treacherous.

(18) *Inner Line Permit* : Entry of outsiders in the states of Nagaland, Mizoram and Arunachal Pradesh is restricted. If any one wants to go to these states he is required to obtain permit from liason officer. This permit is known as Inner Line permit. The Central Government has made this arrangement in order to restrict easy entry of outsiders in these states of tribals. Otherwise the tribals who are in majority in these states may not become minorities. Original inhabitants of Meghalaya are also demanding the same arrangement for their state. This system of Inner Line Permit has its adverse effects also. People from other states start feeling that they have to complete a number of formalities as are required (nearly) to obtain visa for other countries that too when they intend to go to a state of their own country. This gives birth to the feeling of separatism towards these states. Secondly the Border Security Forces become free to do as they like. Transporters pay some money to them and conveniently enter these states. This encourages corruption. Thirdly the tourism industry in these states is adversely affected. In the modern days of globalisation such restrictions give rise to separatism as well as isolation. This again adversely affects the investment by other industrialists to the fullest extent.

Following are some suggestions to overcome this reason of separatism and terrorism.

(a) the word foreigners be properly defined. Non tribals should not be considered as foreigners.

(b) The position of people from outside of the particular states who have come and who want to come to the state for employment or as trader or as Government and other employees, etc., should be clarified.

(c) Identity cards or Nationality certificates be

issued to every tribal living on both the sides of borders of the state. This will also ease their refuge to India in case they come across accidental difficulties as happened in 1971 Bangladesh war.

(d) In order to operate this arrangement the originally settled non-tribal should be taken in confidence. The Central Government should formulate a common policy and date so that this problem can be permanently resolved. Security and protection of fundamental rights of all the people should be provided.

(e) Regular talks should be arranged and undertaken between people of various categories so that amicable and proper environment can be created. An atmosphere of mutual confidence between tribals and non tribals shall have to be created.

(f) The system of Inner Line permit should be withdrawn. This will help the industrialists to come to these states to start industries. This, in turn, will provide employment to the natives and development process will start

(19) *Combination of Student organisations and Militants* : One can not belittle the role of students in spreading terrorism in North east. Students of all colleges as well as universities have their student organisations. The contribution of Assam students Union (AASU) in the Assam movement was very important. The hard core group of students from this organisation parted from AASU and founded ULFA a terrorist organisation. ULFA showered its fury in Assam during the ninetees. The AASU leader had kept mum about the activities of ULFA. They never spoke against ULFA. On the other hand they, every now and then, tried to blame the army for its so called atrocities. This created a feeling in general public that AASU and ULFA are two sides of a coin. They work as AASU activists during day time and ULFA activists during night time. A number of such incidences came to light during police as well as army action.

As it is very clear that students organisations in every state are enacting various important roles in the movements in all North Eastern states. Khasi student union of Meghalaya is seen publishing in newspaper, their orders to so called outsiders to leave Meghalaya. This they do on the lines of militant organisations. They are seen collecting money from smaller or bigger, industrialists and traders, in the name of the student organisation. The people pay them out of fear. There are numerous such incidence in Nagaland, Mizoram, etc.

The Choudhari commission under the chairmanship of retired Justice S. K. Homechoudhari, in its 39 pages report has recorded the fact that All Manipur Students Union (AMSU) has its strong relations with underground terrorist organisation United Liberation Front (UNLF). The commission further discussed the relations between AMSU and UNLF specially in killing and abduction cases. These relations were proved on the basis of documents seized from Premanand Singh the then chairman of AMSU, during a raid on his residence. The same way AMSU financial secretary who was also the member of UNLF was arrested along with seizure of arms and propaganda equipment and pamphlets, etc. The report has further said that the demand for removal of special rights to armed forces Act and boycott of Republic day were aimed at providing help to the said terrorist organisation UNLF. The report says that the contribution collected by AMSU finally is diverted to

UNLF. Large amount collected by AMSU in the name of student welfare is used by UNLF for terrorist activities more and very small part is used for the purpose for which it is collected. Justice Home Choudhary has stated that all the amount collected by AMSU was illegal. The report further commented that AMSU which raised the point of atrocities by security forces as braking human rights, and took it very seriously, did not speak a word against abduction, killing and ransom by UNLF though such acts are more severe than atrocities.

Thus, it is essential to divert the students mind towards their own education and better educational atmosphere. They should be inspired not to indulge in politics and militancy even providing help to militancy. It is, therefore necessary to concentrate more powers in college managements so that they can ensure that the students are not adopting unwanted and wrong path.

(20) ***Role of Media*** **:** People from North East are ever complaining that the newspapers and electronic media do not give proper coverage to them. They say that incidence of killing, abduction etc. in this area are given wide publicity by these media. But they ignore the specialities and goodness of the people. They further complain that such publicity carries negative information regarding the people of North East which, in turn helps the rest of India to form wrong impression.

More than 500 dailies and periodicals in local as well as other Indian languages are published in this area. Every State has its own newspaper published by the tribal in their own language. These newspapers are devoted to their welfare and benefits of their owns. But the area covered by them is restricted to their region. Naturally information and news of National interest do not find place in these newspapers. They elaborate only the regional feelings. Take the example of Assam, it is seen that the newspapers published in Assamese, Hindi and English differ in their view points and nature. On one side Assamese newspaper gives importance to regional feelings where Hindi newspapers try to protect the interests of people who come from outside. The role of Assamese newspapers in making paper tigers of ULFA can not be denied. This is done by the weeklies also keeping in view the increase in sale. Local news are published in exaggerated manner. But then English editors like S. N. Deobarua openly criticises the terrorist organisations. On the other hand the Hindi newspapers placed ULFA with high esteem and glamorous position which caused terror among non Assamese people.

Many proofs of insurgency of terrorist organisations in media have come to light. Some journalists were found working as liason officers of these organisations. This has harmed not only the ethics of journalism but encouraged separatism also. Thus, it is necessary that the newspapers in this area should decide with themselves whether they should glamorise the militancy or not.

Chapter 12

Conclusion

'As the medicine is administered so the disease increased' such is the case of North East of India. Their problems go on increasing though the remedies are found and implemented. A number of economic packages are given to this area during the last few years but the situation goes on more disturbing than improving. The geographical structure of complete

Table 12.1 Estimated Employment in Public and Private Sector 1997-98 ('000)

States	*Public Sector*	*Private Sector*	*Total*
Meghalaya	69.3	7.6	76.9
Arunachal Pradesh	-	5	-
Assam	534.8	566.9	1091.7
Manipur	77.9	2.3	80.2
Mizoram	39.6	1.4	41.0
Nagaland	73.0	2.9	75.9
Tripura	90.7	10.5	101.2

Northeast is such that this area has become a fertile land for the foreign organisations like ISI. These organisations are engaged in misleading the North

East people specially the youth. They want to keep the situation ever disturbed and convert this area on the lines of Kashmir. These organisations have placed an imaginary danger of destroying the culture, identity and self-respect of the simple natured people of this area. These organisations supply them weapons and financial assistance and inspire them to create

Table 12.2 Number of registrations in Employment Exchanges 1997 (000)

State	*Total*
Meghalaya	33.5
Arunachal Pradesh	10.8
Assam	1495.58
Manipur	207.3
Mizoram	67.9
Nagaland	21.7
Tripura	212.5
Total	2049.2
Total India	39200.0
Percentage in North East to rest of India 5.3%	

disturbance against so-called destruction of their culture, traditions, self-respect etc. They mesmerise the people specially by showing them castles in the air. Naturally the feeling that all such destruction is done by the outsiders and they therefore, should leave the area, makes them infuriated. It is a fact that ISI has joined hands with almost all terrorist organisations in this area including ULFA, Bodo, etc. If we look at the situation in five districts of Assam only we can see that the Bangladesh infiltrators have come in majority pushing the original residents to minority. Naturally insecurity feelings cropped up in the minds of original residents. The state of Tripura, which is surrounded on three sides by Bangladesh, has become the entrance gate for the infiltrators from that country.

The Northeast is under such an impact of Western culture that we can no where find India in at least the states of Mizoram, Nagaland, Meghalaya and to some extent Manipur. Drug addiction and free sex has conquered the youth in this area. In totality the situation in Northeast India, though not sensitive, is not good also. Bringing normalcy to this area is as difficult as charming a snake or untieing the silk-knot. As a serious effort towards this, the following 19 points suggestions can be put forth. These suggestions are based on the discussion with Government and Semi government organisations, various educational institutions, teachers organisations, social forums and organisations, terrorist organisations, other organisations fighting for protecting their culture, political parties and their leaders, intelligent, people connected with periodicals and newspapers, etc.

Table 12.3 Central Aid to North East

States	*VII plan (1985-90)*	*Yearly (1990-91)*	*Yearly (1991-92)*	*VIII plan (1992-97)*
Assam	2567.05	632.62	805.00	4662.00
Arunachal Pradesh	384.42	164.69	235.00	1155.00
Meghalaya	531.09	148.18	178.00	1029.00
Manipur	613.24	145.35	195.00	979.00
Mizoram	362.05	104.34	152.00	763.00
Nagaland	699.72	124.55	164.61	844.00
Tripura	619.96	164.17	195.66	1130.00
Total	5778.43	1483.88	1925.27	10562.00

(1) The wind of total revolution is blowing fast in the North East region. The people, therefore, are disturbed because of fear of destruction of their tribal culture and identity.

(2) The local parties and governments always blame the Central Government for ignoring the North

East region. But it is not the fact. Actuelly the centre has sanctioned and declared a number of economic packages for this area. But the state government agencies appointed to utilise the funds, do not properly use the funds. None of the funds ever reached the backward people.

(3) All the Local parties and government in order to save themselves from the blame of backwardness of this area blame the Central Government.

(4) Total North East sector is rich in Natural resources. There is ample scope of generating hydroelectricity. People of this area are very good at handicraft and handloom. But their art is not being utilised properly to bring financial returns to them.

(5) There is a great potential for tourism industry in this area. Tourism of foreign and local tourists to this area can be converted into a good source of income. But there are no proper arrangements for package tours, etc.

Table 12.4 Non Lapsable Amount (1999-2000) from Central aid in Crores

States	*Rs.*
Arunachal Pradesh	12.50
Assam	153.85
Meghalaya	26.21
Manipur	51.00
Mizoram	46.24
Nagaland	31.03
Tripura	32.50
Common	10.10
Total	372.43

(6) Law and order situation in this area is in shambles. The traders are not in a position to do the business freely. The terrorists and even any local

group collect enormous money from them by threatening them.

(7) Looting the people, collecting the ransom, abduction and killing havc become regular profession of the terrorists.

(8) Some communal groups, some student leaders, and leaders of local parties are involved in encouraging some so called terrorists organisations for their own financial as well as political benefits. Some local newspapers are working as His Masters voice for some organisations. These newspapers feel honoured by publishing any press release along with their letter pad. Threatening messages aimed at so called outsiders are given through these newspapers ordering them to leave the area as if these organisations are the rulers.

(9) But the fact remains that all the North Eastern states with the exception of Nagaland and Mizoram have their roots entrenched with the rest of India.

(10) The educated as well as uneducated youth of this area do not want hard work. They are after easy money which they collect as ransom from the traders, tea gardeners and outsiders calling them the squeezers of North East. For this they keep the atmosphere of separatism ever boiling. They start threatening the industrialists or other agencies even before starting any industry or unit, to employ their own men.

(11) Separatism and or terrorism in North East is not the result of unemployment in the youth. But the fact is the youth from this area do not want to go out either for employment or for starting a profession.

(12) They are more interested in sports, music, and dance. Thus, it is desirable to develop and encourage these arts.

(13) Literature from the North East languages needs to be translated in Hindi, English and other languages with a view to have wide circulation.

(14) We do not find the mention of great personalities as well as freedom fighters from this area in the history of India and Indian freedom struggle. Let us take the example of Assam only. We find that the sacrifice and contribution in freedom struggle made by Diyali, Vastukan JiuramBarua Tarum ram Fukan Gopinath Basdole Kanaklata has been either ignored or forgotten to be mentioned and noted by the history writers. Queen Gaidulu of Nagaland hoisted the tricolour with the name of Mahatma Gandhi and was eventually jailed. Name of U. Tirot Singh who revolted against the British also could not find a place in history. Naturally people feel that when the contribution of their leaders is not taken cognisance of, then why should they remain connected with rest of India and therefore should have their free existence. This feeling is further converted into separatist mentality

(15) The system of inner line permit for going to Mizoram, Nagaland and Arunachal Pradesh should be stopped.

(16) It is necessary to encourage the traditional customs, Music Dance, etc., and produce them before rest of India to restrict the impact of Western culture

(17) Administration, Political parties should be made accountable to the people.

(18) The help received by voluntary organisations should be properly used for the purpose for which it is given. It is necessary to supervise and restrict its mis-utilisation.

(19) Cultural troupes from rest of India should be made to perform in North-East. Various sports festivals on National level as well, should be organised in this region. This may help connecting them with rest of India.

Appendix

Assam Agreement

Signing of Assam Agreement on the 15 th August, 1985 is an incidence of National importance. All Assam Students Union (AASU) which was running the movement under the banner of (Assam Gan Sangram Parishad) was ended by this agreement. Main object of this movement was to get rid of illegal infiltrators from East Pakistan (Bangladesh). This agreement brought peace and normalcy to Assam which was totally disturbed for a pretty long period and Assam Assembly elections could be held in December 1985.

The leaders of AASU and AGSP stopped their movement. Responsibility of implementing the provisions under Section 13 of the agreement, meant for all-round development of Assam was given to New Government of Assam which was formed with the support of general public. The centre was supposed to act as nodal agency for this. As a matter of fact the Central and State governments were made jointly responsible for implementation of Assam Agreement in totality.

Points in the Agreement : The movement by AASU and AGSP was mainly aimed at identifying the illegal infiltrators and expelling them from Assam. There were also other objects which were related to the foreigners. For example. Amendment to the voters list which includes the names of foreign citizens which were included illegally in the voters list and removal of their names from these lists. Providing security and developing the linguistic identity and culture of the area by providing legal and administrative security.

A plan was prepared for uplifting the living standards of Assamese, under this agreement. This plan for fourteen sided development of Assam was prepared by the Central Government. It included establishment of educational, scientific and technical institutes. The agreement also provided for ways and means for achieving this.

The revolutionaries during the talks demanded to erect barbed wire fencing or wall along the international border, to construct breakers at proper places, to guard the border by protection forces and to construct road along the international border. This was included in the agreement. This was aimed at stopping the infiltration through the open border. They also demanded to remove the encroachment on government land in tribal areas and to make arrangements to stop the recurrence. A demand for providing restriction on transferring the immovable property of foreigners, was also made. All these demands were accepted by the Central Government and were included in the agreement.

The Centre accepted to instal one refinery plant and to start one Indian Institute of Technology in Assam. This is aimed at fast development of Assam. The centre also promised to restart the Ashoka Paper Mill at Jogidhopa which was closed for six years and also promised to give financial assistance to sick jute mills.

Foreigners in Assam : One has to go fifty years back in order to understand the problem to foreigners in Assam when displaced people from undivided Bengal started coming to Assam in 1920, to Rangpur and Gaimesing. It posed a problem bcfore undivided India that time. But this problem assumed serious nature during the Sixties and Seventies when refugees entered Assam during India Pakistan war. As a matter of fact the central as well as Assam government were knowing this According to both of them they tried to stop this infiltration but to no result.

As a result AASU declared 'Assam Bandh' in October 1979 and restarted the movement. This movement prolonged till the time the Assam agreement was signed.

Organisations Participating in Assam movement

All Assam Students Union (AASU): This organisation took active part in the movement run to expel the Bangladesh infiltrators from Assam. The AASU was declared a political organisation in 1979 by its the then chairman Prafulla Kumar Mohanto and Secretary General Bhrugu Kumar Fukan. This organisation was more active, strong and well organised. It has branches in almost all colleges specially in Brahmaputra valley.

Assam Gan Sangram Parishad:- (AGSP) This organisation also took active part in Assam movement. Purvanchal Lok Parishad, Assam Communal Youth Student Parishad, Assam Sahitya Sabha, Akhil Assam Karmachari Parishad and other tribal organisations were also included in this organisation.

Purvanchal Lok Parishad : Mr. Niwaran Boda was the chairmen of this organisation with communist ideology. Various small tribal parties were working under his leadership. This organisation extended moral support to the revolutionaries during the movement.

Assam Communal Youth Students Parishad: This organisation is supposed to be the father organisation of AASU and was working on the lines of AASU. This organisation is generally known as supporter of AASU.

Assam Sahitya Sabha : This organisation was formed about 75 years ago in 1917 with the object of creating educational atmosphere, encouraging talented authors and poets, publishing books in Assamese language. Well known dramatist and Literature Shri Lakshyadhar Choudhary is its present chairman. This organisation was encouraging the revolutionaries from time to time by giving awards.

Akhil Assam Karmachari Parishad : This is an organisation of all government employees of Assam except from Basak Vally and Karbo Aglang. This organisation is known for its strength and fighting nature. This organisation supported the movement indirectly.

Army operations in Assam

Operation Bajrang : State government of Assam led by Assam Gan Parishad was held responsible for worsening law and order situation in Assam. As a result the government was dissolved on the 27th November 1990. Operation Bajrang was also started on the same day to control the ULFA which was going stronger day by day.

The army could not get sufficient success. This operation had to suffer from the displeasure of the officers as well as leaders. The same time it had to face the fruitlessness of the operation because of the infiltration of ULFA members in the police force and the administration. On the other hand, the ULFA activists killed 58 persons during the operation.

At least 15 ULFA activists and about 2800 suspected ULFA members were arrested during the operation. The army could not lay its hands on any of the important leaders of ULFA. The ULFA declared sease fire on the 1st March 1991 and spoke for peaceful elections. Accordingly the operation was withdrawn on the 20th April 1991 and the army was sent back to its barracks.

Operation Blue Print : Shri Hiteshwar Saikya released all the ULFA activities from Jail by awarding general amnesty on the 30th June 1991 on his acquisition of office as new Chief Minister of Assam. Because of this all the ULFA activists again gathered together and started kidnapping and killing. During this spree the ULFA terrorist kidnapped 14 senior officers and demanded release of its members/ activists who were imprisoned for murders and other serious offences. As a consequence the army was alerted and it was known as operation Blue Print.

ULFA training camps in Arunachal Pradesh were under surveillance. Locating the important strings of ULFA was undertaken under this and a prepared to destroy the ULFA was also prepared.

Operation Cloud Burst : Operation Rhino was permitted on the 15th September 1991 and on the same date another deep operation known as Operation Cloud Burst was also started. Three training camps that were being run at Kopatalli, Chapri in Arunachal Pradesh were totally destroyed under this operation.

All the road and water routs were first blocked by the army and after that the jawans were taken to the dense forest by helicopters. Many secret documents along with rockets, etc., were seized from these camps. Names of the ULFA leaders could also be collected from there. Six persons were arrested during this operation. ULFA's senior leader Paresh

Bauria had visited these camps just before a fortnight of this operation.

Operation Rhino : Army action was operated within the state and along the border area of Assam after 15th September 1991 which was called 'Operation Rhino'. Its object was to compell the organisation for talks along with destroying the organisation to a great extent. Four army divisions along with security forces were employed for this operation.

258 ULFA and its supporters were arrested during the first week of operation along with attacking twelve training camps. The army received full support and co-operation from administration as well as public in general during the operation. Speciality of this operation is in the efforts of the army to gain confidence from general public for which the army had to leave its traditional character and adopt new policy and nature. This fetched good results. A number of ULFA top leaders were arrested and large number of ULFA hard-core activists were killed in the encounters and clashes. Deputy commander of ULFA Hirak Jyoti Mahant was among those who were killed.

The ULFA organisation was totally destroyed and the leaders had to declare unilateral cease fire and preparedness for talks. This was the great success of this operation. The operation was stopped on the 13th January 1992.

Operation Co-operation : After compelling the ULFA leaders for talks the army was deputed to help the public in reconstruction. This was known as operation co-operation. The army Jawans were deputed for welfare work of Assam public in general, Flood control, repairs to buildings, construction of roads leading to inner areas of Assam were some of the works which were done with the help of Army Jawans.

Bodo Agreement

Demand for providing opportunities for the development of Bodo community inspired the student organisation - Plains tribes council of Assam (PTCA). All Bodo Students Union (ABSU) Assam Gan Sangram Parishad (AGSP). All Assam Student Union (AASU), etc., to start the movement. This movement assumed violent nature afterwards. Bodo Security Force (BSF) was founded during the peak of movement by ABSU and BPSC. This organisation wanted sovereign state of Bodoland.

The state government was compelled to give a serious thought to this movement by rising pressures from all sides. The state government put a proposal of autonomy according to Panchayat System. But this was totally rejected by them. After this the Central Government appointed a three member expert committee to study the movement. This committee was entrusted to discover ways and means for providing rights to Bodo community in the areas of execution, assembly and administration without any more division of Assam.

The Bodo leaders brought some lethargy in their activities. But the terrorists camp of these organisations performed a number of violent activities and the situation started going out of control. Afterwards there was an agreement between the government and the leaders of movement demanding more facilities for Bodo community. This agreement was signed by the chairman of ABSU, S. K. Viswamurtiyari, joint chief Secretary of state, government K. S. Rao, General secretary of ABSU Raviram Brahma and BPAC Chairman Subhas Vasumatari. This agreement was signed in the presence of Hiteshwar Saikya the then chief minister of Assam and Minister of state for internal security Rajesh Pilot.

Accordingly an interim executive council with 18 members was appointed. Its headquarters was established at Kokrazar and S. K. Vishwamutari was made its chairman. 38 divisions coming under Bodoland Autonomous council (BAC) were brought under the newly appointed interim 'executive council on the 9th June 1993.

Cease fire agreement with Naga

The Central Government entered into a cease fire agreement with National Socialist Council of Nagaland (Ishak/Muwaia). This agreement provides the following :

1. Cease fire will be applicable to the total population and not to the terrorists and security forces only.

2. The NSCN (IM) shall not give protection to any other terrorist organisation.

3. The NSCN (IM) shall not attack or undertake any activity that may cause injury or death or damage to property.

4. The terrorist group shall not create any road jam or obstruct any development work.

5 Identity cards shall be provided to all activists of NSCN(IM) and they shall not go from one place to other in uniform or with weapons.

6. There shall be no tresspassing of scheduled area of terrorist group by the security/protection forces.

7. No security forces shall be deputed within two kilometres area of NSCN(IM) camps, even then permission can be granted for patrolling within one kilometre area, but the camp in charge should be informed in advance.

The NSCN, NGO and the centre shall supervise strict implementation of these rules.

Bibliography

1. *Assam 2000* - A handbook.
2. *Tribes And Castes of Assam* (Author : Cipra Sen)
3. *Tribes of Tripura : Description, Ethnology and Bibliography* (Author : Cipra Sen)
4. *Tripura* (Author : S.N. Guha Thakurata)
5. *Arunachal Pradesh and The Tribes : Select Bibliography* (Author : Cipra Sen)
6. *Tribes of Mizoram : Description, Ethnology and Bibliography* (Author : Cipra Sen)
7. *The People of Meghalaya : Study of the people and their Religion-Cultural Life* (Author : Captain B.S.Rana)
8. *Insurgency In North East India* (Editor : B. Pakem)
9. *Nagaland* (Author : Prakash Singh)
10. *Guide to Mizoram* - I, II, III, IV
11. *Where do we stand in 2000 : Meghalaya in North East India, and India and the World.*
12. *Assam : The Emerald Trizarland* (The Directorate of Tourism, Assam)
13. *Meghalaya* : The Directorate of Information and Public Relation, Government of Meghalaya.
14. *Socio-economic Atlas of India* (National Atlas and Thimtic Mapping Organisation)
15. *North East India : The human Interface* (Editor : M.K.Raha and Alok Kumar Ghosh)
16. *Social and Economic Development in NorthEast India* (Author : B.K. Ahaluwaliya And Shashi

Ahaluwaliya)
17. *Basic Statics of North Eastern Region* : 2000
18. General of the North Eastern Council
19. Peoples of North East India

20. *Tribales and their Culture : I, II, III* (Author : G. K.. Ghosh)
21. *Tribal India : Problem Development Prospect*- I, II (Author : M.K.Raha And Palash Chandra Kumar).
22. *Single Woman In Assamese Hindu Society* (Author: Jyoti Baruia)
23. *The Chakmaj : Life and Struggle* (Author S.P. Talukdar)
24. *Primitive Triblas Groups In Eastern India : Welfare and Evaluation* (Author: P.K. Bhaumik)
25. N.E. News letter
26. Annual Report 1999-2000
27. *Geopolitics of North East India : A Strategical Study* (Author : Jaishankar Hajaria)
28. *The Missings of Assam : Development of A New Life Style* (Author : Jatin Mipun)
29. *Eastern Panorama* (News Magazine of North East) Editor : Dr. K.K. Zunzunwala
30. *Strangers of the Mist* (Author : Sanjay Hajaria)
31. India's North East resurgent (Author : B.G. Wargis)
32. *Economy of the North East* (Author : Gulshan Suchdeva)
33. *Ulfa : A Political Analysis* (Author Selbi Takkar)
34. *Travelling with the Dreams* (Author : Shrutimala Duara)
35. *For Existence* (Author : Nikhil Khashanavish)
36. *Anthropometic variation in Assam,* Bihar, and Orissa (Author : Arbind Basu and Srinath)
37. Archaeology of North Eastern India (Author : V.P. Singh

38. Assam and Neighbouring States : History Document (Author : N.N. Acharya)
39. Census of India : Assam-I, II (Author C.S. Multan)
40. Documents on Assam-I, II (Author : V.R.Trivedi)
41. Encyclopedia of North India (Author : S.K. Khanna)
42. Garo hills Land and Peoples (Author : L.S. Gassaha)

Index

PERSONALITY DEVELOPMENT

HARI OM GOEL

PUBLICATIONS

KALPAZ PUBLICATIONS

DELHI-110052

Personality Development

ISBN: 81-7835-600-7

Published in 2013in India by
Kalpaz Publications
C-30, Satyawati Nagar,
Delhi-110052
E-mail: kalpaz@hotmail.com
Phone : 9212729499

Lasser Type Setting by: Rudra Computer Graphics, Delhi
Printed at : G. Print Process,Delhi

Contents

Foreword

I deem it a pleasure to write a few words about this book *Personality Development* and the author Dr. Hari Om Goel. There have been some books in the market from Indian authors as well as very well known authors the world over, in the form of context or write-ups in illustrating particular theme. Such books which have been mostly in the form of Monograms, have ventured to bring home to the readers a significant impact by way of what can be called light reading material. Most of these books, however, have focused on western philosophy and therefore the illustrations or antedots have also been drawn from the western way of life. Probably, for the first time an attempt has been made by Dr. Hari Om Goel to bring home the same concept focusing on health, discipline and character and that too in the Indian Context. The title of the book *Personality Development* is particularly meaningful as ultimately whatever one does in life is consciously or sub consciously intended for achieving happiness. It is a different matter though many people may not even understand what happiness is. The topics like "Happiness lies in Compromise", "Understand Realities and try to be Happy", "Happiness means Adjustment and Habitation" etc. etc focus on them without putting the burden on the mind of the Readers. I am of the considered opinion that the book, when in the hands of the Readers will certainly go a long way in making the lives of readers happy and thereby achieving the purposes which the author has in mind.

I have known the author. Dr. Hari Om Goel for several decades and his obsession of trying to do something for the society all the time is the impelling force in taking such projects. Earlier also, he. has written two books titled *Tension - Tension* and *Ten Talks* which were perused by me and I found them to be extremely useful and purposeful in their objectives. The present book will achieve the purpose in a much more magnificent way, I believe.

I take this opportunity to place on record the appreciation of the author and best wishes to the Readers for whom the book is really meant.

K.K. Aggarwal

1

Contentment

Judge your Pain and Pleasure in Own Perspective

We quite often forget our preceding position and aspiration and shorten our betterment by comparing with others. Unless this tendency is checked you can never become happy. Suppose Mr. X has a manual bike and wishes he should have a motorbike. Nature favours him by providing that what he desired and the man is still not happy because he sees all people around him having motorcars. If X on achievement of a motorbike would have felt happy and thanked nature for that, he would have earned the benediction and pleasure of nature as also derived energy to continue further effort for the next target, a motor car. Nature is so benevolent that it does so much for the human beings but the ungrateful instinct of thanklessness and grumble, which is spreading fast amongst the humanbeings, is neither pleasing their own self nor the nature. Man's achievements and nature's contributions are abundant but the small thinking of man turns even his grand pleasure into pathos when he starts comparing with others. Everyday we see people repeating this tendency in different forms. Suppose X is groaning with pain. He is actually in trouble but when he hears some one else suffering more severely he feels relieved Mr. A enters into a deal with B. Mr. A has accepted the deal after careful consideration of his own benefits from it. The deal is matured but A's deriving pleasure from the achievement is marred because the cynicism in him obliterates that thought of own benefit. He has started thinking about the benefit B has achieved from the deal. Suppose a person is one eyed and sometimes feels the anguish of this deficiency. He is very happy when hears an eye loss of a rival as if that way the rival's lost eye sets in the one eyed person to make him have both eyes. There is darkness in the house of X because of the interrupted electric supply. He is crying darkness but his darkness turns into brightness because of the jubilation of dark in the neighbour's house too. Mr. A's son had failed in the examination last year. This time the boy made a mark and secured eighty percent marks. Instead his mother should have patted and exhorted him for better in future; she started scolding her son only because the neighbour's son secured higher percentage. This feeling, which gets aroused in mind, is the root cause of many human maladies. We must learn to enjoy in our own perspective and eschew diluting our pleasure when know about the betterment of others. There shouldn't be enhancement of pleasure or feeling of reduction of own grief when others are in trouble. When there is physical darkness you must achieve light by lightening your inner instinct. The instinct that glows with the grief of others is like a deep dungeon of darkness where there is nothing else than diseases like Tension, depression, Insomnia, Amnesia, hallucination and insanity.

When the Thankless Thanks

Mr. X is very happy today and inviting friends for a dinner to be hosted by him. It was a big surprise to know that the man who was never satisfied and was always found complaining or cursing his luck is happy at something. It was a curiosity in me like others to know the surprising thing that provided happiness to such a fastidious person. I always enlightened him about his possessions and achievements and would advisc against cursing luck or fortune as they have endowed him plentifully which he is ignoring. He would consider nature's contributions to him as his right for which there is nothing to feel obliged or grateful but the absence of that what he lacks is certainly a misfortune for which he is right to grumble. That means such accursed people never find peace and pleasure with or realize their present material achievements whatsoever. They continue crying for more and more without having enjoyed what is already in their possession and without knowing the purpose of that incessant cry of deficiency and bad luck. Mr. X was hosting this dinner to celebrate his recovery from a disease that was troubling him for the last some time. I asked him what is your new achievement the yearning for which had been tormenting you all the time? He replied, 'my recovery from illness'. I flouted 'there is nothing new or more, you have had a healthy body before illness but you never realized this favour of nature at that time. Instead of feeling thankful to nature for the health you were provided, you would curse it for your new demands having not fulfilled. So there are numerous persons in this world who realize the grace and generosity of nature only when they are jerked as in the case of Mr. X.

What Can't be Cured Must be Endured

When something is irksome or an onus is it possible to get rid of it at own will? Is it possible always to cut and discard all that what can't be cured? No, quite often there are persons and situations that cannot be discarded and thrown away or ignored. There is no help at that time to endure the unwanted because of compulsions. That is why it is said as captioned, to endure that what you cannot cure as is done in case of necessary evils. A disease or contingency is not in anyone's control. Neither anybody invites them nor they get averted at the will of a person. Man's duty is to face them with fortitude. Two strangers from different environments enter into conjugal bond to become husband and wife and pass life together. It is not necessary that both agree with each other and there is no friction in their mutual relationship. Is it right to prefer rescission of conjugal bond in an endeavour to cure that friction between the two? Sons or other family members sometimes adopt attitudes and behave in a way that keeps the entire family in tension and nuisance. Cure lies in forbearance and wise counsel or an outright snap of relationship? Similarly happens when your children get married. With the marriage of a son, daughter in law from a new family with different background enters your family and with the marriage of a daughter you enter into kinship with a new man from a family of thinking that may not match with that of yours. What is done in such cases when you have to deal with persons and situations that do not suit your taste, temperament and status? You have quite often to swallow the bitter pill in the form of an unpalatable condition of temperamental and circumstantial incompatibility. Such forbearance is possible only by concentrating on the positive aspects and becoming apathetic to the negative features, as we have to do when accept the necessary evils. Remember that necessary evils or unwanted compulsions of today quite often become absolutely reverse with the passage of time provided you pass the present looking only to the positives of the incompatible. There are instances when either of a new couple could not get adjusted to the circumstances but that became the ideal most couple of tomorrow. Similarly the most arrogant and nuisance daughter in law of today becomes the most loved and endearing member of the family. The wicked or the vulgar son becoming the most dedicated and devoted member of the family. The wicked or the vulgar son becoming the most dedicated and devoted member of the family. In such circumstances undue haste or expectation of an abrupt change of adaptability proves detrimental to the stability and peace of a family. When some acrimony is noted it is better to leave the achievement to time and luck; making best efforts to rectify. Even in the most advanced countries where instantaneous and quick decisions like divorce are preferred in the family matters, the disturbance if destined, completes its stipulated period, may be in a changed form. Waiting and giving time for betterment is not always bad. Some wounds get healed better when no incision or surgery is done for some time. Boils and abscesses cure better after completing their time of maturity. Such conditions that require time to mature as is quite often in case of most of the human agonies must be forborne with this thought in mind that time turns pathos to pleasure and vice versa however no relaxation or laxity should be shown in your efforts and toil to achieve better at the earliest; but that will become more sustainable if the role of luck and time is also kept in mind. This notion of time and luck is not advised to prove a barrier to your efforts but it is a caution against and a viable solution to your facing and confronting the unwanted with fortitude and not frustration. There is no fun of peeving over the situations that are providential wills and must be forborne till maturity of their span of existence. Of course no guilt of lack of own effort should be there as that can itself become more troublesome than the unwanted situation. Thus the unwanted compulsions like that of a nagging wife or a defiant daughter in law or a defamatory family member must be tolerated as is done in case of many more unwanted compulsions like a disease or an accident or the birth of a handicapped family member. They are the providential wills having stipulated lengths whose solutions must come at the right time, the time of their maturity. This idea should keep you animated and hopeful of the expected good to come and make you work vigorously and enthusiastically in the present so far as your own efforts are concerned. Remember that providential makings are not avertable at the behest of human beings whose main duty is to act, work hard for their duty-performance and not try to disturb the system of or dictate to nature for premature happenings.

Many Superior and Inferior to Me

Acceptance and adoption of this fact in life acts as a regulator on vanity in success or tension in failure. During better times, i.e., the time of mounting success, achievement and glory if one keeps in mind that there are numerous far better entities, he will not become a coxcomb and vanity will not rise to his head. Such thought will keep him self-contained and eschew rowdiness due to rise of success to the head. When it is frustration due to failure or pecuniary difficulty the astute thought that many inferiors and more miserable persons are surviving and smiling, why can't I? This introspection saves the aggrieved from tension and stress. It means in plenty this attitude saves from vanity and in penury it saves from dejection. In effluence it keeps you composed and well poised while in paucity it keeps one hopeful and animated. When a person in grief contemplates worse cases of misfortuned others living but still living with smile, he starts feeling ashamed of himself and tries to be his own teacher. When a person in plenty thinks of far better people living gently, humbly, behaving nicely and well composed in their appearance and attitude, he starts feeling ashamed of his low contained and snobbish actions and tries to control his rude behaviour towards his nears and dears. This golden thought if adopted in life will save several social embarrassments. It also saves tensions and stressful conditions due to misunderstandings and nuisance that is generally seen in moments of grief and pleasure due to attitude and behaviour. Suppose a person is groaning with pain and creating hullabaloo of his trouble. He feels that none else is having the trouble like him. This thought aggravates his trouble but the thought or sight of someone in a comparatively worse condition makes him feel the foolishness of his creating a scene and he becomes somewhat calm. Some newly rich or newly modern person boasts his status or bullies his contacts. Such attitude generates wrath and ill will in others' minds and creates problems and tension for the doer. The thought or sight of a comparatively far better placed but well poised and well behaved, makes the former feel ashamed for such indigestion of success and achievement. Like the advice that 'Avoid thinking I am the only aggrieved even this advice that 'I am neither the superior most nor the inferior most' proves very helpful in allaying several delusions about the self that breed tension.

Something Tempting in Every Human Being

It is a general feeling that pecuniary paucity is the only problem in the world and the affluent people belong to the favoured category while the poor are the prejudice product of the providential power. Such feeling is absolutely wrong and betrays ignorance of the thinker. It is decidedly the root cause of most of the human anguish. Everyone born in the world is gifted with something more than the other. In other words it is not only the poor who tempt the affluence of the rich even the rich tempt many things of the poor. In other words every human being born on the earth has got something special for others to tempt. It is a matter of realization and identifying the plus in you. Unfortunately there is a general tendency of lamenting for what others have got and grumbling what is deficient in one's own self. When a person identifies the favours of nature vested in him he starts enjoying life and his petulance is changed into placidity. Therefore what actually lacks in the grumblesome creatures is the sense of gratitude for the magnanimity of nature that has gifted something special which the poor fellow is not caring as if it is his right and what he lacks is the only favour lacking and to be yearned. A healthy person with all body parts in tact and all functional parts of body in absolute health, he can taste and enjoy the savour of everything because of his good digestion, he can enjoy a sound sleep because of no neurasthenic deficiency, he eats, enjoys and laughs with his family because of no material malice or hypocritic element amongst the family members. None or many of these things are absent in the rich who surely tempts these possessions of the poor. The rich inwardly curse their luck. Who is then pleased with his luck? Naturally he who realizes this truth that it is not the few favoured persons but everyone born is having in him some extra favour of nature that others tempt. When a person is asked the reason of his grumble every moment despite all material possessions, he impulsively replies, 'what given? I lack many things. See to that Mr. X laughing, enjoying and spending so much. To hell with my luck, I cannot afford that diet or this dress. Is it just calling such state as 'everything' given by your Almighty? 'To hell such vague convictions', he assuages himself by spewing the residual wrath on luck and god'. The petulant grumbler is taken to a rich man's bungalow for him to decide the plus aspects endowed in him by the Almighty. He is blind to his possessions and sees those of the rich man's. His possessions are tantalizing for the seemingly smiling and lucky looking rich man who knows and feels the pinch of his hidden deficiencies and troubles that were hitherto unknown to the grumbler. At such demonstration of facts and realities of life the grumbler feels satisfied with the unprejudiced distribution of woes and pleasures by the Almighty. He apologizes from his god for having been so rude due to ignorance and exasperation. It is this ignorance of the realities of life and the people around that creates misunderstanding and delusion and makes people unhappy. When a person gets unhealthy he realizes the worth of being healthy, an acquisition that had hitherto been with him but he never thought been endowed with as the nature's gift and favour. Disease or adversity come in life to make wailing people see, feel and realize the contributions of nature and not to dilute every possession in them with one and only one namely the financial factor. An enormity of wealth can bring costly couches but its cushion cannot soothe the lacerated mind, provide slumber or somnolence to the fatigued brain of the wealthy who feels tormented due to rancour nurtured by his co professionals and the nuisance prevailing in the family. That innocence, affection, concern for each other along with the informal and unsophisticated behaviour amongst the family members, along with their health, sleep, digestion, sharing of each other's pleasure and misery are the coveting and tempting possessions of the mediocre person that are so tantalizing to the affluent. Why then these financially scarce people feel scared by the affluence of the rich and add the venom of snobbery or emulation to their so smooth and smiling lives? It is therefore not the material or the means that are creating so much anguish amongst the humanbeings, it is the ignorance about the realities of life, lack of art of living, perverted thinking and an illusive modernization which is thrusting mankind into a dark dungeon of chaos, clamour and cachexy. Such conditions create an allergy for life due to increasing stress and hypertension in people of all ages. Let us therefore gain power and confidence by realizing the truth that there are many aspects of life making humanbeings exceed or recede each other in one aspect or the other. We must realize these plus factors too and thank the Almighty for what has been given to us rather than cursing every time for what lacks in life. The real thing that lacks is the sense of feeling grateful and joining those running blindfolded to unknown destinations and hypothetical pursuits in life.

2

No Month, Day or Time is Auspicious

Present is Supreme

Most of us remain tense thinking about the future or brooding over the past. This is being done for the time which has either passed or yet to come affecting the time in current. Here again you are misunderstanding the word plan and preparation that superficially imply future. When you are distributing your actions or expenditures, a constructive and thoughtful part is advised for the future. Admitted that 'Hope sustains life', aspirations and ambitions are one's tonic of mind but they must be reasonable and not hypothetical or like building castles in the air. That may or may not be fulfilled. Dupe of expectation can demoralize you and affect adversely. An optimistic and positive attitude for the future decidedly ensures zealous approach and execution of the objective but an apprehensive thought for future or breeding imaginary fears can weaken you and create psychic problems for a time which is yet to come and you cannot preominate the actual form of it when it turns into present. Similarly the past is passed and those gone moments are irreversible. What is the fun of wasting time and energy in burning precious hours and energy of the present in lamenting for a period the consequences of which are before you, why not then to augment all potentialities for shaping the things lying before you in the present? A cursory thought of future and past are permissible. A proper and genuine ambition and aspiration maintains your interest to work hoping success and achievement keeping in mind the past errors, deficiencies or the causes of failure and their rectification to avoid repetition in the present; make that thought useful. Conclusively we can say a casual thought of future should have tonic value for the present while that of past should have an educative value for the present but major concentration of energy and attention must be in the present.

Identify the Tune of Time

It is not that pleasures of Mr. A synchronize with those of Mr. B. When there is illumination in A's house there may be darkness in B's and vice versa. Every individual has his own chart of events and the wheel of their occurrence moves at their respective speeds. Do not lament the lumination in other's house when it is dark in yours. Must remember that the reverse either happened in the past or may happen in future. Try therefore to be a part and parcel of the sorrows and pleasures of others and never to mingle or match your own with theirs thus spoiling the sense of humanity and magnanimity. This habit of jealousy and emulation is the worst curse of human beings and only those are happy who have got rid of it, none else of any material status is happy and peaceful in the real sense of word. Why don't you keep in mind that you are to work with full fervour and force using utmost efforts of body and brain for some objective? Rest is not your field to enter i.e. to decide your own and others' destiny. That power rests with the creator and any supersession of power or jurisdiction is nothing else than sowing the seeds of sin for the self.

3

Do Maximum Work Yourself

Do Maximum Works Yourself

This advice is to ease and not to harden your life nor it prevents you from availing astuteness and dexterity of experts. It is a warning against entrusting every little job of routine to servants in a false notion of comfort and status. Getting your works done from others (what you can otherwise do your self) quite often entails more punishment and less comfort besides a compromise with your actual need and aptitude. There is much saving of botheration and time if one is habitual of doing maximum jobs by one's own self. Nature has given head to think, hands to work, legs and feet to walk, teeth to masticate and so on. Sparing these parts due to affluence and 'status maintenance fad' will clog the respective bone joints and subject you to Osteoarthritis or Rheumatism, the horrifying ailments. Can it be called an expedient approach? Suppose a train you want to board, has reached and there are good number of vacant seats. . One little light bag is your journey luggage. Now let us decide the attitude of a sagacious person Mr. A and that of the one who is badly after a false notion of status Mr. B. Mr. A silently carries his handbag and occupies a comfortable seat of his choice, taking a cup of tea and enjoying it waiting for the train to depart. Mr. B, the work shirk due to snobbery and nurturing a higher status feeling, cries out for a coolie to come and carry his bag to the compartment. He waits and repeatedly cries for the coolie. By the time a coolie is available, most of the hitherto vacant seats in the compartment are occupied and the time of departure of train has reached. Mr. B rushes, jostles with the rush at the entrance and manages getting in. He stands in the rush and some important papers fall from the pocket while making payment to the coolie. The sandwiched B cannot move to pick up and the train starts. The plight of high status Mr. B and his condition at that time compared to comfortably sitting and well composed Mr. A is obvious. Similarly it is easy, less time consuming and comparatively comfortable too for ladies silently disposing little kitchen jobs themselves than breaking head with or waiting for the mates to come and do their menial jobs because doing themselves affects their status. It feels very comical when some ladies feel proud in telling to others that they have engaged a mate though the poor fellows have to work all jobs themselves because of the apathetic attitude of the mate. Let us now talk a bit about shopping your own self and that through the servant. Shopping provides an opportunity to see and know the things and people around and come out of the self-imposed isolation. You can get choicest things from a large variety on the spot and can also judge the betterment from amongst the wide scope of selection. Shopping is a stroll, a mood changer and an opportunity to merriment and mirth. It is a time to have little snacks, meet people, share the company and views of many who meet, see the things happening around besides having the better quality at proper rate, weight and measurement. Is it wisdom to get deprived of all these benefits only because of the craze of status? It betrays inferiority and not superiority complexes in you if you feel degradation in doing your own works and not bother for 'diligence of labour'. It is a question one can ask one's own self, whether such affluence is a boon or a curse and whether this habit of reposing little works on servants amelioratcs your peace of mind or deteriorates it? It is ludicrous when we see people missing the health benefits of doing works by own self-inviting ailments due to rusting by rest. A woman can meet her many body needs in household jobs, which are the indirect physiotherapic postures. Women snobs today prefer taking exercise by superficial mechanical devices. They shun the two-fold benefit of exercise, stroll, and knowledge gaining while accomplishment of their household works. A talk of multiple benefits from self-labour, pinches to the status mongers. The compulsions of the diseased, bed confined, the old aged or taking services of the wage paid employees by those in service is understandable but the thinking of those who subject their body to a virtual handicap of rest due to the instinct of status symbol is pitiable and beyond comprehension of a right thinking person. The effect on the nature and life of the children of the one who understands the diligence of labour and the one who ignores it is obvious. Why not then to make life easy, peaceful and enjoy the pleasure of natural entities? Let our affluence prove of actual pleasure and peace and not a curse due to ill thought of superiority in abhorring self work which in fact exposes you an inferiority haunted personality.

Good Things Better Half than None

The proverbial 'Better give the wool than the whole sheep" applies here. Sometimes we find a useful or beneficial thing or a person or an action becoming either loathsome or difficult to maintain. The negative part of it quite often makes one abjure it altogether and feel better without it. It also happens sometime that one covets for a good thing and wants to carry it whole due to avarice that nothing should be left for others. Both these positions are extreme positions and not advisable to be adopted in life.

For the good things or persons that you feel have been useful and potentially useful however pinching in the present, you must not alienate altogether and let the unpalatable phase pass away. In an endeavour to get rid of the unwanted aspect of the present, we repent for having lost the useful thing or person in future. In a bid to control entirely on the presently good-looking thing or a good felt person we sometimes burn our fingers and miss achieving even the little. It is therefore desired that best effort be made to carry that much what can easily be carried and avoid carrying whole. Similarly a thing or a person or even a habit that have proved its utility may be relaxed not rescinded. For instance we see that taking fruit and vegetables is good for health. It is advisable that even in routine a balanced approach be adopted to such conviction. Due to some body ailment or otherwise a restrained use of the usually good is advised. We must feel satisfied with a little bit of it. Neither leave fully due to a contrary advice nor ravenously stick to it ousting other goods, when advised favourably. This is an eccentric attitude that has to be reviewed and refurbished as it may cause and confront you with tension torn situations and moments.

The Really Valuable

When attending a function if one's pent tears a bit, the major saviour is a safety pin or a needle. Its value increases manifold because of the confronting need of the time. When one nauseates at the site of unctuous and heavy meals or suffering from anorexia the materially valuable things lose charm and the value of savoury and mouth-watering pickles becomes more. It stimulates appetite to make one ready for the rich diet. The value of menial value pickles is understandable. Drought of water to slake thirst or a vent for air in a suffocating atmosphere proves like a straw to the drowning. The necessity fulfilled by these things increases their value enormously and the material value loses significance. A gift prepared with love and toil becomes valueless. It ranks highest amongst the materially valuable gifts. The concern and sentiments imbued with the emotional gift are beyond anyone's evaluation. Never therefore try to keep only thc matcrial status in mind. The emotional aspect must be thoroughly appreciated and cared. He who inculcates this instinct saves his own and also of others' tension rather enthuses and animates withered and gloomy individuals. Such people endear themselves to everyone and enjoy benediction of every human being. On the other hand the coxcombs, officious and arrogant whose mental attitude and judgment always revolves round the material considerations, ostentations and snobbery are the biggest nuisance not only for others but also for their own selves. They create tensions; invite troubles due to their vicious approach. Those who are really affluent and realize that now they require the affluence of love, they become sober and magnanimous while the sick and ailing brain of the snobbish and low contained individuals remains around petty material considerations and is deprived of most of other requirements of a happy and peaceful life. Such people are drowned in self-delusion and deserve every wiseman's pity not wrath for their wicked behaviour and preference for material prosperity. Their approach to life and attitude towards fellow humanbeings betray the hollowness of their mind thus qualifying for everyone's sympathy and not hatred.

Death's Day is Doom's Day

Some people remain anxious about their property and children after their death. Some remain worried about their achievements and actions exploited after them. It has been highlighted above invariably that life is a fixed length journey and all agonies or pleasures; comforts or discomforts end with this journey. They are the creation of our actions, which in turn are done to pass this fixed length. If there were no work to do or to remain busy it would have been a hell to pass this fixed length endowed to humanbeings. Also it has been asserted that man came empty-handed in the world and will depart as such leaving behind all makings, relationships, friends, foes, achievements, tainted moneybags and powers. It means life is a fixed length game and all the creations are for the period of stay here. If this fact is imbibed by each and every humanbeing he will live in the world with full sanity. The very thought of this reality would never let him feel intoxicated by any power. All powers and possessions are transitory, no arrogance will overwhelm or obsess such a person and he will behave with other humanbeings like his own self. A person commits excess with others only when he becomes delusive about his own power and position and forgets the reality of life. Also he forgets that nature's rules to contain every person are same; he being no exception to the regulations. He starts spreading a reign of terror and tyranny. Chronicles are the testament to the plight of such powerful monarchs and other individuals who regretted having done so much excess and cruelty towards their fellow beings due to ignorance of these staunch realities of life. All status, seniority and specialty ends with the end of life and every one dealt in the same manner on the basis of deeds done during life. The status of departure (death) and entrance (birth) of all humanbeings is alike and that status is that of being empty-handed. The balance sheet of deeds however accompanies a person after death to decide the shape and style of life in the new birth. None was a warrior when born and no dexterity to fight works at the end moment. You were not a son or a father before coming to this world and you will cease to be so when you leave this world. What is that which humanbeings should worry so much? What happens with their makings, how they are used or misused, what happens to their teachings and lectures, where go their wealth and property, who captures and who surrenders, such like all worries end with the end of journey of an individual. If such is the position, the folly to worry for men and material after death is understandable. Such worry is nothing else than the tortures destined for them or created by them to pollute their charm of a happy and peaceful life of action and performance of duty in the present. He is the wisest who keeps himself busy in work, performs all duties and responsibilities of life to the best of his ability and capability, works in the present and feels satisfied and happy with his present, thus passes life enjoying relationships, tastes all presentations of life and leaves the world empty handed leaving all concerns here never to return to see what happened to some particular thing or person after him. Great men leave behind, the footprints of goodness and morality to be followed by their progeny, fragrance of sweet memories for the world and message of duty with dedication and devotion for the entire humanity. It is also worth noting that such persons accept and intrepidly cross the vicissitudes of life. They donot succumb to stressful conditions in the same way as they do not let any success or achievement rise to their head. In nutshell such people justify their birth by remaining happy in all circumstances doing all that is expected of them. They are like the noble passengers who know their journey is for a fixed length that they pass amicably and by accommodation to make memories for the co travelers who may have to travel further miss them and feel their absence. Only those pass the journey in strife and suffocation who are delusive that it is a perennial act, never to end. Gift the imperishable soul with the noble good deeds and leave behind memories at the termination of journey of life.

Belief in Luck and Time

The three controversies namely, Belief in luck and time, Fear from god and conscience, curse of the aggrieved and benison of the relieved; need attention of the neo moderns, alienating everything in their vague understanding of scientific reasoning and self created meaning of logic and argument. They believe all gabble and egoism as their profundity of knowledge and quite often indulge in a meaningless logic, debate, discussion or argument as if it depicts their wisdom and insight of the subject. It is good to be scientific and reasonable instead being dogmatic or conservative. It is nice to be scientific instead being superstitious. It is however not advisable to be negligent and scornful about the universal realities. An effort to undo a fact by a dexterous debate or verbosity is as dogmatic about modernization as it is to follow blindly the old convictions. Sometimes things are not looking as per their language but their effects are occult or indirect. For instance when it is said that Luck and time are supreme, it is one's own misconception to take it as an advice to stop action and wait for the time to come or the luck to prove its power. It is instead an advice to bear things and results composedly, neither to lament the failure nor to flaunt the success. When worry, anxiety or depression of a failure afflicts some psychosomatic disease to the aggrieved, what is the most desirable remedy with the attendants? Obviously it is the sagacious advice, homily or a psychological lecture that works. If that sense prevails on mind, if that practice preached by a savant or the lecture of psychotherapist works worry and anxiety get vanquished. Similarly it becomes soothing and the affected person calmly bears and passes the time of turbulence and tension if he accepts the supremacy of luck and time. At such stage when any word or lecture is being searched for the patient, if this conviction helps, it is no less than magic. Is it less return of the belief in luck and god? One becomes psychologically wrecked when his thinking is hit adversely. Why not to mould that thinking according to the realities of life instead of remaining belligerent and argumentative every minute to win the battle of orthodoxy and modernization? The entity of luck and time and their bearing on life is not disputable because they are the facts that ultimately manifest their role in the life of a person that is realized and accepted sooner or later. Don't you see around you people born in plenty and others in penury? Some are born beautiful and healthy while some others with ugly figure, diseased and subjected to several surgical needs due to congenital defects, diseases and deformities? What deed, action, assiduity, erudition or astuteness these creatures do immediately after birth that makes them so distinct? At a later stage of life the successful people flaunt their success stories and impute all their achievement to their exemplary toil and astuteness as if those not achieving are sitting idle or are all the nincompoops. Innumerable hard workers and so intelligent people are seen loitering in the streets while the idlers and fools are enjoying the prolific possessions. Also it is frequently seen that a person reprimanded and chided by any Tom, Dick and Harry due to persistent failures and an incompetent person becomes affluent, wise, assiduous and astute overnight. Success eluded whole life despite persistent and obstinate efforts and unexpectedly falls in the lap when hope was left and frantic fight for the same had ceased. A person on board a plane programmes to end his journey while another enplanes due to sudden thought in mind, why? Because this plane is ill fated to meet a crash, the former is yet to live and survived while the latter was to end and boarded the plane without any prior programme. Similarly a person purchases a plot under some compulsion quite reluctantly to become rich lately by its sale at the destined fortunate time of life while another sells due to some whim or thought or compulsion coming to mind because of his destined bad time that is to follow. Someone declared an all time idiot becoming suddenly an adviser of an elite person. An enemy of yesterday becoming the most suited wellwisher of today and vice versa. Expected obedient and faithful persons prove perfidious. The all time suspected enemies coming to succour. Own trusted people leaving in the lurch and some unexpected strangers proving angelic. So fate and time are the hard realities of life around which moves the entire world. So the belief is not false but a reality. It is the subtleness that lacks for its proper understanding and not grasping it in its right perspective. It should be considered as an antidote against levity in success and frustration in failure. Things happen as fated at a time lotted for a particular event but the deeds and actions never stop, as they are indispensable to pass life. This belief gives patience to bear and stomach to digest lest an eventuality due to consistence success or failure necessitates the services of a psychotherapist. Next we discuss **fear from god and conscience.** It is generally argued by the logic masters that this is a vague talk of orthodoxy and only conservative people think of it. What is the need of discipline in life and why strict scaring rules and laws formed by a system to enforce this discipline? If somehow an internal fear pervades that can help maintaining the necessary discipline, what is the harm in accepting and adopting that belief(say, fear of god or conscience) for a life with less chaos and confrontation? God and conscience are the most formidable power sources in despair and regulating forces in discipline. He who argues merely for the sake of argument is losing a golden benefit that demands no cost from the humanbeings but eases their life and its activities to an appreciable extent. Confessedly one must not be dogmatic or superstitious. That is an error, which can enter and erode any aspect of life. One has to prevent it and save oneself from this detrimental stage or condition of belief. What is stressed here is that belief in the entity and power of god and conscience in their absolute pious (not polluted) form pays dividend in the day-to-day life. What the written deeds and papers cannot do is done by the fear of conscience and god just as what cannot be provided by the costly medicines is quite often provided by a homily or a psychological lecture. Quite often physical punishment or other punitive steps cannot achieve that what is achieved by a word or lecture that reaches the conscience of the wrong doer. A conscientious person thinks several times before doing a wrong act. A god-fearing person seldom dares cheat, loot or indulge in unwanted activities for self-gain at the cost of harming fellow beings. If the fear of god and conscience is receding, the peace of mind of the people is vanishing despite exuberant material acquisitions. If fear of god and conscience is alienated, the strictest regulations are being mocked and flouted. Conclusively fear of god and conscience are in the interest of smooth sail of life provided that it is free from superstition and dogma. The third factor **Curse of the aggrieved and benison of the relieved** needs meticulous thought. This belief too invites joke and jeer for the believer and labels him the one of uneducated and orthodox cadre by the perverted logicians. If there were no scare of curse and when it gets vanquished from the world, there wont be anything like pity, generosity, help or philanthropy. It is this feeling which checks and contains the cruelty of the powerful on the weaker. The sigh and sob-wrapped curse of an aggrieved annihilates the most formidable inflictor of woe. While acting in the world and doing deeds, good or bad one must refrain from and eschew committing atrocity on the poor, weaker and circumstantially compelled humanbeings. When they are being punished for their deeds by the Almighty no interference is allowed to those who are fortunate and blessed with mirth and might. It is not expected by the Almighty that the latter should misuse that blessing against the former. It is the Almighty's prerogative to decide the deeds and that power of decision is not vested in any humanbeing. If therefore someone mistakes to misuse his blessed fortune for committing excess on the aggrieved he is considered perfidious defying the providential set up. Thus the fortunate person playing perfidy with the creator of universe becomes a victim of its wrath. This way it becomes the effect and consequence of curse of the aggrieved for the committer of excess on him that he becomes unfortunate from his fortunate status due to this sigh and sob of the aggrieved or the god's wrath obviously due to supersession of jurisdiction by the blessed one. If curse of the aggrieved is so affective on the one agonizing a weaker, the benison of the person relieved or relaxed from an agonizing situation is equally effective on the philanthropist and succourer. A person dying of hunger, benedicts the one giving him meals and the one dying of thirst heartily benedicts a person quenching his thirst and rescuing from an eventuality. When all confidants of an aged and dependent person betray, those coming to his help earn the benison of the needy for having relieved him from the anguish of torment of time. In nutshell we can conclude that the creator and regulator of the world, the Almighty, omnipotent and highly judicious carves the destinies according to deeds, the balance sheet of which accompanies in the following life. Human beings are not empowered to take discipline in their hands. The cry and shriek of the aggrieved remains in the immediate notice of the creator, similarly does the smile and relaxation of the blessed. Persons responsible for creating troubles for the aggrieved out of their folly to forget their duty during good fortune (which is supposed to be deployed for good deeds and not to be exploited to commit atrocities) remain in the notice of the creator. Similarly those who relieve and relax fellow beings in agony, utilizing their good fortune, earn favour of the creator. One must therefore fear from the curse of the aggrieved and try maximum to earn benediction of the relieved by actually relaxing their troubled fellow beings by deploying their good luck in the relaxing and reforming actions.

Positive Thinking

We generally see around us physically deficient or handicapped boys and girls of rich families entering into conjugal bond with physically normal people of comparatively far less stature. What is the element in thought that makes the financially perfect (rich) person accepting a financially deficient but bodily perfect spouse or a bodily perfect person consorting a bodily deficient rich? It is possible only when there is a positive element in thought. That positive element is realization of own minus factor and other's plus factor. Same factor exists when an ugly but talented person gets a handsome consort. The talented is internally handsome though externally ugly-looking while the externally handsome may not be likewise so far as the internal beauty is concerned.. Such instances and entities are clear message to humanity that there are innumerable categories of happiness and sorrow, pleasure and grief in the world. Neither any one is fully endowed with all pleasures nor any one is cursed with all miseries and sorrows. It is a distribution of woes and pleasures. The tragedy is that every person wants perfection and no deficiency. People do not see the betterment endowed in them; they see the betterment of others. Similarly no attention is paid to rectification of own faults. Instead full attention is paid in finding faults with others. Such people will obviously not spare even the Almighty and nature and curse their fortune and god for all their woes. They would never express contentment or gratefulness to the magnanimity of the creator. This is surely shocking on the part of humanbeings who hold others responsible for their woe ships and seldom review their mental inclinations. This is the crux of their remaining unhappy, grumblesome and tension torn despite increasing material exuberance. Positive thinking is to realize what is better in you and to compromise with the deficiency. It is possible by realizing the hard fact that none in the universe is cent percent perfect. He is happy in this world who imbibes this fact, learns to gain power from own positives and strive with pleasing disposition for betterment. He strives for betterment with an attitude that is contented and not contentious. Remember that deficiencies are indispensable to life. If there were all perfection and no lacuna or deficiency or desire to achieve, there would have been no work or action and the plight of an idler, a person without work, is obvious. How monotonous life would have become without work, is horrifying to imagine. The positive thinking therefore makes one-take deficiencies as opportunities to work, to strive and to pass life remaining busy and active. If a life of struggle and action is a curse, a life of indolence and lassitude is an absolute hell leading to meaningless maladies that are beyond the comprehension of treating physicians or the attending beloveds or even the victim himself. If any time there is a thought of incessant misery or misfortune befalling, there is no fun of lamentation, as that would weaken effort to alleviate it. Positive thinking is to take it as process of debt clearance. Debts that are running in arrears in the balance sheet of deeds and also that it is for the ultimate good. A noble person feels pleasure in squaring up the debt overhead; similarly the debt of deeds (misfortune or adversity) must be passed with the satisfaction of a debt being squared up. Destiny and time are the potent figures in one's life. Acceptance of and compromise with the realities prepare a person mentally to work enthusiastically for the better. Acceptance is the foundation on which stands the edifice of action. This edifice shines when paint of prayer is applied on it. The owner's (concerned person's) countenance glows at such sight and he in turn distributes this glow to others to get enlightened. Thus a person with such positive thinking distributes happiness and contentment and becomes a cynosure of all eyes while the one with a negative thinking, grumble some nature, lamenting attitude becomes a nuisance not only for his own self but also for everyone in his contact resulting in peoples' scorn, indifference and shirk contact with him. Some people feel humbled down when they have to go and beseech some one for a favour or fulfilment of some necessity. This is also lack of knowledge of reality of life. As work and action are indispensable, necessity and deficiency are also essential for smooth functioning of life. If one person had not felt the necessity of other, there would not have been any interaction or cooperation amongst the humanbeings. To feel anguished by some necessity or deficiency in own self and lament the compulsion that takes one person to the other for its fulfilment, is also a negative thought due to delusion of ego. It is also due to ignorance with the reality that every one needs other's help in some form. Positive thinking will take it as a natural and normal gesture of life that provides opportunity to a person to go to other, tell his own self and know others. Perhaps this might be the consideration before the creator that no single person is born perfect and fully gifted. If such provision were there, the so-called 'fully perfect person' would have gone to the acme of arrogance. Not to speak of his cooperation and usefulness to society, he would have become a nuisance for all. Snobs, flaunters and megalomaniacs are miniature forms of that imaginary aspect. Thus the positive thinker always considers work and labour as a boon, need and necessities essential for mutual contact and cooperation amongst people and adversity as the best education. They consider this world as the fields wherein good quality or bad quality seeds are sown in the form of similar deeds by the people and the fruit of deeds are savoured during this life, arrears are carried forward in the next life which gets shaped and destined accordingly.

4

Discipline

Happiness Lies in Compromise

See around you if there is any person materially all perfect and happy that way. You won't find any and an outwardly most affluent is under tension and torture of a type that may never have come to your mind. Are you in a position to fully satisfy and do everything for what every individual member of the family wants? If you say it is impossible, how do you expect it from the creator to whom you curse despite his having endowed so bountifully in you? Everyone laments one deficiency or the other how can one feel happy? Even if you are the most loved and most favoured son of your father he can at the most oblige you in having the first option to select and pick up the most beneficial part. You will be ambivalent as every pile will be deficient in one thing or the other and no choice can fully please you. Similarly the creator may ask the most favoured person to select his platter of destiny first; there will be both, the things of liking and those of disliking. None is allowed to have a platter of selected things because even that selection and consequent pleasure of perfection is not possible. What is then the way to that pleasure? It is the

Compromise with the achievement, which is the best way to pass life in a happy healthy way. You will have to tame your desires you will have to acquire the skill to know your achievements, you will have to learn the art of relishing your possessions and you will have to compromise with what you achieve and what you already possess. Trace the positive qualities in your acquisition for congenial coordination with happiness. Do not get incited by the proverbial saying that 'grapes are sour' or label of a Pessimist and frustrated man's attitude foisted by some logicians or neo moderns for such happy life-thought. Once you feel that what was in your control or expected from you has been done, it is none of your business to ponder over the result. Those who are mocking, in fact those mindless moderns are themselves confused and know not the purpose of their franticity and fastness. If ever they try to introspect they must laugh at the futility and frivolity of their actions in the name of achievement and progress. What remains for an astute personality to imbibe is, knowing the objective of an action. The agile moderns seem to be unmindful of the objective of their reckless materialistic race that fatigues them ultimately. In the long run they rue over the futility of their thinking which creates frustration and makes them run hither thither in quest of peace of mind and get relief from tension caused by their own deeds. Perhaps they forget the saying 'Haste makes Waste' which seems the most pertinent reply to their sneering and jeering the astute people by calling their sagacious approach as an indication of 'Grapes are Sour'.

Understand Realities and Try to be Happy

Reality is that it is your labour and not luck which is in your control. It is the effort part for an action that should be your sole concern and a matter of thought. Having done efforts to your maximum possible capabilities, your job is over. It is not justified and even of any use to worry.

Remember it is not that much the good or the bad parts which trouble a person as much the feeling of guilt, when some deficiency of effort is felt. So when that deficiency is not in question, there should not be any reason to worry for the result. It must be left to the will and jurisdiction of destiny.

Reality is that you brought nothing when you were born; nothing is there what becomes yours to be carried after death. It is the action part to keep you busy during life and feel happy or unhappy with the gain or loss during life and it is the good deeds which accompany a person after life, it is the memory of his virtues which is left behind. All material collections or makes and breaks of relations are deeds for which one acts during life and keeps himself busy, exclusively for a limited length of life given to man. Keeping this reality in mind one must act, do duty and feel relaxed having justified his birth. Afterwards no worry due to rue or loss of any type should come to one's mind. Why to worry after having done the job of your purview namely duty and why to worry for the worthless piles when you know that all makes and breaks were created here and will remain here. What is that for which one should burn one's heart and poison life in the present? The third reality is that time and fate have their independent calendars and never move with the directives of human beings. Let them do their jobs and human beings to do their's. Do not try to dictate in an endeavour to change time and destiny, they will not change rather your persistence can excite their wrath. Imbibe this reality too and let the sorrow or pleasure come according to the mutual consent of destiny and time. Unwanted moments in life are the debts of own deeds. Try to pass placidly the turbulent times with that feeling of relaxation as you do when you square up the financial debts. Your work is duty and acceptance of what is bestowed in your favour and not to burn for the expectations or coveting and weeping for one thing after the other.

The Real Rich, Brave and Trustworthy

There is a general feeling that a person of pecuniary perfusion is **rich** but the fact is far from this notion. A person with little heart is not rich though he has tainted moneybags. A miser, frugal or thrifty person cannot be called rich because he can spend neither for the self nor for others. His happiness lies in augmentation of money and he seldom bothers for doing anything to help his fellow companions in pain or penury. The real poor he being, he cannot part with his money to spend little bit on his own self to ameliorate his condition. Confessedly nothing or no virtue is totally banished from the world. The presence of virtuous people proves a wimple for the wicked misers, called rich, whose wantonness remains veiled and not exposed to society. Such people to whom parting with the pennies pinches, are not to be considered or called rich because their riches is meaningless as it is fake and flaunty. It is the generosity and magnanimity that entitles one to be considered and called rich. The rich people have rich heart that makes them spend lavishly. So a person with a rich heart is rich. Who is **brave**? Does it represent a bulky or voluminous person? No. A gutsy and intrepid person with strength of heart and thought deserves to be called brave. The one who nurtures several apprehensions and seeks shelter in others cannot be brave despite his big body. Slim and frail people perform feats and exhibit examplary fortitude in adversity. This is all because of their valiant thought that doesn't allow timidity. Who is **trustworthy?** A person with noble deeds, actions and intentions is trustworthy. Long talks and tales of self-praise and trustworthiness is merely a trick to ensnare the naives in such honeyed talks and play perfidy afterwards. Unless a person possesses and performs acts of trust that are visible to each and sundry, sheer boast and talk of trust, belief or fidelity doesn't make him so. It is the actual deeds that authenticate the veracity of his claim. He cannot be entrusted works and responsibilities that demand bonafide workers and not sheer claimants.

5

Character

Think Before you Speak

Proper mastication before swallowing ensures rumble free stomach, proper thinking before speaking ensures tension free brain and peace of mind. Speech has a very deep impact on your routine life. It is some utterance that brings a person from plenty to penury and vice versa. Words emanating from the lips act either like an arrow on the normal mind or a balm to the lacerated. Like an arrow shot from the bow which never returns back, bitter or sarcastic words emanating from one's lips do not fail in affecting the listener and causing an irreparable damage to the speaker's cause and cordiality with others .It is also some peoples' delusion that some particular person remains undeterred even by my worst words. This notion should be expelled from the mind, as it will not let your wisdom review and repair your offending attitude. Consequently you go on augmenting animosity and alienisms by sticking to such detrimental actions. Every person has an inner conscience. It is another thing that some people are enough astute to understand the tide of time and pretend having digested the poignancy of remarks, language or words uttered. No doubt the sensitivity of individuals matters, but it does happen that your speech or utterance changes quite often your life altogether. One soft and sympathetic word can make you master of your destiny while bitter, despicable or scornfully spoken words push a person in a dark dungeon of despair, disappointment and destruction. There are instances when words or utterance made about a menial of the past resulted in the death sentence in the present when that menial has become superior and free from the pressure of tolerance of excess. This is because the bitter utterance pricked the occult conscience of the menial of the past (but a big pot in the present) who was nurturing rancour for the afflictive till the time of avenging the excess. One should therefore avoid such attitude even for the most depressed of the present which arouses anguish in others simply because of your arrogance Speech is an art no doubt but that is required for acquiring better aspects in life. Normal life doesn't require special speaking and any person can exercise a restraint on his language and behaviour that imminently feels pinching others. Ego, arrogance, anger, revenge and hatred arouse acrimony in mind and acridity on tongue and speech while magnanimity, love, selflessness, sincerity, service and a sense of sacrifice yield smile and satisfaction and prove soothing to the extent of endearing you to many rather a cynosure of all. It is in one's own hands to decide whether to justify one's existence in the world as the one most abhorred or the one most loved, liked and remembered.

Abstinence from Snobbery

One of the stalwart vices responsible for human misery in the present times. Life or its support is not that difficult, as it has been made by this tendency of the neomoderns. The snobs have in fact created a nuisance for the genuine stuff in the society. It is these people who have spread the venom of hypocrisy, swindle and ostentation in the peaceful people and pushed them too in the dark dungeon of moan and mourn. Snobbery turns an easy, light and pleasant life to a costly, complex and cumbersome process only to satisfy ego and faddishness. In the name of status maintenance the snobs cross their limits of money and might and remain floating in delusion of their being great, extraordinary and elite category with special status. In this endeavour these people alienate all consideration of affection, emotion, sentiments or relationship and become absolutely materialistic stuff susceptible to any change that gives them special status. There was a time when people hesitated in telling anyone some fatal, infectious or contagious ailment afflicting them, thanks to these snobs who not only boast their wards being sent in status schools and medical treatments from status nursing homes, but even boasting the status disease that is ailing them. The foolish fellows feel shy in telling anyone about their disease being of a routine nature like an ordinary coryza or a simple stomache. Getting ailed by such little ailments of little people does not behove to the snobs who should have the elite ailment at least the Diabetes Mellitus or Hypertension or some cardio vascular trouble or carcinoma so that they can share some moments with the elite group of patients. This would enable the fool maintain status of his trouble and boast the status treatment being taken. They do not bother rather mock a sincere sympathizer who is healthy, disease less or tries to tell them a simple, easy or indigenous approach to cure which these delusive people laugh away as the poor man's thinking. Getting cured does not seem to be their target because their becoming normal will snatch a platform of equation with the status people. This position of mind is self-explanatory and makes any reasonable person pity their position instead of admitting their hegemony. Do you want such type of status and the style of life which keeps you awakened at nights and makes temptable and tantalizing any savoury eatable, comfortable attire, easy and short cure of a disease, sincere and selfless love, dedication and emotions of own people in the name of status? Do you want to keep yourself tied in the shackles and fetters of nauseating status diet, loathsome dressing, irritating formalities, hypocritic relationships and insomnious conditions? Any person of wisdom will obviously opt for the former life of simplicity and savour and abhor the latter which is nothing else than an expression of inferiority complex that prevails in the snobs who try to compensate by such like overtures of false assumptions. If we conclude that snobs are the mentally deficient people and they require lectures of psychotherapists, why should we follow them in the name of a mindless modernization the deleterious effects of which can turn us from normal human beings to nincompoops? We must therefore prefer self-conviction and eschew snobbery in our behaviour and attitude. Snobbery engenders wastage of money and might for a false feeling of better status to maintain. This way one implicates oneself in a chain of social and family nuisance, the extrication from which becomes very difficult. Also it is in no way a sign of superiority rather it betrays the complex of inferiority that haunts a snob's mind. Why not then to bid adieu and dispel this stigma of personality?

Gentleness versus Cunningness

Here also people have misinterpreted tactfulness and exploiting it to justify their cunning and hypocritical actions. Similarly cleverness has exceeded its limit to make people become over clever. Admittedly one cannot live life dumb driven. Tact and cleverness are the essentialities to live with this life where all men and women are declared actors to perform their respective roles during life which is a stage for the drama. There is an increasing inclination to evil and the gentleness seems to be trampled by the skullduggery, hypocrisy and cunningness. However it is the gentleness that survives and proves prolific in the long run. The short-term or immediate gains of evil are like the immediate gains of gambling but the ultimate favour goes with the gentle and the principled. You are noting in the day-to-day life how much stressful one feels when happens to tell a lie or play an imposter's role. To conceal one lie one has to tell several lies and this habit obviously keeps the liar mentally estranged. No doubt when it becomes a part of life the liar or the hypocrite loses sensitivity to such things but it cannot be taken as a token of clearance. They suffer two fold. On one side they find themselves engrossed in social upsets, scolds and strictures and on the other side they are under an occult state of tension which makes them addicted to alcohol, drugs and other narcotics so as to achieve a delusive peace of mind.

Sleep, Smile and Savour Devoid is the Poorest

Conventional thinking considers money and material as the only thing that decides a person being fortunate or unfortunate. It is not so always as it is a matter of consideration because money makes the mare go but making it the exclusive factor of human happiness is a matter to be considered. Imagine a very rich person having every amenity and comfort at his disposal but some life threatening disease has confined him to bed. There is no dearth of money to call the physicians at home or to carry the person to the best nursing home for treatment. Plentiful people wait their turn to attend and serve the ailing 'man of money'. Medicine of any cost or scarcity can be arranged from any source. Now look at the actual plight of this person who tempts to eat something but cannot because of the dietary restrictions by the doctors, he cannot smile at the most funny events and epigrams because the pain of disease and the pricks of drip and injections are torturing him from within, he experiences sleepless nights and can sleep only after having taken some somniferous drug, he tempts to go out in the open and see the world around in a free atmosphere and free will but he can't and is confined to the costly bed in a beautiful, well painted room of the palace. In nutshell the man cannot sleep at night or speak at will or smile during the day, all the time there is a loss of taste, anorexia or nausea and vomiting. On the other side is a man with meagre means of livelihood. He is having a well working body with all vital organs functioning normally. This person is busy performing routine duties however feels difficulty to meet the expenses required to coup up with routine problems due to pecuniary paucity. He can relish and digest a delicious diet, he sleeps well at night, enjoys and responds the happy and laughing moments, moves freely in the open and at a place of his choice. No doubt he is little uncomfortable due to financial hardship. This deficiency however does not keep his body and mind gripped all the time as does a serious disease to the affluent man of means and might. A scrutiny of these two instances will easily reply the conflict in our mind regarding fortune and the preferred option to be given if the fortune maker asks us to opt. Is there any thing for the financially rich to boast and consider himself 'fortune maker' of others? When his own fortune is beyond his control, when his savoury and delicious diet is for his menials and servants, if he is not in a position to attend functions and use so precious and costly dresses, his condition is pitiable and deserves all sympathy but the arrogance and ego in him do not let him compromise with the realities and remain deprived from relief due to self delusion. The way he earned riches is best known to him but he rues when realizes in the end that it were better to earn noble deeds which would accompany him. All that he has earned and piled up will remain here; all those 'own people' for whom he committed sins whole life will be left along with the material stores. He rues for having lived a life of delusion and disease but Alas, it is too late, 'It is no use crying over spilt milk'. We must therefore be aware of the meaning of happiness and the purpose of our actions. Blindly following customary and prevalent tendencies of amassing money by any means leads to committing crime against your sect and society. If one is doing so for the welfare of the family it is also a delusion. Because bequeathing the sinfully earned money to the children means bequeathing languor, lassitude and lust, which will not earn even their gratitude in the long run when they indulge in wanton acts. Wise men who want to have a peaceful and pleasant life always work with certain objectives, which are decided after having known the realities of life and the purpose of coming into this world. A purposeless and emulative approach leads to tension and depression during life with plenty of sinful acts to be carried forward and scores settled in the next life.

The Three Tips

If you want to lessen your tension and curtail causes of anxiety, you must imbibe three features in your personality. These are, **1.Think before you speak, 2. Assess your back, arms and fist before you act, 3. Know your contribution before expectation.** A meticulous thought will make you know the worth of these worry- vanquishing words. Most of the tussles, trifles and scrambles amongst the humanbeings develop due to an error of speech or utterance. You must be seeing in everyday life people objecting to someone's comments or words. The speaker explains at length the actual intention that was not to hurt anyone. The trouble obviously was owing to misunderstanding. We can't have control on others' minds, the sharpness and pickup of their understanding but we can have a control over own action and think well before letting some words exit from the lips. It is well said that 'easy to heal a sore of sword, difficult to heal that of a word'. It becomes therefore imperative on a person desiring less hazards and tension to think well before an utterance and speak after due knowledge of the person, place and purpose where one happens to converse. A word uttered wrong or misunderstood wrong by the other side creates problems of unlimited magnitude. Thus it becomes rueful to speak in a way that proved detrimental to the extent of creating deep differences in relations and friendly bonds and sometimes creating animosity of a serious nature. Therefore think well before you speak to avoid repentance or apologize afterwards. Second tip, 'Take an action after thoroughly examining and assessing own back, arms and fist'. Back stands for financial and administrative influence, arms stand for support and cooperation of well wishers in time of need and fist stands for own guts, stamina, prowess and perseverance. Mostly people engage self invited troubles due to their delusive knowledge about the self or emotional and sentimental inclinations or instigation by a hypocrite or adulation by a sycophant. The result of this no assessment or misjudgment or misguidance happens to be embarrassing and humiliating or quite often subjecting to troubles unbearable to ones physical, psychological and mental capabilities. There is an adage 'Cut your coat according to your cloth'. This dictum seems quite pertinent if applied here in cutting one's coat (taking an action) according to one's cloth (assessment of back, arm and fist). How ludicrous it looks when an actually gentle person of sensitive temperament engages some situation requiring callousness, stubbornness and tough heart but the weak minded sensible person gets engrossed or implicated due to either misjudgment about the self or misguidance by some hypocrite. Similar positions and ridiculous conditions are seen in matters pertaining pecuniary matters or aspects that require sincere support and backing. However hollowness in time of need makes mockery of the person. Everyone born on the earth bears an ego and self-respect. All time victory is every one's desire but it is never possible in one's life. One must be ready for the defeat if he wants to win because none in the world is complete in all respects. An egoist, arrogant and officious person considers victory and self-imposition his exclusive rights. He faces anguish and anxiety quite often and remains involved in some tension-bearing problem. If he were aware of his factual capabilities, reality of life (that no one is absolutely accomplished to be victorious every time) and the art of living, he would not have subjected himself into a state of perennial nuisance of one type or the other. The third tip, 'Know your contribution before expectation'. This has become a top necessity of the society because of the mushrooming social problems coming in its purview. The word contribution must be understood in its right perspective before discussing this tip. Contribution under compulsion is different from contribution for a duty and contribution to satisfy own pleasure (love, sentiments, emotions). The expectation of parents from their grown up children especially in old age is an example of troubles and problems brewing in the society. Parents give the plea that their sacrifice and contribution in upbringing the children deserves due dividends while some children defiant and indifferent to the old parents, counter this plea by saying that parents did so because of compulsion of love and emotions and a duty which they could not defy because of their weakness of love for the children. It means they admit that it is the feeling of love, attachment and emotions, which got it done and this may be considered a causative factor for what the parents did. The plea of such children is that they don't have any moral binding for reciprocation. If some children have that weakness factor (love, attachment, emotions) for the parents, they do their share in turn but the children devoid of this weakness factor cannot be reproached and the situation has to be accepted as the one lotted as in other aspects of life. Love and respect are the factors, which become charm less taken by coercion or undue influence. They are the instincts that develop in mind and manifest intuitively. Their charm lies in their natural and inborn form. They don't give that effect taken forcibly or done under compulsion. The real pleasure in such cases must be felt in having accomplished the duty that was due (for instance upbringing the children born) and to assuage own feelings of love and attachment. All that is done is an obligation on none but the self-emotions. Most of the people, who become tension torn because their expectations in many aspects have been duped, must analyze well and see whether their lamentation for 'having done' is really genuine. Introspection quite often will reveal that their expectation was false and delusive and what they think to have done for others was primarily for their own satisfaction. It was for self-appeasement. If it was for others' appeasement and the expected return or reciprocation is absent, there must be some deficiency in your own action or duty performance. When one satisfies oneself having received the return of contribution, the grumble and lamentation of dupery gets dormant and tension recedes. The ultimate thought of luck and fate is the best escape from anxiety at least for the situations that are beyond human control.

Individuality of Temperament and Traits

Some people feel irritated at the varying natures and attitudes of people in their day to day life. They react to many perhaps in an effort to change them or to make them speak, act and behave in a way of their own liking. Is it ever possible that a person can change thinking of all? Is it ever possible that nature had born people with similar traits and temperaments? If it were so, where from a reaction would have started? By the law of nature, an action gives rise to a reaction. When there are varying tastes, traits, temperaments, behaviours, attitudes, thoughts, prejudices, inclinations, liking, disliking in the world there are consequent reactions, the constitution of this world and the jumblement of human activity. If variety is the spice of life and if the multiplicity of human attitudes causes activity, why should one peeve at such situation or remain grumble some for someone or the other? Those who remain tense and grumblesome for the speech or action of the people they meet in everyday life are the chronic sufferers and more aptly the chums of tension. We must accept the reality of life that the world was constituted in variety to create multiplicity of goodness and badness. This was not possible unless there were different action by the individuals and the consequent variety of reactions by others. Until and unless someone's utterance or attitude is a matter of sustained nature detrimenting one's cause there should not be any effort to invite tension or trouble for the self by embroiling in to an argument or a tussle in a bid to change. It must be thought that there are as many natures and temperaments in the world as is the number of individuals and that every individual bears his or her individual personality. A person who reacts to every one's actions or is extraordinarily sensitive even to the casual effects is a chronic patient of tension and depression. Such person himself needs some psychological changes instead of changing everyone who meets him. If someone asks you to see greenery all around, you will feel baffled trying to change everything green. Why not then to wear the green glasses as this single action will serve the desired purpose and create greenery all around? This lecture does not mean that one must not try to guide a misguided or a disgruntled person and move in the world like a useless burden. This prescription is to be applied only on the sticklers, supersensitive and fastidious people. Such people are never pleased and seldom enjoy even their prettiest possessions sheerly because of their desire to change or impose their own liking on others. They even expect everyone to meet them daily failing which they either indulge into a debate or a fight. They augment their stock of grumbles for the society; the world and ultimately life itself and curse god for having created such and such like creatures. They seldom feel that the real curse lies in the creations of creatures like their ownselves who or the likes of whom not only keep their own life tension torn with futile affairs but also their families and the people in contact. We can't call them as the gifts for the society. The world and its people in their respective natural tones and types are unacceptable to such people who are the virtual slur on the society. Enjoy the variety of people and their varying natures, their tastes and temperaments. Guide only once what you feel can benefit the other side as an overture of service to mankind and your duty as a welfarist but do not impose or expect change as per your liking unless it affects you every minute due to frequent contacts and dealings. Leave the final and full changes to different agencies working in the society for this purpose and let the person change himself learning by experience. Let the saints and their sermons and the homilies work on them .At least you have not been exclusively authorized by nature to do all works of many agencies and shrink the world by shrinking its versatile people with different natures. If you do not contain and control such attitude you are inviting tension, depression, frustration, mockery and despise from the society and a hellish life with sleepless nights for your ownself. Ease yourself by taking life as it is. Try best to meet its challenges and accept the realities of life. Do all action in life, may be a humanitarian or a welfarist job only to a desirable and possible extent and not to surfeit yourself to the extent of becoming tension torn. Such instinct to change people talk and think the way of your liking is not social service, it is labeled as lunacy or feelings of a disgruntled mind. Try therefore to refrain from such cause of tension the abandonment of which is in your own absolute control.

The Shadow Character of Lust and Materialism

What is the character of shadow? It flees the more we follow it and like wise is the material lust which fleas when we follow it. Its evasiveness is mistaken as its preciousness or rarity and this thought creates more lust thus frantically to follow it till achievement. What happens when such frantically followed and hankered after thing becomes a possession? It starts looking small and there is rue and wrath for the fad that obsessed mind before its achievement. We hear great kings and power wizards dying with the anguish of crime committed during lifetime to augment that what remains here, nothing going along with but the sins and slaughter committed for its achievement make the dying big pot rue and rave at his such power crazy pursuits. You must have experienced that till a thing is far from your reach there is a craving for it .The aspirant feels and declares it as his ultimate mission on achievement of which he would feel his life a great success. Its fulfilment would slake his thirst to achieve and satisfy his appetite to emulate. However it is not so when the lured objective achieved. It starts seeming small and man's lamentation starts for something else that seems better because it lies at a distance and not in possession. It means it is the distance and difficulty to achieve that creates yearning and greed to acquire. The much-aspired big thing became small the moment it was pocketed by the aspirant. What is this tendency? It is the lust that follows a fleeing object, thinking it a remote possibility; a thing of beauty and rarity. All thoughts and imagination about it get punctured when it is acquired. Similar is the position of a person about other human beings. The good and great are those who are remote and lying at a distance. A close contact and proximity makes them small and creatures to be criticized for one thing or the other. Here the adage 'distance lends charm to the view' feels pertinent. Money and material are confessedly indispensable to life but a faddist attitude that makes distant objects tantalizing and present possessions small and unimportant is responsible to arouse tension in humanbeings. It is a mistake to feel that it is necessarily gold the glitter of which is deluding. Even if it is, the entire gusto and charm about it calms down invoking some new lure at a distance. Intense thirst makes the thirsty man feel the remote sand query as a water source, a mirage that it wants to capture and that will make his mission of life fulfilled. Does it ever? No, rather it further aggravates the lust to achieve and augment more. This is stray thinking that needs rectification. To rise above this tendency and know the realities of life is a path to peaceful progress. Work for your actual needs with dedication and integrity then feel the pleasure of achievement. Like little quantity of a delicious thing that gives more savour and a yearning for it remains in tact for the future, similarly money and material of actual need achieved by toil and integrity is more pleasure giving than the tainted moneybags by wrong means. Lust in man can be compared with a dog sucking a bone. What happens? The dog cannot satisfy its hunger but is blind in lust to cause bleeding of mouth due to lust and goes on shaving the bone piece in lust for meat. A person, in whom there is lust, is the one lying in absolute darkness. He is in fact having dearth of good deeds to go with him after death and also paucity of money and means to be used before death. The lust in him doesn't let him enjoy his possessions in this life or do deeds of goodness for the life to follow. Thus this shadow character of lust and materialism, its mirage nature, its similarity like the dog biting the bone, bleeding itself without satisfying appetite, must be imbibed well. It is advisable therefore to stop following the shadow. You will note that shadow starts following you the moment you turn your back. Success and happiness will be after you the moment you get riddance from lust.

Over Health Consciousness Makes Mind Stressful

Suppose you are told the presence of a snake in your house , how will you feel? Till the snake is caught what is the ensuing position of your mind? Obviously a stressful mind that remains scared all the time. This knowledge of presence of the snake made your life so tense and full of fear. If it were not known things were going as usual. Numerous risks and dangers move around us but knowledge of anyone scares and horrifies. If you see the snake yourself, your fear and concern are understandable but making hell of your smooth sailing life due to some hearsay, is beyond comprehension. It is good to be cautious or to take a precaution when something comes to knowledge but doesn't it quite often make a person sceptic, whimsical and fearful? There may be many snakes under the ground, have you insured yourself against every potential trouble? Little knowledge of everything is bad, it were better to remain ignorant because ignorance is a bliss. Deliberate ignorance or negligence is not advocated but an over indulgence in health matters may never let a person become bodily or mentally relaxed. In the name of wisdom and sagacity use of thermometer to know the body temperature, measuring blood pressure in the name of precaution, routine checkup of different body and blood parameters without any complaint, all the time measuring calories and vitamins, remaining extra cautious in the matter of using butter, sugar and salt without an ailment in the youthful years as anticipatory precautions are not the signs of a healthy or more sagacious mind. Precautions in proper limits are a good thing but excess of restraint and over astuteness can spoil the charm of a carefree life. Over attention to precautions and abstentions for health fitness affects adversely. Likewise it is the over use of salt, sugar or butter that may be affecting deleteriously may be more restricted for the old people or diseased persons. There is however no wisdom to keep mind strained and scared about their required use by the normal persons during childhood and youth. If excess creates troubles deficiency of these requirements can create physical troubles besides the mental strain due to phobia created against them. It makes one to conclude that in the name of giving health consciousness, fears and phobias are created and the benefits of a relaxed and easy style of life are being intentionally veiled. Unless there is a specific complaint or disease one must obey the normal dietary discipline and abstain from the real nuisance factors like the excess intake of preservative and chemical added tinned items and fast fried foods. We are very liberal in matter of the real troubleshooters and ignore them deliberately but in the tension torn fake whims of some commercially motivated clever people, we flaunt having become extra cautious and more health conscious. This is also because of the craze of status and to be considered amongst the elite, the more civilized and sensible people. Let us not assume fake astuteness. The real facts for a healthy body and brain must be obeyed and the snobbish signs left. Regular checkups of body, temperature, blood pressure, sugar, cholesterol and other blood and body parameters should not become routinism. It is worth mentioning that these parameters and many blood ingredients exhibit changes with your every little action. In certain persons they are inherently and congenitally different troubling least to the concerned person, no panic should arise from such observation. Most of the vitamins and minerals are provided by the daily diet, a neat and clean life style of prevention, observing the well-known precautions and good things like exercise and morning walk. Such observations are enough to keep your body fit. Childhood and youth in them are the best antidotes against any irregularity because of the natural vigour and vitality of this stage. Unless therefore one feels some physical trouble or complaint, one must refrain from such acts of snobbery or self invited whim and tension.

Think Before, No Rue After

Some people, mostly perhaps those who inculcate a habit of worrying as a pastime, worry for an action before doing, remain tense during its execution and remorseful after having done it. Can we expect such people remaining peaceful any time? They are fearful before starting to act, frightened during action and frustrated on completion of action. It is due to their worry habit and lack of confidence. They always see success in every action of other people just as they feel everyone except them lucky. This is a grave deficiency of thinking which is one of the major causes of their worries. To feel that every one other than him is successful and fortunate, betrays the extent of negative thought in a person. Admitted that confidence comes by success and recurring failure causes frustration, the reality to be kept in mind is that success and failures are destined with everyone. It is the patience and fortitude in failure that leads to success. Such person seems successful to others as happens in the case of those who enjoy the present with satisfaction and strive for the future betterment with composure. Remember, this is a way to achieve endearment of god and also worldly contacts. It is a fact that an all time complainant with a weeping countenance becomes despicable and abhorring. His misery seems pretentious. In today's world if people are jealous of smile on others' face they avoid and run away from gloomy and glum faces because of their brains already surfeited with tension. Persons who remain lost in the world of thoughts, sit philosophically or go on brooding without any action and result are the brooders and inactive people who should not curse god or people around for having failed to achieve. One's own role in making life bloomy or gloomy cannot be overruled. Luck is a feeling. Good luck is the feeling of pleasure while bad luck is the feeling of misery. Feeling is in one's own control. There are people who remain happy with little and enjoy even an adversity. There are people who are unhappy even during material exuberance and keep creating or confronting nuisance in their most accomplished or fortunate periods. The real version of luck is self-conclusive. The pleasure of thinking lies in acting on the thought and giving it a practical shape. The pleasure of life lies in witnessing the results of actions that generate further action and hence goes life. These lovers of tension and meaningless brooders provide variety to the world no doubt (Because world is comprised of human groups of different varieties) but they are worthless creatures for their own self or even the society and sect to which they belong. Obviously their family members (if they succeed in deciding to marry) live in stressful situations. These brooders, spreading meaningless tensions live a parasitic life imploring and expecting well-wishers to act for their family responsibilities by pity and compassion. No self-respected person prefers such type of fortune that is clearly carved by the person himself and none else. Such situations too develop because of ignorance with the realities of life and the art of living. Life must be taken in a joyful and sprightly manner and enjoyed in all forms. He is happy who is endowed with or who nurtures the instinct to accept life in every form. When there is a matter or a problem requiring action, one must not afford sitting complacently in apprehension of something bad or adverse. This is one's own weakness, the weakness of negative feeling and is not the way of life. One must think the best viable action and take it without bothering for the aftermath. The thing in human control was a good thought and plan before taking an action. When that has been done, there is nothing that lags and now the result, positive or negative is the way of life. Every person cannot have the results of choice, results happen to be as per destiny which expects people to accept it and move ahead for the next needful. The habit to regret an action after its result is wrong. Action has to be decided and taken. Consequently positive or negative result has to come. Life cannot move if some person goes on brooding an action that would guarantee him only positive result. He would remain thinking without action whole life. Whom will he hold responsible for his plight due to such thought inclination? After the result of an action having come, Uttering words like 'it would have been better had I done so, it would have been better had I not done or said so' is absolutely wrong. Of course, a lesson of betterment from the past action is a necessity indispensable and mark of wisdom. Good thinking before an action ensures good result. The question that arises before persons who regret their action after the result is, whether the action was taken without having thought about the best result. Did you not consider the likely consequences and made arrangements to handle them? Could you afford the work without an action? You felt this action taken to elicit favourable result, if it has duped your hope how can you vouch or guarantee for the favour of an action that is now being deemed fit? The present dejecting result can prove a boon in cognito and the imagined golden action could have proved detrimental in the long run. So this thinking to disregard or degrade or belittle an action taken, a thing in possession or a person in contact in itself is very dangerous and seldom lets any one to step on the platform of peace and serenity. How strange it feels when a husband finds faults with his wife and regrets for not having consented to some other proposal from amongst the many at the time of marriage? Similarly regret some wives. The physical distance between the lover and beloved fancy both to the extent of conjugality and is called a love marriage. Near contact breaks the lure and charm of conjugation. The knowledge and glimpse of realities after marriage subside that fervour-giving vent to detracting feelings culminating to consequent severance that is divorce. Here again the same factor works. The present relationship was considered preferential and accepted. If it has exposed realities and proved unsatisfactory after action (marriage), how can we talk about the unaccepted proposals better? They seem better till we have seen or dealt with them like the present that seemed most preferable till a close proximity of all aspects dismayed and disgruntled. Now a substitute too is not a thing of surety. None can vouch for the prospective substitute to whom the exploitable precedence is known or revealed. If it proves worse and makes the person regret having left the first, what will be the plight of such a wise person? If his plight is miserable, then the real wisdom lies in accepting the results of own actions and never to rue when the outcome is there. The best one can do is to think well before an action and act well for the most favourable outcome. After this, the consequent effect is accepted with pleasing disposition and further steps taken after thinking meticulously. Thus remains the circle of action in life. Life span should thus be passed in creative action and not in lamentation or remorseful actions and expressions.

Accept the Realities

Acceptance of realities is the best way to happiness. Almost all troubles in the world are due to prevailing propensity to please and win everyone. Also it is due to the fact that everyone should satisfy you or come to your expectation. None of these two is feasible. No one has succeeded to win or woo everyone and the avidity for such achievement should be abandoned. One may do anything to the best of one's efforts, still many critics and faultfinders are found and everyone will not be found admiring your action. Those sensitive people who bother for everyone's reaction and attitude, can never remain happy as their desire to see admirers of their acts all around is never fulfilled. One must therefore do the best of efforts from one's own side and never bother for the people's attitude afterwards. Similarly everyone cannot please and satisfy you. There are points of clash of thought, action and attitude and consequent dissatisfaction. This is again an infeasible aspect to expect. If both situations namely to satisfy and please everyone or to be satisfied and pleased by everyone are infeasible, what is the way to live peacefully? The best way is to adopt a policy of acceptance, reconciliation, accommodation and adaptation. Some people call such policy as a weak man's tool. Such people seem to be convinced with their style of life namely fighting, arguing, debating, criticizing, backbiting, chiding, bearing reprimands of others, mud flinging on others and so on. A very mention of all these tendencies creates an irritation to the mind. The friction and consequent heat created in the brain can be well imagined. To talk about peace of mind adopting such attitude is absolutely paradoxical. When we do not bear and accept others or their attitudes and remain dissatisfied, we are left alone in the world, a horrifying picture to imagine. Even here some people criticize and talk of weakness. Do they find their might in complaint and grumble about everyone? Do they seek peace and find sagacity in aggravating little matters that can be averted?

Astuteness lies in reducing resistance to smooth sail in life. Confronting impediments and interruptions at every step is very unfortunate. A habitual critic who condemns everything and every person is the most despicable character and seldom liked. Accommodation, acceptance and adaptability is the best choice left with the aspirants of mental peace and a care free life.

6

Health

If you Grumble, Peace and Pleasure Crumble

This habit of grumbling something or the other makes a person despicable and keeps him tense and peevish. There is a grumble for others' betterment or own deficiencies. Whenever there is a bit inconvenience or a little displeasure, a grumble some person starts lamenting his lot and holds the Almighty responsible for his agony. He does not remember or recollect any moment when he has thanked god for having magnanimously endowed in him numerous capabilities however seldom misses an occasion to grumble for every little twist in life. It is an advice to such grumbling personalities that unless they inculcate a habit of expressing gratefulness to god and acceptance of achievement that accrues after performance of duty to the best, they can never become happy and enjoy any material possession or acquisition. The real cause is this element of complaint that they harbour as a plus point while it is the worst negative part of personality and the crux of their problems. One's contentious and fastidious nature never lets peace of mind come to him. 'Lotted cannot be blotted' and destiny moves its own way. It never changes at the behest of a person who dissipates his energy in grumble and lamentation holding others responsible for his woes.. If these potentialities are harnessed for duty and action, the brain batter is replaced by brain betterment that makes one think positive and pertinent.

The Addiction

That instinct or action, the missing of which creates malaise and discomfort, is called addiction. It is in one's own hands to select the addiction. Some people are addicted to alcohol while others to the use of narcotic drugs. Most of the people are addicts of collecting money while some are addicts of earning name and fame. Some enjoy vandalism while others enjoy serving and helping the poor and the weaker. Some people are addicts of gossiping or prattling while some are addicts of eulogizing the creator of the world through hymns. Some people are addicted to cursing their luck or god for their troubles. There are some others who nurture the addiction of worry. They are always busy in worrying for one thing or the other. We can say they find or create a topic to worry, because they are the worry addicts who feel uncomfortable without a matter to worry. Some people have the addiction of good name and reputation at the cost of their entire material resources while some prefer money and material and stake their all honour and dignity for financial benefits. The habit to know human psychology and inclination of thought or to know life and its realities and impart guidance to the perverted thinking is also an addiction. A person who inculcates addiction of glimpse of the self, searches happiness from within, he forgets all other addictions. That does not mean that such a person becomes indifferent to his worldly responsibilities or renounces the world and his responsibilities. He becomes truly responsible and performs his duties in life with pleasing disposition. Such a person is free from the delusions of ego and snobbery, emulation or jealousy and he is not a coward. He is not fearful because he is not nurturing false aspirations and is fully conversant with the realities and purpose of life and also the secrets of happy living. This addiction of glimpse of the self and quest for peace from within when comes to a person, his life becomes happy and cheerful. It becomes free from the burning and emaciating flaws of one's personality that create stressful situations and make life hellish instead of making it happy.

7

God is Right

Think 'All that Happens is for Betterment'

Man's lamentation starts when he does not see the things in their proper perspective, he is prejudiced and lacks farsightedness. If one glances anecdotes of life, he would realize some particular happening or effect, which he disliked and thought detrimental in the initial stage but it proved a saviour and a boon in the long run. For example if someone cancels your programme to accompany some people on a site seeing tour, it feels quite irritating but the plane crash of those who boarded makes you realize that cancellation of your programme was for your ultimate good. Something so savoury if snatched by a person immediately before putting in the mouth infuriates however you feel obliged when find that the users of that thing died because of food poisoning. You had some money for some domestic necessity and scolded the person who pressurized you to invest it in some lucky draw. You become indebted to the person whom you declared unfriendly at that time when later on you find that the reluctant investment fetches amazing achievement. You are put to some assignment due to conspiracy of some jealous colleagues with an intention of harassment and humiliation You curse your luck and grumble to the Almighty for such happenings with you but after some time when it is declared that those assignees including you would be given extraordinary promotion, you jump and feel ashamed of your earlier attitude of concluding that 'it is all wrong happening with me' however you had to change your utterance and say 'it is good happening with me'. Remember, your gentle and generous attitude, genuine intentions and sedulous nature never go unrewarded. One of the golden keys of happy living therefore lies with the positive thought that whatever happened in the past, that was for my benefit, whatever happening or will happen is entirely for my betterment the remote effects of which are unknown to me but the all prescient Almighty who is deciding destiny according to deeds is just and fair. He who challenges the providential will sheerly enervates himself and invites dissent of destiny. The verdicts of fate do not change at the behest of human beings. The fury of fate can however calm down for the people who raptly perform their duty with pleasing disposition without grumble or care to count the reward of work done for a duty which ought to do. If so, why not then smilingly?

What Happens that is for One's Ultimate Good

We many times declare some happening as bad when it actually happens and after sometime we change the opinion to call the same thing as good. The Indian mythology is right in guiding humanbeings that what happened in the past or happening in the present or to happen in the future is for your ultimate benefit. It is true and if imbibed well perhaps most of the rue or groan of humanbeings may get subsided. Logically only a person prescient with the actual effects may be competent to comment or criticize an action of nature. When one does not know the future effects or repercussions of some will of nature, he has no right to condemn the action of nature by its immediate appearance or effect of the present. The creator knows the actual effects and objectives of its actions and only he knows whether they are going to prove beneficial or detrimental for the concerned person. The creator may have taken a step for the ultimate benefit of a person while the person starts condemning or disparaging the creator due to his short vision and in view of the immediate effects that may not seem beneficial. When the same action proves beneficial in the long run and in the overall interest of the person, he repents for having criticized a favour of the Almighty due to misconception of its being a curse. One feels ashamed due to his own action but there is no way to withdraw or replenish the wrong committed towards the creator in the form of ill utterance. Still, the so magnanimous god never minds the rudeness and ingratitude of humanbeings and laughs away their follies giving bountifully even in the time to follow. Can this attitude be observed amongst the humanbeings who expect great returns for little done towards fellow beings? That is why it has been said that he is liked most by the creator who does his own duty with utmost diligence and intelligence. The Indian mythology boldly gives this message in the essence 'Work is thy duty reward not thy concern'. Sometimes a man feels very happy and fortunate with an action of nature while the latter laughs at man's folly because that seemingly fortunate action not to prove beneficial for the joyful person at a later stage. It means that one doesn't know which action of nature would prove beneficial or harmful in the long run. Thus the ignorant humanbeings must remain innocent and concerned with their own duty. They must refrain from adverse comments, complaints or criticism for the actions of the creator. He remains happy and cheerful who accepts the verdicts of nature with pleasing disposition, prays for the creator's benevolence and benefaction to live happily and tension free during life. The quintessence of the aforesaid thought concludes in the message that what happened or happening or will happen, is for the ultimate benefit. One must continue doing one's duty with sincerity without fear or expectations and accept the results with pleasing disposition, not grumbling for every action of the creator.

8

Work is Worship

Avoid 'Putting off Today's Works Till Tomorrow'

A row of works and a rush of jobs sometimes demand streamlining and scheduling of works but the development of the habit of putting off today's works till tomorrow only because of sullenness or wantonness is not a rest but a disturbance to your peace of mind. Compare the feeling of relaxation you have by disposing the works of today right now with the tension of pending and piling today's work till tomorrow. Do you think that tomorrow will be so vacant as to allow space for adjusting yesterdays' works? Do you expect importing more wish, vigour and willpower tomorrow?. If your reply to this query is no why then to inculcate this bad habit of deferring works ought to be done today till tomorrow?. Have you seen tomorrow? Are you sure about the circumstances of tomorrow? If tomorrow proves more rushy and hectic what will be the consequence of your procrastinating attitude? All this will aggravate tension in the mind and make you depressed and diseased. It is a boon to remain busy, it is more important to work with plan in a way that uniformity is maintained. Remember it is not the excess of work that troubles a person. In fact it is the mismanagement and confusion that creates the trouble and tension. It is the lack of interest and will power and lackadaisical attitude that creates tension. Never therefore feel that excess work torments instead it is the work sense and work management that matters so far as the peace of mind is concerned. Shun therefore the habit of deliberately pending today's work till tomorrow. Do it today rather right now without delay and get mentally free from its onus

Dress Covers Body, Profession Covers Inherent Nature

How sophisticated, elegant, suave and sagacious people look in their professional chairs. If we happen to enter their actual life, we are surprised to see a reverse picture of their real nature and vice versa. It means, to live with life, one has to maintain a balanced approach towards professional etiquettes and family manners. How about those people who curse their luck whenever they happen to strive more in their professional work? They feel as if they are working for the family. When such perverted thought occurs and they remain ignorant with the fact that they are professing and gaining for their own selves too. It is not the families only who are to avail the benefits. This feeling of obliging family members and remaining irritated with them is wrong. It generates nuisance for the family and tension for the professional. Unless a person feels that what he is doing is for his own self too, the work will feel like an onus. The best achievement to self is the enjoyment of having done a responsibility towards the family and also remaining busy to pass a peaceful life. Life without work is the real onus. Work without the feeling of achievement is an onus. To realize satisfaction derived by doing duty towards family makes working more enjoyable. Remember, idleness is the worst punishment, which makes passing of life very difficult. No doubt one professes for augmenting means to maintain life but it is also to maintain one's own self, health, prestige, position and also an opportunity to project oneself in a graceful formal form. One may remain simple, unsophisticated and inactive in the family life but profession makes him active, smart and sophisticated. Profession brings forth a person's latent features that remained hidden. Thus one professes more for the self-pleasure and benefit and there is not much to feel irritated with the beneficiaries namely family members or spouses. One loves a child out of attachment and emotions no doubt. It is actually done to satisfy one's own appetite to love, pat and kiss. A philanthropist shows generosity to help those in need but he does so actually to satisfy his own instinct. Parents upbringing their children, Patriotism demonstrated in one's actions, duty done with dedication and devotion, worship done to the Almighty and all other virtues, they are not all the obligations or gratitude on others. It is basically to appease the feeling that develops in one's mind and satisfaction of that feeling is the real factor that urges one to work for the seeming benefit of others. Similarly profession is a costume that covers one's faults and provides an opportunity to present oneself in a different shape for the people to see and even his own self to surprise, is it actually me? We must therefore be grateful to nature that if it gives life, it has created work and professions for the people to pass life that would have been hellish if there was no work or there were no professions. Why then to weep or wail and create a clamour and nuisance in the family when one finds some difficulties in profession? He who walks will find some impediments and he who works will face certain difficulties. But feeling that profession an onus creating all problems is a cynical thought, which must be eschewed as it breeds many psychological troubles. Normally all human beings have the same traits, emotions, negative and positive features that are seen in their personal life. It is the variety of professional appearance that provides variety in the society and a make or mar of image other than the actual one according to one's professing, presenting and acting on the stage of a profession. In our daily life we see people being different in reality but looking absolutely opposite in profession. Thus profession provides an opportunity to act, to present, to cover and conceal the faults of personality and personal life. Profession is a cover to clad the originality. Some people do not require a profession for earning purpose because they have ample money to spend sitting idle at home. Even they start some profession because idleness is a curse, boredom and devil's workshop. They prefer the boon of profession, an opportunity of self-grace to an idle sitting which is a slur and slander. Profession is also an opportunity for learning varying aspects of life and attitudes of people due to public relations in profession. Sitting idle at home and feel thriving in idleness is a perverted thought. An idle man's brain on one side is a devil's workshop and on the other side it creates stagnation and stereotyped style to live. There is no place for the dictum 'variety is the spice of life' in the life of a person without a profession. Stagnant water starts giving stench after some time, similarly is the condition of those who invite stagnation in life i.e. monotony in life which is a definite path to depression and frustration. Whatever may be one's level of affluence or financial capacity, one must pray to 'die in harness' except under compulsion of an inability. It becomes tortuous and humiliating for a sensitive person to sit idle or sleep at home. This feeling of lowlessness creates tension. One of the major reasons of geriatric tension is their confinement to bed or cottage and becoming profession less. The condition of a rich man sitting, sleeping and eating without enjoying a professional grace is obvious. So idleness is a compulsion for a rich man due to some physical problems but a curse if he prefers so with the delusive thought that I have ample money, therefore no need to face the fluctuations of a profession. He is not heading towards relaxation, infact he is heading towards tension, depression and frustration. Thus for a person of limited resources, profession is a compulsion to arrange two square meals and family support. Idleness is a compulsion for a rich man due to some life style or bed confinement disease or disability, it is never an escape from, rather it is headway towards tension. Idleness or sinecurism is not relaxation but absolute tension.

How to Move in Life

Like good and bad, action and indolence, there are mainly two ways to live with life. One is an aggressive attitude for the affairs of life and the other is a submissive attitude. Former is the approach of a belligerent and the latter that of a Complaisant. One is that of claiming and snatching and the other is that of waiting and winning by wisdom or coming due to compassion. One is adamant while the other docile. The rigid, fighting, adamant, belligerent, snatching and aggressive attitude means engaging friction for mind and consequent tension while the other that is, submissive or docile, imploring and waiting is calm and peaceful, but questionable in the present scenario when it is taken as weakness and stolidity rather than greatness or gentleness. Nature and temperament are inherent factors that can be moulded a little bit but the basic quality cannot be changed altogether. Moreover waiting and imploring neither reveals action nor honour and dignity. The shameless, callous and selfish people of today's culture would never let a docile person have even his meals. If docile attitude is weakness and inaction, belligerent attitude is tension torn, what is that which is moderate and saves one from undue stressful situations? No doubt the adage is that 'Might is Right', it is also an admitted fact that complaisance ultimately pays dividends. Also it is difficult to cheat or gulp a noble man's right, it remains with him or restored to him in the long run. This is a controversial advice that may perturb anyone and many people may feel reluctance to accept it. If an action packed gutsy approach creates friction and consequent stress; a state of helplessness often smacks weakness and lack of guts generating peevishness, blood boiling and consequent stressful situation. The best attitude is that of wisdom, sagacity and prudence. One should decide an attitude as per confronting person, circumstances and an unprejudiced assessment of own material and mental potentialities. An ambivalent nature is the worst enemy of a person as it neither lets one act forcefully nor lets him sit silently and see like a spectator. Such condition also creates depression and frustration. An instance is worth mentioning here. There are two persons X &Y.Both are servicemen and each is having two sons and one daughter. X is seen grumbling, cursing luck and relations and holding them responsible for his miserable plight. He feels himself the most unfortunate person on the earth. His factual position is that he is a well-placed and well-paid employee but his over ambitious nature doesn't let him feel satisfied with whatever he achieves or his luck endows in. Contrarily Y is an erudite, philosophically natured very sensitive person who realizes the facts of life and is more practical in facing vicissitudes of life with pleasing disposition. The Y couple is ingenuous while the X couple is ingenious. Mrs.Y is a sober and docile lady while Mrs. X is a belligerent, over clever lady nurturing delusions about her foolishness and bellicose nature. Both X and Y marry their sons. Mrs. X due to her over clever overtures, sceptic and cynic nature takes her son's conjugality to courts, thereby making the elder married son a divorcee and the younger one a chronic bachelor. Mrs. Y too weeps the snatch of her elder son by his wife to the extent of even sentimental segregation from the parents and inciting the younger son's wife too against in-laws. Both sons with their wives are living in different cities away from parents. The Y couple is no doubt anguished with the situation but they find solace in one thing that as parents they have done their duty and the sons are at least adjusted with their families, let us leave our care to the Almighty, fate and time. Any aggravation of conditions by us can detriment the family life of sons therefore it is wise to leave them in their own world. Realizing this truth that children are ultimately the independent entities and not the whole life assets or ransom of the parents, they leave the matter on destiny and time. In these two instances there is decidedly anguish to the parents. However the repercussions of the X couple thinking can create more problems only to appease their fear psychosis, egoism and fastidiousness and a delusion that sons' life decisions are parents' prerogative. The Y couple weeps, laments quite often but tries to understand the realities of life and feel solaced by the pleasure of having accomplished responsibility of life enabling children settle satisfactorily in their life. Rest of the things will settle with time that is a great healer. Here while the X couple is ingenious, Y couple ingenuous and imprudent, a third couple Z is very cunning and shrewd. They are enough callous too and making their way to stay in their both married sons' houses with action, wisdom, diplomacy and moving with the tide of the time. Conclusively they are right using wisdom and prudence that seems the solution to live in the world. If thought well, in the above instance Y couple is in the real and right gain. They are living their own life and letting the children live their own. They know that superimposition and interference generates undesirable results. Moreover love and respect must develop within and not to claim or get forcefully. Also the sensitive nature and erudition of the Y couple justifies their approach to this matter. An erudite person decides as per need and demand of time using wisdom, prudence and astuteness in confronting matters and problems during life. A sagacious action leading to easy solution and not a hectic approach that may aggravate and multiply problems is the right way to deal with life matters.

Stop Adding Worries and Works

If a person starts counting the weight of flour he has eaten or the quantity of water used or the amount of money spent or the quantity of milk consumed since birth, he will die of burden that such feeling creates on mind. If however he thinks that he ate, drank, consumed and spent as per needs, demands and provisions of the time as per my duty, way of life and a matter of routine, he never minds having done anything special or surprising. Similarly if you go on collecting your worries and the adversities of the past and synchronize them with all worry-creating situations of the present, it will be hellish to live life. It will be a horrifying exercise that would weigh heavily on health, head and heart creating tachycardia and sometimes even breathing problem. Insomnia and petulance are the first consequences. Life is passed in accomplishing its duties and augmenting resources for a smooth sale. Works and duties that fall over are done as they appear. It is the time and circumstances that suggest the solution. A premonition or imagination of the quantity of jobs and their onus makes the things irksome while their actual performance and disposal is done without feeling the least pinch of having done. This is again another form of the previous suggestions that do not get terrified by seeing the mist or the fog. Move ahead and you would find the way. Similarly it has already been suggested that do not pre imagine the difficulties .In order to board a train or embark on an adventurous journey, start, work step by step. Apply the principle of working in the present, thinking of the present and what lies ahead. Do not inculcate the habit of brooding over everything, piling up worries, acting least and giving no performance. Think more about action, creativity and output. Thinking that is prolific in breeding worry, anxiety, fear and apprehension leads to self-annihilation. So do not inculcate the habit of counting your works, duties, and liabilities of the past, present and the future. This by its sheer thought seems brain bursting; the actual effect of such tendency is obvious. It is said ' do good and forget' lest the addition of your goods done weighs heavy on your mind generating expectation and returns. These expectations if not fulfilled produce stressful conditions. Routinism makes one do one by one what is impending and imperative in a cheerful manner but the habit of their simultaneous ponderance surely irks and makes one gloomy, withered and tension torn, the causative factor should therefore be kept at an arms length.

9

Shed Five Evils

Five As, the Hub of Human Agony

Almost all human misery revolves round the five A, which means Attachment, Amativeness(Amorousness), Anger, Avarice and Arrogance. All forms of unacceptable human behaviour are the ultimate products of these five As. Even the preceding and the following writings are only the varying manifestations of these five basic enemies of human happiness. For instance jealousy, which can be considered enveloped in Arrogance, depicts itself in numerous shapes. Fear. The crux of several problems is merged in Attachment. Effect of Anger is an open secret. It is the anger, which quite often culminates into annihilation. It is the amorous thought that astrays from the righteousness and takes one to any depth of moral turpitude. Amativeness therefore leads to multiplicity of complications for the humanbeings. Avarice i.e. greed that never lets a person enjoy the achievement in hand, hanker after more and resort to any means to appease the rapacious instinct obsessing brain. Like blood in the human body, these five elements are present in the human nature since birth. Like the variations in the blood constituents, these elements also vary with the circumstances and environments of birth and support. That is why a bad company or a deleterious lecture should be abstained from while a good company and teaching proves conducive to formation of a good character and personality. When the normal limit of any blood constituent exceeds, it gives rise to some physical ailment and when any of these five A exceeds in the human mind it germinates maladies of mind resulting in several personal, social and family problems. Isn't it wise to keep these necessary evils in controlling limits to avoid mental agonies?

Vices are Voracious Vultures, Virtues are Gold Mines

Today's man is behaving like a voracious vulture to meet selfish ends and forgets all norms of morality, duty , service or sacrifice. For him money is everything, which he goes on piling despite tainted moneybags already lying uselessly but the lust for more pecuniary benefits is increasing. Such vicious thinking in the name of progress and modernization is giving rise to modern ailments, tension, depression and stressful conditions of body and mind. Everyone is stewing in one's own juice, i.e., everyone is looking after one's own purpose. Does it mean that virtue, magnanimity, charity and pity are altogether vanquished? No, it has enormously decreased because of the delusion that a virtuous nature is non-paying while wickedness and vices are the ways to progress and prosperity. In every prayer to the Almighty wisdom and sanity is the first demand of all human beings. If one's thinking is in the right direction such delusions like 'prosperity in vice and wickedness' do not come to mind. Money needed for necessities of life is everyone's compulsion but the pastime of pecuniary piling for the posterity is not the thought of a wise man. The dividend paying methods of virtuous nature and the vulture culture of wickedness are seen in our day-to-day life. Money made by wicked means is wasted in vain while that earned with virtuous means and toil is utilized well. Nature diverts thinking accordingly. Ups and downs come in the life of every human being .The method of handling and tackling becomes different because of different thinking made by nature depending upon the type of earnings. Suppose a corrupt person collects money by wrong means. In the event of his physical indisposition his thinking will be moulded in such a way to make a mountain of the molehill. He would feel horrified more and become mentally imbalanced. This torment and nervousness will make him move to persons and places of costly cure. Thus the treatment that entailed heavy expenses swept all that he augmented by sin and wrong means. On the other hand the virtuous man's biggest troubles too get cared without even the knowledge of their gravity, he is thus saved from the panic of the trouble and gets rid of it in a play way method by homely, indigenous or petty treatments. The man with vices justifies his means to collect money saying that if he were not having that much money, he would have been deprived of the necessary treatment while the fact remains that nature strayed his thought to the extent of his sins so that the voraciously earned and piled wealth, is swept by the physical indisposition. There is an adage 'Cut your coat according to the cloth'. Here nature makes the disease cut coat (sweep money) according to the cloth (the type of earning and the person, virtuous or vice). Similarly when it is a matter of children's admission in professional colleges, the wrong way earned pile is deposited in capitations or other expenditures while the virtuous man's child gets admission without incurring any capitation fee, donation or other type of expenses and on the basis of good performance. When it is a matter of setting in a profession, the virtuous one's child gets settled by the benevolence of someone or gets a job without incurring any undue expenditure while the child of the one with vices prodigally spends and wastes father's money before getting settled. Some people may differ with the foregoing views and remark that they see everyday poor men dying due to dearth of necessary treatment and the genius children of people with paucity and penury deprived of making their careers. The reply here is that lack of pecuniary facilities is an easily available excuse for every mishap of life. When the rich men and the kings getting the best of treatment die, when the children of people with high access and authority are deprived of some opportunity despite their offering tainted money bags or when they do not settle in any profession or don't accept and enter parental business and prefer loitering idlers and the children of virtuous people are not facing such nuisance, why not then talk of money? Is there still any doubt about the quality of action and the consequent outcome? If in the matter of visibly poor person one excuses penury as the cause of every woe, what is to be imputed for the failures that are afflicted on the affluent? Society therefore is a mingled fabric where high and low people are to exist. It does not mean that all the high status people are high exclusively due to financial capabilities and the low status necessarily low due to paucity of funds at disposal. Nurturing such notion means to exaggerate the importance of money. Such thinking encourages and justifies all means good or bad to augment money. In an endeavour to change luck by accumulating material possessions, a person resorts to all methods fair or unfair. Such instinct to carve himself or change luck is the basic folly of today's over enthused, over smart, clever and cunning people. Man's duty is to act in the best possible manner and adopt the virtuous ways in life for a peaceful living. He should accept his lot with pleasing disposition and leave the rest to the judicious ways of the regulator of the universe, the one who creates and carves destiny of his people. Virtuous style pays the first dividend in the form of a carefree life while a life of vices for money sake is tension torn with an obsession in mind that perhaps money will carve or change the destiny, which is never the case. If it were so, the rich men and the all-powerful kings could never die and faced no trouble of any type. Is it ever seen? If it is not possible, why then there is ado for money by any means? Money is a necessity like other necessities in life however it must not be mistaken as the one that should become exclusive for which all virtues of humanity and suavity of nature are sacrificed. Virtuous thoughts and deeds are doubtlessly gold mines that ultimately pay dividends.

10

Steadfastness

Will Power and not Age that Matters

A person is a child if his acts are childlike or is naïve and ignorant to worldly affairs while some smaller aged persons become precocious and prudent. Similarly some children grown up in penury and adversity behave in senile and desperate manner due to frustration, while the actually old persons living in affluence are fostered and cuddled like children. A dejected young man of withered spirits cannot be called youthful but an age-old person of high spirits and nimbleness aptly suits to be called a youth. It means that one with the youthful heart and spirits is a youth irrespective of age. Similarly it is the will power and intention to do which makes a thing easy or difficult. It is one's affordability that makes a person take rest in indisposition and he can shelve his duties and responsibilities. Adequate attention and medical care make the onlookers realize that he is truly troubled while a poor person or the people who can't afford they are on the road for two square meals despite so serious ailments afflicting their bodies. Only those people are retired who can afford their living without responsibility of work otherwise there are people who strive to survive in the old age and their output is more than the so called youth. Why so and how is it all that? Obviously it is due to a feeling and compulsion before them that does not let their will to retire. When the will and intention gets retired the person is actually retired at that time. **What is fatigue?** Do you think it is an absolutely physical phenomenon? Not so. Suppose there is a wage paid gardener and he is asked to work a bit more than the stipulated duration. He will tell you that he is fatigued. Now an officer after having worked so hard in the office, returning home after the day's toil feels enjoyment and relaxation in gardening. Why? A work that was irksome and weary for the gardener is a source of relaxation for the rest-seeking officer. Obviously it is the feeling and the intention that makes a thing loathsome or lovable. Strong intentions make strong persons. Don't you see so many people yielding to little pressures while there are so many others who confront the most persistent or recurring failures valiantly? Those who imbibe the essence of life face the adverse moments of life with fortitude, an instinct which cannot develop unless one determines to do, strengthens his will power, becomes fully conversant with the realities of life and the secrets of happy living. A person, who remains in self-delusions or the one who keeps his eyes shut to the realities of life and never bothers for theological gains, seldom achieves true happiness. We must not remain deaf to the common findings of all cultures and mythologies. Theological guidance keeps your thought and mind balanced and cool. The gems of wisdom contained in the scriptures strengthen the will power which in turn makes the intentions and determination strong to make one fit to face any challenge with pleasing disposition thereby keeping tension and stress at an arm's length. The health that such positive thinking and attitude provides is quite obvious. When a person is mentally happy, physically well, his life is naturally happy and charming and worth living in the true sense of word.

Stage and Status of Comfort and Discomfort

Every stage of life namely; childhood, youth, middle age and Old age have their respective problems pertaining to life, its activity, worldly affairs, family and health. Healthy body and brain ensure happy life. Every stage suffers from some major health related complaint. Namely Dehydration in Paediatric troubles, Genetic problems or diseases of genitals during puberty and Alzheimer's disease amongst the geriatric diseases are the likely torments of these stages. Similarly there are troubles regarding expectation of love or respect from different relationships in life. These expectations are more from those in propinquity. When these are not fulfilled, one feels depressed and anguished. With the changing trends of life, culture and viewpoints these also demand a change. If this change and mental preparation is not done there is lot of nuisance and tension amongst different relations when adverse attitudes are observed and cherished hopes get duped. Even in the former times when they were generally observed and on that basis expectations were formed, it depended on circumstances of a family and differed from culture to culture, people to people rather family to family. There was a general feeling of commonness but no hard line could be drawn. For instance a general feeling harbouring peoples' thought was that parents look after and up bring children who in turn care the parents in old age. Due to the fast changing trend of peoples' attitude towards human relations and the ravenous materialistic approach, the expected old values have fallen into oblivion and obliterated from peoples' code of conduct. Also wantonness that haunts the minds of all elderly and younger people has made people of the type that neither the parents are that way truly dedicated, as they ought to be nor the children are responsive to their expectations. Of course there is more clamour, ostentation and hypocrisy but sincerity has decayed enormously in the present life and there are no such overtures as are cunningly pretended. In the older days children were in the laps of mothers and old people were under the shelter, sympathy and support of young children, now the children are quite often in the crèche and the parents in the geriatric home. An argument to justify these acts may be given that because of the costly life both husband and wife have to go to respective duties and because of the style and responsibilities of life the old parents' interference cannot be tolerated and their responsibility is not possible to be borne because of own compulsions. How can one change this notion and bother head with the arguments that smack the lack of 'will to do' on either side? There is thus a need to review such expectations that can torment our minds afterwards and lead to tension and depression. Similarly happens in other relationships where from the expectations of affection, respect and regards have become the things of past. One has therefore to be mentally ready for all such developments because most of the family tensions seen around are the products of the nuisance that breeds from such non adjustments. Similarly there was a feeling that childhood to play, youth stage to act and earn to the maximum and old age to retire, rest and enjoy the care and love of children. Now with the change of thought from sincere devotion to false ovation these propositions of stage of pleasure and pathos are changed. There is neither anything for anyone to bet or boast nor there is anything to feel, fail or frustrate. There is now no specific stage of toil or retire and rest nor there is a cause to frustrate that the stage for such and such thing is passed. No one can claim nor anyone can declare emphatically the people and relations who will come to succour nor there is a stipulation and surety of some faithful and trusted person of today prove insidious tomorrow or a staunch enemy of today proving an angel of the future. This is all in vogue because of the moral values and virtues of personality getting dissolved in the materialistic and self centred thought. Therefore it has become all the more necessary now to act only in the present and deal with the present people according to their attitudes without nurturing any type of prejudice. One must not feel frustrated with the failures of a stage or attitude of a trusted person in whom confided most. Because any one can change any time and the moral bindings are replaced by the material bindings. Anyone, even a stranger can appear as a well-wisher and a saviour if a relief is destined for a person. If it is not destined no power on earth, even a brigade of well wishers and helpers cannot resist the wrath of nature. From this side one must do what is supposed of him in the present and leave everything else to nature. There is no fun of lamenting the loss of well wishers and opportunities. If you feel that some adverse reaction is there despite your best effort and actions and even a review of your attitude conveys the same, do not worry about the loss of such fake and hollow opportunity or a person. They were like a mirage. It was a false hope that would have ultimately duped. It was delusive to consider such persons and possessions your own. There is no fun of worrying or entreating such people or beseeching such occasions. Worry will only weaken you without changing the things even a bit in your favour. Remember if your efforts are sincere towards a person and actions right for an occasion, it is your mum ness and indifference to the missing that may retract the person or opportunity in your favour if even a bit of genuine attachment exists otherwise thank the Almighty that the delusion is over at the earliest with little pain without further loss and more painful infliction. The deeper it would have penetrated the more painful it would have been. There are frequent instances of some people having a childhood deprived of its charm. They sometimes get those missed charms of love and fostering in the subsequent stages. People who enjoyed whole life and could never think of a stage that befalls in the old age when it was a time of rest. There are people who have to strive hard in the old age while their youthful stage was the one of mirth and merriment. Therefore never worry or get frustrated thinking of a stage or time having passed. There is now no hard line on the stage and time of pleasure and sorrow. Never let your spirits dwindle if some expected helper turns face, there is no replica of his being the only one to help, any one will be created by the will of nature and destiny. Relationships are man's makings for nature all humanbeings are alike. Do not worry some expected helpers turning face or finding baseless faults with you. This may be their excuse to get rid of you and such people are better exposed at the earliest. You are in the delusion of their power to be of your use in the time of need and they are in the delusion of being your godfathers and destiny makers. Both are mistaken. You must not bother or beseech such meaningless turn faces and rely only on the magnanimous nature that has entire humanity at its command and create many helpers for you if it wants. Therefore bother and worry for the resentment of nature and the Almighty. Try to keep your conscience and the creator happy, none can spoil anything of yours and no work or accomplishment that falls on you will lack the requisite resources and potential. Never worry lack of performance or loss of an achievement, there is no limit to it. If you have sincerely done your best, think that sky is the limit for achievements what special they get who carry achievements in abundance, after all these are also for satisfaction and pleasure of the self, where that pleasure comes there is the fulfilment of the goal and if that pleasure is missing, all what you achieve living in the world becomes meaningless. Also never worry the time to come or apprehend the things of the future, which must be having most of the present parameters, changed when it turns into the present. Judge its compatibility with your potentialities at that time rather than worrying right now, weakening and demoralizing the self. It is not therefore advisable to pend jobs of a stage to some other stage of life; try to dispose the duties of that stage looming large on your head. This is because the shape of the stage upto, which you are pending some duties of today, is unpredictable and unreliable. Any stage of life can bring sorrows, pleasure, toil or turbulence. They least care the making in your mind. Similarly refrain from bad word or behaviour that may pinch a person of any rank or relationship with you due to false notion that more powerful and better placed status relations are enough for your needs and that would never leave you in the lurch. Clear your thought from such intoxicating delusion because you can't predict the status and rank of relationship appearing to your succour or proving insidious when fidelity and help is required.

Good Actions Pose Difficulty to Start

Do not get perturbed with the initial difficulty that irks at the start of a good and useful habit. Once it is assembled in the routine, its non-performance starts troubling. For example, a wristwatch of a large size feels and looks awkward, proves irksome and loathsome too. When you become in tuned to it after some time, its absence pinches. It is very difficult to get up early morning for a walk or meditation to start with however after sometime it starts giving pleasure and missing it proves pinching as if some important aspect of routine is lacking. The initial stage is no doubt irksome but when accommodated in your routine it becomes a necessity. It is like accommodating a person when you are feeling sitting comfortably, you hesitate initially due to tigtness but after sometime when the person alights from the train and vacates the seat, that looseness troubles for sometime. One must never therefore feel disturbed with the initial difficulties because a new start always takes some time to get adjusted. There are some habits that are very pleasing to start with but they prove detrimental in the long run. Do you think that initial pleasure is the one to be relied forever? No it is only transitory and when you adjust it as a part of your routine it may prove wreckful for the ensuing period. Here we can mention gambling and drinking. How pleasing they feel in the start but when you accept and assemble them in your routine or become an addict the results do not require a mention. Must therefore identify the right and the wrong things, people, places and habits. Here you may raise an objection. You can plea that one man's wrong may be another's right and vice versa as is the case with other aspects of life. Here the suggestion is that there are things which are the universal truths based on the majority opinion. One man or few men may be prejudiced and have different options of right or wrong or good or bad but the majority based universal realities cannot be ignored or considered at par with an individual's liking. No doubt when a person takes an action it is only when he gets convinced with it propriety, aptness and feels justified after doing it. Even an assassin bears justification for his act but the good or bads of universal bearing cannot be lied at the instance of some individuals or a particular person. His act will be adjudged and declared good or bad on the basis of the universally established list of good and bad habits, acts or human traits.

Wee Hours' Worrying is Terrible, Avoid it

You must have felt the effect of thinking in the early hours of the morning. Brain is so active, fast acting and sensitive at this time that it can prove both advantageous and disadvantageous depending upon the topic of thought and its concern with your benefit or detriment. Early morning worrying is so grave that it makes one lose sleep for the rest of time and if lost in the chain of that worry consequences, one feels awfully disturbed. It is therefore advisable that in the early hours if some anxiety strikes, try to avert it and remain out of the anxious thought till the normal awakening time in the morning. Do not invite sleep disturbance by brooding over or thought domination due to an unwanted matter. Let us take an instance of daily observation. When one thinks of ghosts or apparitions early morning, it creates an appalling atmosphere around to make him shudder with fear while during the day, listening or thinking about such things becomes a normal affair and all fear that pervaded early morning seems to have lost in the hullabaloo of life. When there is a bad dream or a nightmare it makes one tremble with fear and apprehension while during thc day things pass normally. So it should be one's effort to avoid thinking awful or worrisome matters in the early hours of morning. Pleasant thoughts, happy plans, joyful events can be thought which quite often prove soothing and conducive to sleep. For students and intellectuals the early hours of morning are the boon hours because the wit, wisdom and memory are at their acme at these hours. The right value of early morning hours must be identified and used accordingly. This time is for the pleasant thought or learning and memorizing, it must not be misused by deploying it for a bad dream, thought, or an embroglio. Early hours to be utilized for sensitive matters of pleasure and achievement purpose while the eroding events, thoughts or mesh matters be put to the rough and tough life of the full day when the brain has to work in a noisy-cat-race atmosphere and thoughts. Worthless matters or futile anxieties erupting in mind horrify in the wee hours while they pass in routine scathing least during the hectic day.

Tips to Pass Three Types of Odds

These odds pertain to **bad time**, Dearth **or deficiency** and a **confronting ordeal.** The best way to pass turbulent times is to relish the good times and the pleasant moments you have had before the present trouble or sometime in the past. Also one can evoke sagacity and strength of mind by the fact that the pleasant moments and its pleasantries were my exclusive privilege. Life is a texture of ups and downs, if I saw and enjoyed the ups surreptitiously and exclusively, I should feel ashamed in creating clamour for others to come and face adverse moments on my behalf. Such thought betrays our ignorance about the realities of life. He, who wishes and wants positives in life, must be prepared for the negatives that are inextricable as both are covalently bonded. Thus the best way to pass odd times and situations is to relish the enjoyable times of the past. Be sure that like a revolving wheel, the unwanted moments too pass giving way to the awaited charms. This hope should be a potent weapon to stand and not to yield against bad times. Second odd is that of dearth and deficiency of some type that torments a person. Basically this trouble is the consequence of seeing others' visible pleasures and inviting an inferiority complex without knowing the hidden aspects. All that glitters is not gold and everyone's circumstances are different. So breeding a grumble by the apparent sight of materially rich, becoming sure of its being that what it seems, and the habit of comparison; aggravate the situation and make a problem of no problem. This tendency must be eschewed. Most important in this regard is the knowledge of this fact that everyone has some betters in him. It is a matter of exploration. The tragedy with the worry workers is that they always explore the pleasures and possessions of others and dearth and dejection of their own self. This fact of life must provide power to any worrying person that the sorrows and pleasures are of many types and they are distributed amongst the humanbeings. If some is rich monetarily, he may be poor from health and may be tempting for some savoury eatable which he cant because of some disease. He must be cursing his wealth which he cannot use and may be tempting for a health like yours who is lamenting for financial deficiency and feel your healthy body as your birth right and of no importance. One must therefore remain assured that there exists some gratitude of god in him, which may not be present in others. He should therefore concentrate on own self and explore the plus provisions in him instead of pondering over the minus factors or the deficiencies and dearth. The third odd is that of an ordeal overhead. A bucketful of happy moments is our right but an ordeal overhead becomes ado and a lamentation for others to listen and know. How ludicrous it looks when we want to enjoy the bouquets hidingly so that none should see us enjoying more. We however come out with bands and trumpet of cries and shrieks during unlikeable situations to make everyone partner in it. Whenever there is a confronting ordeal, keep in mind that it follows an era of happiness. So pass it peacefully observing fortitude. Remember how scaring and irksome it is to prepare for an examination and a competition, which come many times in life and are indispensable aspect of life. Similarly there are many ordeals in life, which have to be crossed with a firm belief that it will pass and its success will open an era of happiness. You must however be ready for failure as well if you want to succeed because single pole is non-existent and unstable in any aspect of life. Must therefore hopefully wait for the positive aftermath of an ordeal and fight the one overhead fervently.

See to the Realities Lying in Front

When a person loses teeth, he is sure to face difficulty in mastication and the one losing eyesight feels problem in seeing the things. To lose either is a big loss no doubt but who wails and cries more when such loss befalls? The one who could not perceive the difficulties or noticed the effect at the fall of hammer. These are the naked realities everyone knows and no expertise is required. The man crying abnormally now remained floating in fantasies forgetting the basic facts and when the things came overhead, he started making a hue and cry. Similarly people, who become habitual of enjoying the comforts and commodities exploiting chair and their official position, forget the fact that this instinct to exploit for augmenting amenities will pose problems for the self. It will make the exploiter habitual of spreading feet beyond his sheet besides addicting him to many vices that spoil the family peace. Their actual entitlement and provisions of rank do not include or afford such prolificacy. When such exploiters of positions retire, they find all illegal amenities absent. Their wail after retirement is attributable to their not realizing the fact that the exploitations of chair are not possible all time in life.

Only those can live a tension free life who did not inculcate this habit of exploitation even during its prime possibility but preferred cutting their coat according to the cloth. Similarly, those are peaceful, well composed and placid who prepare themselves with the fact that on losing teeth, taste will be affected, on losing eyes, charm of life, on losing power and post; the control, command, influence and when the youth is passed, that vigour and vitality of old days is no more there. Those who talk of maintaining will power must understand that the maintenance of will power is possible only when the realities of things are fully imbibed and one gets mentally prepared for the negative that dwindles one's strength of mind. A strong brain conduces strengthening of will power. Unless one gets convinced with the aptness and propriety of a situation and accepts the realities in front, will power and obviously morale is difficult to be boosted.

Persevere with the Imposed People or Problems

Is there anyone in the world inviting disease, disaster or other contingencies? Perhaps none but they do come destiny based. Can we avert or curtail their span by getting irritated? Perhaps no one could do so. How this feeling affects our body and mind? It will weaken the power to act (face) and offshoot different physical and psychic ailments. What is then the best course left? Decidedly to observe perseverance and face with fortitude what befalls on. Difficulties and disease are no one's pleasure. They are the inseparable parts of the bipolar life comprising misery and pleasure. Worldly troubles are to be borne by the worldly people who enjoy the pleasing aspect of life. How smooth life and things are going on in ones life but a misery or misfortune never knocks the door and suddenly changes the entire scenario. One must not get broken instead muster courage and wisdom to resist the nauseating misery, feel placid and composed, get stabilized and start enjoying it while confronting. It should be considered an act to pass life and an event of a fixed tenure that cannot endure long, must go to give way to good times. Like the unsavoury incidents and anecdotes in life, there are people who are not engaged but imposed. Imposed because some relationships namely conjugality where some time matches are uncongenial but the impositions have to be accepted. In some families, the wives of sons are often held guilty for spoiling the affectionate atmosphere of the in laws' family by her separatist tendency breeding tension and nuisance amongst the hitherto amicably adjusted family members. What should be done with such an element that becomes a compulsion? Squabbling in a bid to solve is an utter folly, an invitation to nuisance and consequent tension. Observing perseverance in compulsion is the best remedy. How particular and abstemious some people remain in their routine in every matter still they get engrossed in unpalatable, dilemmatic and enigmatic situations of health and family life. What will their sagacity and abstemiousness do when they are destined to meet particular situation, which never gets averted, as lotted cannot be blotted, it has to be borne? Similarly even the most astute person errs in match making during conjugal relationships resulting in nuisance and clashes of obvious nature. Who then decided these things, the disease, the disaster or the disturbing contacts? It is the destiny that decided and it is the time that will cure and repair by the acts and efforts of the aggrieved. These are neither the invitees of man nor are they the pastimes and pleasure. They simply come uninformed and create work for the aggrieved. He who works positively i.e. faces their effect boldly and with pleasing disposition will not feel the length of their presence while those who work negatively on the onset of such position make a hell of their and others' life. These grave moments seem never to end to a person with a negative thinking. Such people get afflicted to psychosomatic troubles or succumb to their fatal effects. It is therefore always advisable to bear with patience and perseverance the imposed situations and persons, face their effect with fortitude to let them fade and vanquish with time.

Adaptability, Acceptability and Accommodation

This three A phrase if adopted in life proves conducive to a happy living. Some people remain fanatic and fastidious and seldom agree with others' choice, inclination, aptitude or circumstances. They are the people who impose their own will on every person in every matter, the possible cause of such obstinacy seems egoism and also apprehension of some detriment to their set convictions. Orthodoxy, conservatism and conventionalism are also the reasons for such fanaticism. An obstinate person with no latitude in his style of life is problematic not only for others but also for his own self because of nervous strains due to such attitude. A person, who adapts, accommodates himself to the existing circumstances and also the type of confronting personality finds it easy to live a life of cheerfulness. A person who knows his own nature and limitations can take a better and more appropriate decision than the one who flies in imaginary thoughts and delusions. Like the one who 'cuts his coat according to the cloth', a person who has a thorough knowledge of own nature including weaknesses cuts his coat of insistence according to the cloth of endurance and power at his disposal. He who accepts the realities of life, judges what confronts in the proper perspective is said to be an astute and wise person. Decisions of life taken with wisdom and prudence create less problems and hence less tension for a person. An egoist or an arrogant quite often subjects himself to unavoidable troubles and his uncompromising nature becomes the cause of incessantness of unpleasant and unsavoury situations in life. It is therefore essential that the meaning and applicability of the word 'Principle' or belief in the axiom 'courage of conviction' should be understood in their right perspective and not misconstrued to betray fanaticism or stubbornness. Even in our everyday life we find persons of an accommodating nature more acceptable and cynosures of all eyes. Every one likes such people and they endear them selves to anyone in contact. On the contrary the hardliners and fastidious people who remain in the delusion of being 'principled personalities' are despised by the contacts. Before making ado of principle or convictions one must judge the event, occasion and the effect of your accepting and accommodating a situation. Sticking to a principle or conviction does not mean keeping alive nuisance and acridity amongst humanbeings. It is therefore utmost essential that life be kept smooth and serene and the factors within human control must be kept in mind to avoid or lessen resistance in cordiality. This conduces peace for mind and prosperity for life. Avoiding rigidness in every little matter and adapting to circumstances create less resistance and hence tension in mind.

Haste and Hypocrisy

These are not necessarily always paying. Rather they ultimately prove detrimental and devastating. It is good to 'make hay while the sun shines' but the right identification of shine must be there to make hay. A habit of haste without time-judgement justifies the dictum 'Haste makes waste'. Today's youth is agile, hasty, flaunter and wants to become affluent overnight. Sophistication, shrewdness and hypocrisy have become the marks of success. These are not the natural instincts or the inherent features of everyone but they are the part of modern success techniques. The result is, oppression of the free will and thought. This action subjects the brain to self-invited stress. To be nimble and fast is good. No one will advocate sluggishness but to behave like or become a machine is not in the overall interest of any one and such attitude troubles in the long run. An ingenuous style free from hypocrisy keeps a person light hearted. A pause to think proves paying as it revitalizes for better action. This notion of the conventional thought to remain mentally running all the time is very injurious. Even a machine requires some a pause for better working and smooth running. If we have preferred a mechanical style of life for material progress, the human machine too requires pause for revitalization and better working. The over enthusiasts of today however consider even a short nap as the wastage of time or sign of languor and laxity in their zest to misinterpret the adage 'rest is rust'. The best way therefore to peacefully enjoy life is to work intelligently and diligently for the set objectives but keeping an absolute control on our speech, tongue, body and behaviour so that the brain too feels housed in a wise and sagacious person who knows its proper use. Your brain must feel endowed in a wise body that takes rest when needed and not used savagely. This way even the brain housed in such personality gets rest and stability providing suavity in the temperament of such person. Those moderns running aimlessly and frantically in the delusion of progress in emulation can become temperamentally different manifesting petulance and frustration in behaviour.

How to Live (When Paucity or Scarcity Irks)

Whenever paucity of funds, scarcity of needs or deficiency of some requirement torments, Indian mythology proves very helpful. It is good to set higher targets and see to the more progressive people in life but it is not the exclusive, indispensable or an all time specification. Most of the troubles of humanbeings today are that everyone sees to the higher side without bothering for his own capabilities or circumstances. The result is an all time obsession by inferiority making even the achievements above expectations little. Most of the hue and cry of scarcity today is because of seeing to each other and a desire to equate or to excel. It is not that the troubles are more or the sources are less but the tendency to see to the higher group is not letting anyone feel satisfied and pleased with his or her achievement. If a student failing in the examination for so many years gets 60% marks he will be very happy when judges his achievement in his own perspective but start belittling it and diluting the charm of his achievement by seeing to the person securing 80% or more marks. It is like a blind man weeping despite regaining one eye vision but losing that pleasure and weeping with the thought that others can see with both eyes. He can enjoy his achievement and thank the Almighty first by seeing in his own perspective that is, benefit of light gained for one eye instead of regretting the residual blindness of second eye. The man has a delusion that all others except him have both eyes well. He is blind to the fact that all people except him are not perfect or enjoying both side vision. He can also enjoy by seeing to or thinking about the people who cannot afford treatment even for one eye and are blind from both eyes. They are accepting the reality and are certainly the better people living better life in more scarcity. Isn't he better than numerous those who are more deficient? It is good to set high targets or to see more successful people of higher achievements but this setting of targets should prove a force to invigorate your efforts and not those weakening you by creating inferiority. One must therefore remain practical while setting expectations that should be according to one's actual potentialities and not hypothetically framed in emulation of others whose circumstances may be quite different. If a tumbler is half filled with milk the positive attitude is to thank for the portion that is filled and not only see to the unfilled portion and start grumbling. The negative attitude is vented with grumble of deficiency. Such complainant weeps about the empty part but does not relish the filled part. If a person is to remain weeping despite that achievement of half measure, nature regrets having wasted even that for a thankless creature who would have exhibited the same attitude if his entire tumbler were left empty. Do not therefore try to make your life hellish by negative thoughts and resent nature by showing such thanklessness or ingratitude.

Who Gets Rid of Fear

In the starting chapter it has been told that it is the fear that is the root cause of most of the troubles of humanbeings. Dauntlessness and intrepidity comes in a strong conscience. It is a moral force that regulates one's life and makes him live life gayfully without vague and meaningless scare in head and heart for a person, a position or a situation. That makes a person die as many times as he fears from persons or situations. If strong conscience is the key factor for fearlessness then one must concentrate on making his conscience strong. When a person steals something or tells a lie he becomes under mental pressure to save him from getting exposed. That instinct to save is the weakening of conscience due to undue pressure exerted on the thought. He is said to be fearful. When a lie is told for an act of morality, like saving the truth or philanthropy like saving an innocent whom we know confirmedly like innocent but being penalized for some intricacies, errors or legal lacuna it is right to lie for the noble cause, there is nothing to save from our conscience that should weigh heavy on mind. Rather there is a feeling of relaxation and pleasure for having done a right job. This feeling bears a tonic and soothing effect on the conscience. There is no fear in such case. Apparently we find a liar or a thief concealing his act from others but actually it is one's conscience that is the first master and scares the person due to his wrong act making him behave accordingly. Conscience therefore is enough wise to judge the cause and consequence of the lie told. The five evils namely Avarice, Anger, Amativeness, Attachment and Arrogance; each of them generates fear. When fear is there, it is hellish to live life. Let us first talk about **avarice** that is different from desires. Desires are linked with man's coming to this world. Man desires something and then acts for the fulfilment of desires. Our desires and subsequent actions give our lives their unique shapes and identities, as does a potter when he moulds clay to give it a shape and identity. When these desires exceed to the extent of grabbing more than necessity using any means, it becomes avarice. When a person becomes avaricious to acquire more or whole of a thing of his liking he will adopt illegitimate methods to appease his rapacity. He wont shirk telling any number of lies and also steal or usurp that what is not his right but the avarice in him makes to commit that what sometimes even his conscience may not agree to do. Obvious result is the fear of getting exposed and the tension of concealment. What is the pleasure of such achievement that cannot be freely used or enjoyed and entire life is passed in fear and tension of its concealment and safety? Thieves possess enormous material possessions of loot and dacoity. Do they enjoy that possession? Their life is passed in a delusion of achievement in fearful 'hide and chase' strategies. Worldly things are worthy and lucrative only if and till they prove their utility and impart peace and pleasure. If they generate fear and tension they are the worst curse and must never be coveted and yearned. Similarly **anger** generates fear rather fear generates anger. They are thus complimentary to each other. When a person remains fearful, tense (under pressure of conscience) due to a misdeed, he will become peevish which betrays the tension that pervades his mind. Out of that peevishness and anger he becomes friendless and invites animosity of many. In a fit of exasperation (anger) he can physically harm someone or even commit a murder. Not only others but he harms his own self more due to this anger. He would become tense and may succumb to anger due to cardiac arrest or a stroke. Anger can take him to the extent of his own extinction. The third constituent of the five evils of human agony is **amativeness**. If we look around us in an unbiased way, we will find this instinct as the root cause of many troubles in society. Amorous inclinations that are fast growing in today's youth are making all other things of necessity bleak. Elopements, enticements, rapes and more crimes are being committed due to increasing amativeness. Young boys and girls are surreptitiously indulged in amorous activities culminating quite often in committing suicides due to what they call as dupery in love. Thus this amativeness is creating fearful situations for all giving rise to tension and depression amongst the youth and their families too. The fourth evil that is **attachment** is a very important factor that creates fear. Fear of loss of the thing or person with whom we are attached more, whom we like more and what we enjoy more. One feels pain when a thing or person of his attachment is detached or snatched thus duping his aspirations. Almost all attachments are made due to nurturing some desires and aspirations. Even a savoury and palatable thing becomes the one of attachment and attraction only because it is relishing to the mind. Even the poorest person strains himself to the maximum possible extent to make his children achieve that what he could not, to feel the pleasure of his unfulfilled desire fructifying in his child. He cherishes hope from his child becoming his shelter and help in the old age. The more he goes on doing for the child the more fearful he becomes of the child getting enticed away by someone. The child is heading towards youth and professional settlement while the father emaciating in all respects due to senility. This is the reason why in some parts of the world there are numerous troubles and problems after a son's marriage when the wife feels herself the exclusive custodian of man and would bear none's interference or advice while the parents lamenting their love, association and the aspirations nurtured since his birth. So this fight of right becomes the cause of several troubles and the underlying reason is the scare of either side about the man getting biased to parents or wife. The other type of attachment is with the material things which we want to remain stuck and cannot bear their parting. Wailing at the time of death of a beloved is also an instance of attachment. Attachment with own body and shrieking at a little pain, pinch or prick or malaise and a malady are instances of attachment with the self. Thus attachment of any type generates fear of loss, harm or separation. How many precautionary measures man takes due to fear of some torment on the body? How many measures and prophylactic medicines taken due to fear of some harm to the body and prevent occurrence of an ailment? It is all due to one single factor and that is attachment. Fear of accident, fear of injury, fear of theft, fear of loss; all these are there owing to attachment. The fifth evil responsible for many woes of humanity is **arrogance**. This is also due to fear of someone else exceeding in elegance, superiority or ego-maintenance. Here from crop up jealousy, emulation and animosity due to which fights, antagonism and conspiracies are mushrooming in the world. There is an easy way to get rid of these evils and consequent fear borne woeful situations. That way is that of sagacity and reviewing our thought in the light of facts of life and human existence. To argue or indulge into a debate merely to win lip fight is a useless exercise. He is great who has a will to listen, learn and adopt. If a person is self-opinionated and is absolutely biased not to let thought pertinence prevail or alternative measure of riddance from tension to approach, he cannot and must not aspire for peace. He can learn only with time and experience. He would get surfeited with material means and scientific logic that would fail to provide peace of mind. His observations and realization of the realities of life will take him around the world in quest of peace and no profusion of worldly possessions except a glimpse of the self and the life in its proper perspective would prove conducive. It is therefore worthwhile to adopt a holistic approach to life, an approach of listening, learning, thinking, appreciating and accepting and not sheerly gabbling due to prejudiced thought of science, reason and logic. A physician of right intentions, who is sincere to the patient and cares 'cure of case' as his first priority, would never hesitate accepting and adopting every effective and beneficial measure of any system of medicine. He feels satisfied with the cure only while an egoist and arrogant will remain tethered with his limited conventional knowledge and go on arguing its virtues at the cost of the patient's life. Similarly a genuine aspirant of living a life of peace and pleasure will have a holistic thought and avoid stubbornness or more pertinently, 'fanaticism of thought' and a prejudiced outlook for such achievement. The shortest way to live a life of thrill and joy is:

- To accept achievement and outcome with pleasing disposition after having done the best possible action and labour in one's control. It is only the action part that should be one's concern leaving the result to destiny.

- Destiny decides the life of a person and it is according to the deeds. This balance sheet of deeds continues following the soul in the next attire (new birth). Good deeds yield good fruit. Noble deeds and prayer provide strength to and generate energy in a person to pass the turbulent periods of life with fortitude. Wail, shriek or cursing destiny during turbulence and despair cannot scare it or change it rather it weakens a person to pass peacefully the aggrieved moments.

- Everything occurs according to the destined time. One's action helps to keep him busy and happy but haste cannot change the time of occurrence of despair or repair.

- It must be imbibed that Adversity is the best education. One should not wait smooth surface every time in life as that would make one slip and make the movement of traffic on the road of life very difficult. Life is like a river. The twists and turns along the way are meant to guide us not to stop us. Like a surge or a tide in the ocean, vicissitudes of life cannot be tamed or subdued.

- Ignorance is a bliss. After having worked sincerely and with full might under control, it is god's turn to decide. No cunningness or cleverness of human beings can change the providential makings. It is a sheer delusion which gets broken when the over clever persons see the innocents and ingenuous people being prized bountifully, of course sincerity and labour take time to show their worth which is enduring and positively enjoyable. Sincerity and labour are therefore the basic constituents for seeking the creator's pleasure.

- Happiness or pleasure should be fathomed in one's own perspective and not in comparison with others. The tendency of judging things in comparison to or emulation of others', mellows even great achievements and magnifies little losses. This makes one's life scary and hellish.

- Learn from the past as it has an educative value. Future has the hope value. Hope sustains life so remain hopeful and optimistic for the future while acting in the present because it is the present that produces results conducive to the formation of a bright future.

- Strive for better and more with contented and not contentious or voracious spirits. Do not live in the delusion that agility, agitation or excitement yields more while contentment can satiate efforts. No, it is rather the reverse. An action with contented spirits yields pleasure that acts as a fuel for one's power to act. An action with voracity or ravenous (rapacious) approach hammers the cardiac and cerebral functions resulting in their malfunctioning quite often even before fulfilment of avidity for profuse material achievement.

- Every situation and condition high or low, rich or poor, big or small; involves positive and negative aspects. Single aspect is not sustainable because life is bipolar like the two poles of a magnet or two ions or two electrodes. It is one's thinking, positive or perversive that holds the reins to decide and run the type of life. Likewise every individual comprises positive and negative qualities. To live a happy life of amity the positive aspect of personality of contacts and the positive position in the confronting situations should be explored and contempt, cursing or criticism avoided.

- Like the best effort to act for duties and responsibilities and avoiding fear for the results, best attitude and behaviour for the fellow beings be adopted moving in a rightful way. One must never stray from the righteousness in a fake endeavour to win favour or appease some misguiding person. Winning self-conscience is supreme and it is that intrinsic force which rids a person from fake fears, phobia and complexes. Virtuousness pays perennial dividends while the vying and trying people leave in the lurch. Fear of any type is a serious shortcoming of a person. It weakens the stamina to face and fight the vicissitudes of life. Right thinking and virtuous actions are the best antidotes of fear. Fear is the betrayal of one's deficiency of virtuous acts and noble thoughts or it is advertently and intentionally committing wrong acts. Innocence is fearless as is in the case of an infant. It is a delusion to think that cheats, cunning or thievish people thrive; they are the ultimate losers. Gains by hanky-panky last least.

- Keep in mind the fact that the present birth and provided ambience is the result of deeds of the previous lives, this is also a fixed length life, which meets mortality when the stipulated period expires. Like the time of birth (when came empty handed carrying deeds), the time of end and departure will also be carrying only the deeds done during the allotted tenure (life length or age) leaving every material possessions and relations at their respective fates. Why then worry the loss or gain of men or material? If birth and death is a recurring process of transformation and transmigration of soul, why not to sow noble deed- crop during every life, work dutifully and beautifully not woefully, sinfully, arrogantly, snobbishly flauntingly, peevishly, with hue and cry or cursing people and lamenting luck?

11

Shun Ego

Avoid an All-time Self-opinionating

King Bruce imputed his ultimate victory to a spider. One can pass a better life if listen and try to learn from everyone. Self-opinionating is good but listening to none's opinion proves harmful for the self. No one is born in the world without need of others' opinion. It is not advised to agree to every Dick Tom and Harry but it is an advice against the prejudiced feeling that a person of small status or small age cannot give a better opinion. Wisdom is not the exclusive right of the affluent and status people nor it is fully dependent upon the age. Little people of little age and status solve such problems that elude solutions from the recognized masters too. Decisions decidedly should be taken on the basis of own wisdom and assessment but heed and hearing must be paid to the opinion of others. A little clue solves sometimes very important problems. If this habit of no attention to anyone's advice is inculcated it multiplies problems in life and hence disturbance of peace of mind. Such a person will not care for the life experience of parents. He won't bother for the advice of the teachers and even the doctors treating his disease will find him a defiant, self-opinionated and an obstinate patient. The consequences of such an attitude are obvious. If yielding to any opinion, advice or tell tale is detrimental, listening to none entails an isolated and limited knowledge. If a self-opinionated person cannot listen to his elderly well wishers, teachers or doctors, how will he bear the opinion of savants? The sermons of the men of profundity have deep-rooted impact on the mind and soul and quite often they pull you out from enigmatic situations. When a person becomes mentally sick he requires the opinion and lectures of a psychotherapist. If he has been an impatient listener and an egoist relying exclusively on own wisdom, he will neither gain from the medical psychotherapists nor from the spiritual saints. Who will then rescue such a person from the moments seeking second opinion? Moreover if a person is a known obstinate who had listened or cared none before taking any decision, he will not find anyone to save him from some embarrassment and complication at a later stage. It is therefore concluded that to keep the problems and tensions in life under control and check a balanced attitude in matter of opinion too should be adopted and self-opinionating all the time should be avoided

A Glimpse of the Self

It is a general instinct of the human beings that the thing in proximity or easy access is taken lightly, indifferently and negligently while a remote item becomes tantalizing deserving proper attention. How many people think of seeing their country first before going to a foreign country? Born in some corner of a vast country is considered as having seen the entire country. Sheer birth at the place certifies all sites having seen. Therefore a site seeing or tourism means going to a foreign land. This is reminiscent of a person claiming having seen all the cities that were there enroute a remote city during a train journey. A family head or a member claiming that he knows every member and his thinking internally may prove wrong. He may be enough astute to identify the external friends and enemies but his delusion to know his own people troubles at some stage when he is trapped in a conspiracy of own people or those in proximity and propinquity. Only because he could not actually know what was internally going in the minds of those amongst whom he is born. Parents surprise and declare remaining ignorant about their children or failed to judge them rightly on their doing something extraordinary at a later stage. People feel as if they know everything of the mother tongue and they need not know and learn more about it. Such over confidence and vague convictions prove embarrassing for the self at some stage. It is like living near the church and farther from god. Similarly a person feels that he knows his own self because his everything belongs to him including his thought and personality. He advises others, judges others, finds faults with others and criticizes others. He never tries to bother his own self or think even a bit or peep in to his own self. His only endeavour all the time remains to peep in to people around in the proximity . If he glimpses his own self, he can save from many problems and complications that confront him everyday and can also find a solution to several problems for which he runs from pillar to post and which create hellish conditions for him quite often. When one inculcates the habit of peeping into the self and have a glimpse of the self he can come across such rarities as were not found elsewhere. Also one can rectify oneself, prepare for some overhead confrontation and repair some consistently irking factor in one's life. All this is possible only if and when one decides to see ones' own self instead of seeing and criticizing others. The farce is that we are very liberal in giving our attention on others' affairs and stingy in attending to our own matters. In matters of material gains however our attitude is absolutely reverse. The position instead should be otherwise. We should be very selfish in regard to looking to the faults and analysis, repair and improvement of own self and avoid being meddlesome or uninvited advisers in the matter of others. We must be selfish first in repairing our own family affairs and children instead of meddling in others' or advising others uninvitedly. Self glimpse, self-analysis rather selfishness in suggestions, advice, repair, fault finding, criticism should be our first choice. Self-improvement should be our first preference.

It is the Feeling of Inferiority

When a person boasts, flaunts or prefers ostentatious style of life he feels himself superior to others but this in fact is the feeling of inferiority that torments from within and makes one manoeuvre this way to pacify the chagrin of inferior feeling in him. To learn from someone is good but to follow without assessing self needs, circumstances and temperament only to emulate, exposes one's weakness and not power or competence. The intolerant and jealous persons also suffer from inferiority complex. The credulous people are confessedly the worst sufferers of this complex. It is worth remembering that the real charm of life lies in courage of conviction and adopting a fruitful and thoroughly convincing approach. A person suffering from inferiority complex and prone to crying in matter of dress, diet and habits has to suppress his innate action and inherent inclinations. Can one relish a palatable eatable or savour it heartily when sitting amongst the so-called elite people whom he wants to imitate or follow? Some people craving foreign items and abhorring own country's, are also cases of inferior feeling. Such people are said to be suffering from xenomania. When thinking becomes exotic lover and everything that belongs to own country or culture feels inferior, it is an obvious case of inferiority complex. An ostensive outlook and attitude is also sign of inferiority complex. This inferiority complex goes to such extent in some people that when a thing or a thought is said to be from their own country or culture it is not accepted but when the same thing is said to be imported or some theory and belief confirmed by a superior country, it becomes a binding belief. No doubt the matter of credibility and taming of opinion comes here, as people believe a person or an institution that has the credibility and conquered opinion about its reliability. Mostly however it is followed due to social status to give an impression of superiority but in fact it is inferiority. Crazy and faddist behaviour quite often betrays inferiority complex. There are some beliefs that have been the customs and traditions of India but they were never bothered, cared or taken seriously rather mocked till they were routed through some developed country or after getting approval from a super power. Many herbs, shrubs and culinary items of India like Ocimum, turmeric, Garlic, coriander, mint, licorice were eulogized since long by the Indian prophets as the boons for health but they became worthy of peoples' care and attention when the advanced countries accepted their superiority. The mention of today's aeroplanes, rockets, and missiles are all mentioned in the Indian scriptures. They mocked away such mentions calling them fabulous and fairy tales. Their eyes opened when they were appreciated, accepted and controlled by the superpowers. The importance of morning walk, exercise, yoga and many more things are the age-old recognitions for fitment of body and brain. Also they have always been highlighting the negative effects of non vegetarian diet and preference for the vegetarian diet but the inferiority afflicted foolish elite of this country delusive of entire wisdom being their hegemony to set signs of superiority, would make this diet a symbol of low status and the non vegetarian diet as the one of higher status. Such inferiority-ridden superiors of this country did not accept these things till they became costly. They became costly and acceptable when the replica of a superior country was put on it in the garb of scientific realities. Like the old wine in new bottle, the age old convictions and customs of routine Indian style of life and thought are accepted by these big flaunts when labeled by a super power. Something hitherto unbothered appreciated on getting the replica and recognition of a big country. Some person and his talents mocked at, jeered and joked to take him on the verge of frustration. He becomes so dear and appreciable when the big boss recognizes his capabilities and boosts him. This tendency betrays nothing but brains replete with feeling of inferiority and lack of confidence. Manners and etiquettes are good to learn however we must imbibe their real meaning. Some people having rapport with and following the elite, feel proud in making maximum inferiors follow them in the matter of manners and etiquettes since that is the only sign of status and pertinence. They feel as if imitating their way is final and according to the latest trends. Such self styled bosses and neo moderns or neo rich in fact get afflicted by a feeling of inferiority and spread their infection amongst the credulous people in the name of fashion, custom or status. Under such circumstances even the best of own culture, custom, costume or culinary preparation seems conservative, backward, illiterate or substandard. This way such mentally ailing people invite tension and stress in every matter, it may be the way of eating, attiring, talking or behaving; every time they will be found formal and faddist for a particular style to follow. Result of all this happens that to eat the unwanted things of other cultures pretending savourily relishing them, eat own cuisines and specialties in a super nation's style of eating because the style of nativity seems savage and uncivilized which the faddist of modernization can't afford. Sit, sleep, eat, dress, talk, behave, walk and deal in the forced, imposed and copied ways to look moving with the world. To such people, taking Indian diet in that style or using some comfortable Indian dress is a sin. The grotesque appearance that these imitating moderns some time give, speaks the tension, stress and effect of inferiority complex that obsesses their mind in the name of latest fashion, design, custom or modern trend and etiquettes or status and smartness symbols. All such manifestations betray their proneness to inferiority complex in the delusion of superiority and higher status. Even otherwise it is a matter of commonsense that whatever is eaten or worn with freewill and without any formality or strain is enjoyed, relished and felt relaxing while anything eaten or attired under fear and stress becomes loathsome, weary and onerous causing stress and tension. Thus a perverted thought of superiority and delusive status hood leads us to stress. In fact excess or extra ostentation and show of any thing or tendency is an expression of inferior feeling. This feeling may be of money, knowledge, status, caste, religion or achievements; it tantamounts to boasting which itself is the prime depiction of inferiority complex. Why not then to remain poised and refrain from such exercise as it creates tension and stress and embroils a person in troubles, embarrassments and other problems.

Keep Your Mind Neat

Human brain is the drawing room of the building called body. The living style and standard of inhabitants is known from their drawing room. It is kept neat, tidy and no unwanted or superfluous item is placed in the drawing room. The more light, neat, clean and soberly decorated a drawing room is, the better image it gives about its habitants. Similar is the position of human brain, the drawing room of human body. It must be kept free from the rubbish thoughts, the loathsome ideas, and the burning or blood- boiling issues so that the body behaves in a suave style endearing such person to everyone. When a drawing room is comfortably and pleasantly decorated it gives a feeling of relaxation to the visitor or a person sitting therein. Similarly when a brain is free from the sarcastic, petulant and viperical thoughts, the attitude and consequently human relations of such a person are excellent. It is so, because he exhibits appeasing qualities of behaviour that endear him to everyone in contact. He becomes cynosure of all eyes and earns goodwill of everyone who meets. Those aspiring for peace and tranquility of mind and a happy life must therefore keep their brain free from unwanted and emaciating thoughts and there should be no room for the vices of personality like jealousy, ego, backbiting, conspiracy, cheating, perfidy, sarcasm and other such flaws. A gentle and innocent style of living life though seems unacceptable in the present day society replete with conceit and contrivance but it pays dividends in the long run. It conduces peace of mind and lessens unwanted or avoidable stress that is eroding humanbeings because of their delusive thoughts. They may have become erudite to any extent and possess profundity of material knowledge they are becoming hollow and blank so far as the psychological and spiritual knowledge is concerned. Peace of mind comes when the mind is convinced about a thing and becomes acquainted with the facts of life. It is then that the astuteness prevails on the mind and the prime guiding factor that is sagacity rules the brain. A sagacious person does not lack suavity and this helps him understand the things in their right perspective thereby reducing tensions and stressful conditions that confront uncalled during activities of life.

Cause and Crux of Troubles

Almost every human trouble centres round either of the two complexes, the Inferiority or the Superiority complex. Despite having so much in life most of the people are found weeping for one deficiency or the other giving an impression as if the regulator of this universe was prejudiced and has not justified with them. If protracted and not checked, such feeling brews lamentation and consequent complex of inferiority in such individuals. There however exists another form of individuals in the world. The flaunters, who are obsessed with or have delusion about their own power. Such tendency if inculcated causes complex of superiority in an individual. If there is no dearth of people weeping for their deficiencies despite bountiful gratitude of the Almighty, the position is no better in the latter category where people are blind with a feeling of their being superior and fortune makers of many. Thus most of the vows of today's man are owing to either of these complexes, which is on an alarming increase due to increasing egoism. The avidity for material advancement has shrouded the so vivacious element of contentedness in humanbeings looking alive and seeming stalwarts who are breathing, arguing, walking, gabbling, boasting or lamenting but actually suffering from severe psychosomatic ailments and psychopathic manifestations. An affliction by either of these complexes is the genesis of different titles amongst human beings. Some people are snobs and coxcombs while others are grumblesome and pessimist. Tendencies like Megalomania, Xenomania, Schizophrenia, Paranoia, Scepticism (skepticism), Cynicism, fastidiousness, eccentricity, various phobias and fads plus many more are the creations of these complexes inflicting humanbeings. Emancipating our thought from the captivity of these complexes is a straight path to mental peace and tension free life. This is obviously possible by imbibing in word and action the golden thought of contentedness that is 'striving for higher target by refueling with the contentment of preceding achievement' and learn to derive peace and pleasure out of that what is there in our platter of luck instead of belittling it. Thank god for that what is endowed in you and pray for more in future instead of cursing god for the present to invite misfortune for the ensuing period.

12

Learning is Endless

Avoid Becoming Mr. Know All

It is good to opinionate, argue or stick to your viewpoint or convictions due to profundity of knowledge or expertise about some matter or subject. Some people make a problem of no problem by imposing opinion and arguing on a matter, which does not belong to their profession or expertise. Suppose a question arises in a family that the best solution of this problem is making a wall here and partitioning this portion. Giving a casual opinion is the right of every concerned but botheration brews when a person who is least concerned with artisan, architecture, engineering or masonry matters starts floating fears like ' if this happens, it will pose this problem' ' if that is done that will harm some other part' and other apprehensions impeding final solution and execution of work. The best way is to call the concerned master of the profession say an architect or a mason in this case, seek his opinion and feasibility of fulfillment of the desired requirement. You will find that thing that seemed absolutely impossible to you or the solution that never occurred to your mind or the betterment that was suggested by the professional expert, proved very beneficial. Similarly some people start imagining probabilities and problems when someone in the family is ailing. Without least concern and on the basis of their little knowledge some member of the family starts talking about the futility of a medical expert and raise apprehension about the professional physician's intentions and sincere approach to the case. The patient's condition deteriorates and the well-wishers' anxiety increases during such 'waste time technique' of 'Mr. Know All'. Wasn't it better to call the expert doctor of your confidence and seek his opinion instead of meddling in the matter and creating clamour as done by Mr. Know All? Beware therefore from such Mr. Know Alls around you as their little knowledge or first aid like wisdom may prove useful sometimes if they remain well poised but proves detrimental when such Misters exceed limits of propriety to become egoist and start behaving as 'Mr. Know All, the perfect master'. This tendency proves similar to preimagining fears and getting dissuaded from an action or a solution. It becomes appalling if you imagine consequences of the trouble without embarking on the solution. Similar becomes your position when some egoist 'Mr. Know All' exists in your relation circle detrimenting your interests by making you deter, delay or defer your benefits.

Regard of Elders

Today's culture seems to differ in this regard and feel modernized to the extent to which it can defy and disregard the elders and their opinions. Of course the hypocritic actions and pretensions are seen even more the sincerity of respect for the elders has vanquished like the respect for discipline in society. The net result is seen in the shape of chaos and confusion in families and individuals. Confessedly every time and age has its plus minus, so do the elderly people and their advice but a complete alienation of the matured advice and experience is proving deleterious to the physical, mental and social health of today's agile, flaunting and ostentatious youth. To talk of luck and time is declared frustration, to talk of respect for elders is declared conservation and orthodoxy to talk of discipline is called suppression and to talk of mortality and satisfaction is called dejection and pessimism. The results of such perverted thinking are obvious. The rampantly increasing Chaos, confusion, clamour, tension, depression, stroke, suicide in proportion to the material acquisitions testify this observation. The major trend in vogue is the maddening lust for selfish ends abnegating morality and embracing fake-vague faiths. No attempt is made to know and cure the cause of fast increasing tension in every age group but a blind chase of a misconceived modernization is being followed. When there are holes in the bottom of a bucket, it can never fill despite increasing the number of water taps. Caring and curing the real cause only can solve a problem. Solution of many problems of the present society lies in acquaintance with the facts and realities of life. Such knowledge may be presented to the modern generation in a form and style of their comprehension but it must not be forgot, flouted or abhorred, as it is the actual saviour and guide of today's psychologically strained civilization. Elderly advice and experience sometimes puts such constraints that prove boons in the long run. Respect for elders elicits so precious benediction that proves powerful protection against any potential eventuality. Presence of elder in any state of health quite often serves the best guard against any external mischief or detriment to the family interests. Tragedy is that we only see to one aspect of a thing. It is felt that the elderly people are nagging or interruptive and never let the things go forward. It may not be altogether wrong but an unprejudiced thought will bring fore even the positive aspects of the elderly presence and positive value of their advice. This advice quite often serves that purpose or solves such problems, which the most precious medicines or measures could not. The elderly advice may feel like quinine but its benefits bear enormous value, their words and advice quite often saves mind from severe tension and depression and a family from many problems of modernism.

13

Till, Toil and Treat

Body and Brain ; Not Money and Material

When some part of your body is painful, do you and can you enjoy the pleasure of costly cushioned cot? When you are anguished by some appalling event, can an achievement of any pedestal provide pleasure? If your reply is no, what are then the priorities for a pleasing and peaceful life? Why not then realize that the arrogance of material achievement may be palliative but not curative. The perennial pleasure of life lies in enjoying a pain free, disease free body and the fear free, anguish free brain. Why not then to concentrate all your potentialities in these achievements? Some people remain in the delusion that even these are achieved with money and material. If this were true there would not have been hue and cry or stroke and suicide amongst the rich. See to the atmosphere around with an unprejudiced mind and realize yourself the adage 'All that glitters is not gold'. We ignore or we are not aware of the occult feelings, the intrinsic position of the apparently affluent people. Money is decidedly a major means to human happiness and existence but it is not the only thing that decides happiness and peace of mind. Peace of mind is not a thing on sale to be purchased by paying more; it is a state of mind to be acquired after enough sagacity of thought and realizing the facts of life. An ignorance of life and its realities troubles human beings when any of those is confronted with. A person is blindly accumulating wealth by all means. He is ignorant of the fact that life is a fixed length facility, which snatches all material collection on maturity or expiry of its tenure. This fact acts like a thunderbolt on the hitherto ignorant fool, blind in perverted acts of hoarding, cheating looting, usurping and all other wrong ways .If he were aware of the stark reality of mortality he must have channelised his actions accordingly and may have refrained from blind blunder of piling up sins and conscience-killing actions. He is blessed in the real sense of word who has a healthy body and a happy brain, the hallmarks of happiness. Confessedly money is required for providing these adjuncts to body and brain; premonition here is against blind piling of money by blunder and plunder and not against its earning by fair means for necessities of life. Thus a person realizing this fact of real happiness and getting acquainted with the stark realities of life will have to leave the tendency of blind emulation for material pursuits. Similarly people preferring mental freedom will have to sacrifice physical comforts. A lion in a circus or pet animals in a house are the examples. A person preferring willfulness will have to leave the idea of a wage paid employment because it involves discipline and dictations of the seniors and superiors. A person of fastidious nature cannot entrust many jobs to others because he will have to sacrifice his fastidious traits and also liking or disliking for quality or quantity if he gets works from others. If he cannot sacrifice his instinct of quality and quantity consciousness, he will have to search and strive himself. The simultaneous availability of mental freedom, temperamental nourishment and physical rest or comfort is a remote possibility. Some people prefer comforts, amenities and security of a wage paid employment, they are mentally ready to meet the requirements of subordination while some very sensitive intellectuals miserably fail in subordination and prefer physical toil, scanty provisions to reprimands and humiliation by the seniors. In nutshell, plenty of mental freedom possible by penury of physical and material provisions and vice versa. Unfortunately people are voracious to acquire everything, which is not the law of nature and an awareness of such laws means, satisfaction, and hence a tension free mind.

Will Makes the Way

Fog scares one from starting a journey. If stand and see the way, nothing is visible in far length. Quite often such condition scares and makes one stop starting till visibility. If you knew that the invisibility by fog is false and scares lest you tread it away, it becomes meaninglessly created fear. Moreover if one is determined to start and do something, little matters seldom obstruct movements. Some people nourish tension before doing anything because of the imaginary fears and impediments that scare them. Such thinking makes every little work of routine onerous. If they are to start a journey, starting problems scare them, if they are to shift a house, packing and dislocation becomes irksome, if it is a matter of hosting a party or a function its preparations horrify them. In nutshell, such people get disturbed whenever they are to move even a bit from their position of rest. It is not that they shirk work or are lazy and lethargic, it is the impression of something 'difficult' that scares them. No doubt such people comprise mostly the habitually worry lovers; it includes even those lacking initiative and preferring easy life or spoon-feeding. Challenging jobs are difficult for such persons. The compulsions of old age, disease or frustration due to some tragic event is comprehensible but the youth and those in the prime age thinking and acting like that, need psychological approach to rectify this serious impediment in progress and prosperity. The condition becomes worse for the sensitive and supersensitive people who start anticipating imaginary fears and their own contrivance about the potential reaction and fear approaching the person and place and execute an assignment. Some people indulge in colloquialism because of their habit of imagining reactions and attitude of the person to be approached for a work or plan execution. Such thoughts and attitudes are certainly detrimental to one's heading towards a destination, an objective or an achievement. The basic example of fog is given here to adopt that practice while embarking on some important plans and projects in life so that little matters don't matter. When you start your journey in fog, you don't find any difficulty in tracing the next step. The preceding step points and makes way for the next step and you cover a long foggy trail without much difficulty. Now if you see from the other end, you will feel surprised at you ability and ask your own self is it that I have covered this foggy way? Yes, you have and you can any foggy or misty track of life too, provided you have got the determination and a will to do, to perform and to achieve and remember the proverbial fact that 'Where there is will, there is a way'.

14

Awareness is Limitless

Ask Yourself if it were Better Without

Some people are found grumbling about the attitude of one relation or the other. Sometimes they are found to lament the apathetic attitude of their consorts another time they lament the trouble created by the children. It seems quite often, none is free from pricks of varying nature. Is it in one's control to reduce these pricks? Surely it is if one becomes astute and matured about the realities of life. Whenever you have complaint from someone say a wife having complaint about the husband. She must ask herself if it were really better not to have got married and if the spinsters and widows feel happy? If plight of both married and unmarried is pathetic who is then happy? A life of all time sweetness is nauseating as is a road without friction that becomes a nuisance causing accidents. Happiness is therefore a feeling that is generated by positive thought, acceptance and accommodation. Adopting this attitude, one finds it in every condition it is only a thing to be explored. If conception of happiness is a ready to achieve commodity then it is a delusion that has to be cleared from the mind. Happiness is thus a condition to be explored. Whenever we start weeping or worrying our troubles we must call ourselves the work shirkers who are waiting idleness. When that idleness comes to one's life and he does not find any adverse condition or circumstances in it, one loses the charm of life. Life devoid of vicissitudes will be the one of monotony and living such life will also become charm less and an absolute boredom. If and when introspection concludes that some relationship not proving up to your expectation, it is indispensable too and even without it there is trouble, then acceptance is the only solution. A reluctant acceptance is not desirable, it should be an acceptance by mind because you yourself have scanned and probed conditions, the condition of being with that relationship and also the condition without it. Here again comes the question of perfect satisfaction, which is not possible in any aspect in any one's life. Those in whom such satisfaction is noted it is so due to their persistent efforts to glimpse the self and after having realized the realities of life.

The Three Attachments

Blind attachment with self creates fear of harm and sense of insecurity, in his makes a person scary due to apprehension of likely harm in his every action. This makes such person coward, sceptic and a paranoid. Second is the attachment with own things. This makes a person self centred who is waiting an opportunity to augment as much as possible, indifferent to the needs of others and apathetic to the effects of his actions on others. Why has he become so? Obviously, due to the blind attachment with own interests. The third is the blind attachment with own people. 'He is my son, she is my daughter'. This feeling of my son, my daughter and a blind attachment with these whom one calls 'Own', gives intolerable and a protracted pain when the hopes cherished are duped. When the expectations are not fulfilled or when these loved blindly, leave in the lurch. When they prefer their own interests after marriage or run away to a distant abode to settle in a more lucrative career their parting is painful for the parents because of attachment. Why not then to control the extent of attachment before such occurrence? It is only the whim of mind to nurture special feelings about the self-formed special kins, alicnating all morals and abjuring the idea of love for humanity and universal fraternity. Most of the troubles in life are the creations of these blind attachments that make a person selfish, cheat and an usurper. Almost all fights and frustrations are owing to the failure or non-fulfilment of the nurtured hopes or when the aspired objectives are duped. In the mediocre families of oriental culture most of the rifts and differences that crop up in the nearest relations are after the marriage of a son. The over attached parents who cherish high hopes from their sons remain scared lest their son and his sentiments for the parental relations are snatched or embittered by the new comer, his wife and her parents, boy's in-laws. It is the fear that works on both sides. Boy's parents are scared from the girl's parents while the girl and her parents are scared from the influence of his parents on the boy. They therefore try best to undo the natural love and concern of boy's relatives by the superfluous and sophisticated love tactics and pretentious overtures for the boy. The exclusive purpose is to entice the boy and detract him from the parents' side. Also the longly nurtured thought of free living, thinking and doing as per his desire makes the boy less responsive to the wishes of his parents. Thus the concerted efforts of the new coming girl, her parents and the looming desire of the boy to lead an independent post marriage life causes a jerk on his parents' faith. Those who are blindly attached, feel the worst and sometimes even succumb to this unexpected development while the more practical and realistic parents compromise with the situation and accept the things as they find them in the actual form in the present. One must therefore exercise a restraint on attachment with the self, with the material things and with the worldly relations because all these are temporary and endure for a limited length. That does not mean defiance or negligence in performing duty as per extent of relation, that only cautions against blind attachment forgetting human relations, facts of life becoming prejudiced for the own people and own interests and committing all sins for their enhancement. Wale or rue in the event of segregation of the yearning built by the blind attachment or dupery of cherished aspirations due to apathy of the one with whom blindly attached; affect health, mind and sometime prove fatal too.

15

Disceretive is Better than Values

Review Your Attitude

Sticking to your belief is good. Having courage of conviction is good but when it is a matter of interaction it should be reviewed. There shouldn't be obstinacy when some contemplated success points are not working to your expectation. We are not advising to change the universal truths. For instance it is not advised to become a liar if truth is not working or indulge in immoral acts if morality is not working or start cheating and looting if truthful ways are not working. The intention here is to advise, review and change of some routine activity that is affecting your life. Intention here is to suggest change of an act, which is affecting exclusively to you and not others. This need arose because of some people so obstinate as to stick to some instinct because of some whims or belief of that style fortuitously proving right while it may actually be detrimental. If one finds that some way of life or attitude, behaviour or temperament is not working well, there is no harm in reviewing it, remoulding or repairing it. When one finds that a particular profession or trend is not giving two square meals, he will have to switch over to another profession that can provide minimum necessities without the set convictions of a hereditary profession or a profession of training or long tenure. The basic purpose must be kept in mind. The basic purpose of a profession is to provide minimum necessities of life. If the time, tone and tune of peoples' liking is changed there is no harm in thinking about a change as per demand of the present instead of remaining conservative or fastidious and remain stuck to the old to starve. Similarly you believe in some attitude towards some people out of some expectations or your convictions but the results are contrary, there is no harm in reviewing this attitude. For instance Mr. A believes in sobriety and meek dealings and is very placid natured. In the present day life everyone neither understands nor appreciates these qualities that are mistaken as weakness of Mr. A. He needs reviewing of his dealings and attitude. Some person is very rude and habitual of getting works accomplished by officiousness and coercion. Such a coxcomb will only exploit and mistake as weakness the meekness and placidity of Mr. A, who has to deal a person in the way he deserves and the language that he, understands. This attitude may not work well with such a coxcomb for whom suitable and deserving attitude is therefore required. What is the gist of this discussion? It suggests that as your profession depends upon the type of people and place of your habitancy and not dependent exclusively on your own bend and trend of mind-thought, similarly is the position of your dealings, nature and temperament which depend upon the type of person you are confronting or dealing with and has to be moulded accordingly. The circumstances of the society you are living in, the varying natures of the people you are dealing with, the changing times you are passing through, all these affect your attitude vis a vis other humanbeings and your stubbornness in the name of beliefs or convictions only makes you a conservative sometime complaining about the humanbeings and another time the living conditions and atmosphere, a habit that breeds tension and stressful conditions.

None can Win Everyone

What ever measure one may take and as much intelligent or prudent one may be, no one can please and win everyone's pleasure, applause or gratitude. Some people are left unsatisfied and criticize despite the best having done for them. There must not be an attempt or expectation to please everyone and stop dissent. The almighty is so bountifully giving to the world, who seems satisfied and feels obliged? If people do not recognize the magnanimity and benefaction of the supreme authority for its abundance of endowments how do they bother for benevolence or contributions of fellow human-beings that seem too short in comparison to those of the master of the world? According to the Hindu mythology, Lord Rama, an ideal of morality, respect and obedience returned to his kingdom after fourteen years' exile. To convince his subjects regarding the chastity of his wife during imprisonment of the kidnapper Ravana, he desired his wife Sita, the symbol of sacrifice, dedication and fidelity to husband;] to pass through an ordeal to prove her chastity. The mother earth appeared from within the flames holding Sita on the arms strongly avouching her chastity. Despite all this, the over judicious king Rama heard a washer man's flout. In an effort to appease even him, he lost goddess Sita (who went in the lap of mother earth) and subjected to subsequent remorse. It must be kept in mind that there are as many thinking and natures as are the number of humanbeings. Every person therefore acts and thinks in his own way. What seems good to one man may seem bad to other, what hears melodious to one person may hear jarring to the other and what feels pinching to one man may feel soothing to the other. Major aim of a and not to do with an expectation of return or appreciation of what has been done. The first satisfaction should be that of own conscience that duty is done. Even in one's own family every member is not necessarily satisfied despite best efforts of the family head to do best and to give maximum pleasure and comfort to every member of the family. Mr. X had a desire to prove himself fully accomplished towards relations by doing his best possible for them. He wanted to be a good son, brother, husband, father, senior, subordinate, social element and a friend. He also wanted a lovable relationship with every relation, a good humanbeing and endearing position in his profession. Because of such yearning in mind he did whatever best was possible and tried best to win everyone's favour. Luck however wished otherwise. Every person and relation of his rapport and contact would appreciate his achievements and abilities at the back but never accepted so at the face. However love and personal attachment were pretended at the face but rivalry at the back and within heart. The result of all this making of destiny was that he only toiled in life but seldom happened to enjoy the fruit of his toil in any aspect. Some robber of relation, an enemy of assiduity or a perfidious person, a foe of cordiality and justice or some jealous person would crop up to robe the fruit of his labour. The wrong elements fated for him tried to assuage their hearts lacerated by jealousy by detrimenting his interests. The smile, satisfaction and pleasure of X were intolerable for the jealous elements. Not only people in society, profession or propinquity even his own people were not satisfied despite having done the best and the most and having fatigued from head and heart while performing the duties of life and meeting its challenges. Thus every group broke the most dedicated, laborious person of rare fortitude in their respective forms. X had the delusion of winning the favour of all for whom he was enduring till date and not bothering even for his own health but beneficiaries in every aspect were dissatisfied and nurturing one or the other complaint against X. Similarly happened in regard to his other contacts and rapports. It therefore became an every minute tension for the super sensitive savant, X, a genius, rewarded adversely for his labours and talents. A glow of self-awakening made him imbibe the realities of life one amongst which was that 'do your duty, judge well the perfection of performance, if find having done the best possible, forget the result or the return. 'Work is thy duty reward not thy concern' is the essence of great philosophical sermon of the Hindu god Lord Krishna. When one imbibes the truth that satisfaction and pleasure of everyone and winning every one is not a possibility, one remembers only the duty part and relishes its performance without feeling or becoming sensitive to the reactions or attitudes of people. People are mostly self centred and opportunistic elements who have entered into a new title of relationship with you in this life to settle their arrears of credit of preceding birth relationship hanging in your balance sheet of deeds. Hence there should be no regret of the people appeared or appearing in different relationships taking their respective dues in the form of your duty and service. Feeling squared from the debt burden is a big achievement. No yearning for the pleasure, satisfaction or thankfulness of the beneficiaries when own conscience feels happy and satisfied.

16

Humility

Success in Struggle

It is possible provided there is love, sympathy and encouragement from the accomplice. Chides, reprimands, criticism, contempt or aspersions aggravate tension of a struggling person and never let the target or success come near him. The best contribution and support of a well wisher to a person in quest of success is the encouragement, appreciation and morale boosting. These are the concomitants of success. When one enters into conjugal relationship, maximum success is seen in couples with such understanding while a nagging consort spoils the gusto of family life. The family atmosphere becomes tense and nuisance pervades if either of the couple is of a nagging or fastidious nature. Some women are so good wives that they never let the husband get demoralized, boost his spirits by accepting his failures as parts of life and face penury or paucity of any type with fortitude without least indication of dearth or scarcity to the man. Infact they are not only strengthening and ensuring success to the struggling husband but also building strong base for their family and children and endear themselves to their husbands. On the contrary women who peeve over the failures of their husbands or make them feel belittled or reprimand, flout or allege husbands or curse them for making their destiny dark, are themselves responsible for not only their own bad luck but also of the entire family. It must therefore be fully borne in mind that love, sympathy and encouragement are the accessory means with well-planned action for success in any walk of life. They can turn a person from zero to hero. A true and sincere well wisher as is wife in this case, should never think these requisites of success as something pampering husband's ego which she can't at the cost of her own ego. No progress is possible and no peace in the family be expected where such notions exist. No one can enjoy bitterness every time especially after having done the best of toil and thought. Successful people have friendly boosters behind them who never let the struggling and scrambling one get lost in dejection. Exhortation, pat and encouragement are tonics of achievement while Nagging and criticism are bosom friends of failure and frustration. If the person is of a sensitive nature the deleterious effect of chides, criticism and derision prove more injurious causing sometime even nervous breakdown to the sensitive temperament. An already fatigued and frustrated person feels relaxed, recuperated and rejuvenated by sympathy and encouragement. Those who commit such blunder of demoralizing a person in despair, in fact create acrimony for their own self in the mind of the struggling individual the consequences of which are not beneficial when he becomes successful. He may be broadminded enough to avoid harming the critic of his dark days but his experience of dark days will not let helping thoughts come for his adversary during adversity. The importance of love, sympathy and encouragement for a person struggling and scrambling for success is of vital importance. The sensitivity gets sharpened due to struggle and little or no success. It awaits morale boosters who pat and encourage. No material gift or thought is so precious and valuable as is the consolation, affection and encouragement of wellwishers.

Moderation and Humility Pay

There is a general feeling in some gentle people that those who are clever, smart and brisk in action achieve more. They feel that these are the natural gifts which may be lacking in them and becoming the cause of their lagging behind their counterparts. It is however a whim because like briskness of action and cleverness, temperance and modesty i.e. moderation and humility bear dividends to be paid in the long run. The story of hare and the tortoise has remained a good homily for the children. The increasing use of psychotropic medicines is an example of hasty and hazardous life style. Most of the physical diseases these days are having an emotional origin. In other words the psychosomatic nature of many troubles these days is because of the hasty thought and action that initially seems prolific but proves fatal ultimately. This attitude is becoming responsible for the genesis of many psychopathic manifestations. It is not that the group comprising agility, fastness and cleverness proves always paying rather it is the group comprising of moderation (temperance), humility (modesty) and meekness that mostly pays. The proverb 'Haste makes waste' is proving its pertinence when applied on the lifestyle of the modern youth and the consequent effects. Like the adage 'Adversity is an education', 'Ignorance is a bliss', 'Scarcity is a boon' another gaining credence in the present scenario is 'Moderation and humility pay dividends'.

Grumble and Boast

When do they enter one's mind? When a person is ignorant with his own possessions and others' pains or when he looks only to his own deficiencies and others' achievements; he becomes grumblesome and starts cursing luck or god or holding other humanbeings responsible for his plight. Can such lamentation of luck prove conducive to its betterment? Never, however it can create depression and passiveness in the grumbler. Such attitude generates a stench in one's personality thereby making him abhorring amongst the fellow beings. If it entails such heavy cost, why not to refrain it and prefer the habit of satisfaction and pleasure? That is possible by seeing to and remaining thankful to the creator of the world for what he has given instead of complaining for the deficiencies. The second aspect is boasting by some people. When a person boasts something? Obviously when he is ignorant of others' potentialities and own deficiencies or when he feels own acquisitions supreme or superfluous and others' possessions menial and meaningless. Both these situations create delusions and lead astray any person infected by either. Here again the erudition of natural realities comes to one's rescue. Natural realities being that one must work intelligently and diligently, perform one's duties with sincerity and dedication, lead a truthful life of morality and idealism, justify one's coming to the world by doing maximum for the fellow human beings, observe maximum abstention from the five standard A sins (Amativeness, anger, avarice, attachment and arrogance). One should keep in mind that life is a fixed length journey that allows nothing but virtuous deeds to be carried after the completion of this journey, whatever therefore achieved or endowed with, should be happily accepted and enjoyed. Living in the present one must strive for the better and more however feeling satisfied and happy with that what is achieved and not to shorten the charm of every achievement by keeping the fire of discontentment alive or remaining grumblesome every minute. In this long list of natural realities no cause seems inciting jealousy or emulation hence the question of grumble or boasting should not arise in the people who have imbibed the inner truths of life and peaceful living.

Gentleness Pays

There is no doubt in the conclusion that most of the troubles in the world are owing to fear. If there were no fear from each other, snakes would never have bitten men and men would never have killed snakes. It is that fear to be killed that makes both to spur to the moment and play the first fiddle. In the present day world suave and saintly ways are mocked at because anyone can loot and cheat a gentleperson. It seems as if vandalism is the order of the day and everyone wants to surpass every other in cheating, looting, over cleverness, cunningness and lying. To hoodwink and show legerdemain in day to day dealings have become symbols of success. If these are on an alarming increase, their offspring or the consequential effects are no less. The ingenuous and innocents seem to be losers and the clever and cunning seem to be gainers. However, it is not factually so. Over cleverness and cunningness create misunderstandings about the person. Cheating, looting and skulduggery create mistrust and fear for the doer. They may be seeming beneficial initially but prove detrimental in the long run because a person losing trust of fellow beings becomes wingless and hence unable to fly in the world of success and happiness. In the present day world it is seen that the increasing material status has proportionately increased human agony. Why so? Man aspired material prosperity for mental peace and freedom from tension, why then the reverse effect is noted? Obviously due to the vicious, venomous and viperical ways adopted for achieving these targets. If the ways were virtuous, the results couldn't be that agonizing as they are found today. The varying types of nuisance, tension, disease and disaster and everywhere prevailing atmosphere of hue and cry wipes and wastes the charm of affluence or material acquisitions. Such material progress alienating all ideal values, preferring moral turpitude to any extent, leads to an obvious decay of mental faculties and astuteness. This results in tension and depression. Fear is the main cause of woes that afflict human beings. Inhuman or immoral acts weaken a person mentally thus aggravating fear in him. It is therefore wrong to think becoming powerful by indulging in clever, cunning or cheating acts or gaining in life by hanky panky. This is obvious from the fact that once you tell a lie you have to strain yourself manifold and tell many lies to keep up the first wrong utterance. Once you tell a lie or conceal a fact or steal something or seize someone's right you remain under fear and tension of the fact getting exposed. Similarly over cleverness and cunningness cause enormous harm to one's own self. Though apparently they seem proving beneficial, their latent negative effects are felt after some time. It is therefore a delusion to think that the gentle, sober, meek, unsophisticated, innocent or ingenuous are losers and the shrewd, cunning or over clever are in a better position. The gentle, plain hearted and straightforward personalities enjoy tranquility of mind and their little material possessions too while the cheats and clever though materially better, remain under mental stress and tension that evades the best medical treatment and depriving them from relishing their far better possessions. While the clever, cunning and cheat fears being caught because of such acts, the people knowing such traits of a person fear from him and feel betterment in evading him. The innocent and unsophisticated person endears himself to everyone and becomes worthy of anyone's trust. No one fears any harm from him nor is he having any fear of others. It is so because he does not manipulate or think the ways to cheat or loot by legerdemain or over cleverness. Such attitude keeps him mentally light and relaxed. It is therefore fear from each other that is responsible for the human agony. Some people fearing to be ensnared by the hanky panky of an over clever person who fears his skullduggery and cheating plans getting exposed. Why not then prefer an ingenuous and gentle life so that the unnecessary tensions created by over cleverness, like losing credibility and becoming doubtful, are no longer seen and a peaceful sublime life of equanimity and enjoyment is ensured?

17

Knowledge is Supreme

Explore the Good in the Apparently Bad Three

The tnree i.e. **A person, An event, A situation**, looking apparently bad may envelope goodness as per the bipolar theory of nature. One has to explore this good aspect by turning the will to do so and mould own thinking and sight accordingly to explore the hidden goodness. That is why some persons, events or situations that prove quite detrimental to one may prove very beneficial to some other. Besides other factors it is the attitude and will of the person that works. If one's inclination is to see and find good, he must succeed and if his approach is negative or nagging, there is ample scope even in this respect. So one has to select a mind-set to befriend or to alienate a person, event or situation. If it is to seek good, success is not remote. There are frequent events of gold in mud, genius found in the shanties, Silver lining behind a black cloud, a dacoit proving a deity, ruby (gem) in the rubbish, lotus in the mud and so on, why the presence of good in bad should seem strange? These are bad looking positions but goodness is wrapped within. It has to be evoked or explored by the aspirant himself. Even otherwise, if big looking or a magnanimous person can prove adverse i.e. if 'Great cry and little wool' is possible why there should be ambivalence in accepting the fact that apparently bad looking person, situation or event can have latent goodness. Explore with raptness and interest, apply full wisdom and sagacity and then see how you succeed in searching plus in a minus looking or felt situation, event or a person. Such astuteness and attitude pave the way for success and good luck. Every thing, event or situation is not so different as it looks to different human beings. It is because of their different attitude, nature and temperament resulting in a varying approach and thinking about them. Why we say adversity is an education? Is it so? Yes, it is. Rather it is the real education. Now apparently it is adversity i.e. an unpalatable situation but the ultimate reveals its utility and we achieve goodness even in it. When one achieves this goodness or positive thought? Only when one is inclined to accept that adversity happily accepting that there is some goodness in it, which requires one's intention, attention and search. The moment this thinking is there, besides getting the educative value of adversity one forgets it is adversity, takes it usually and enjoys even that. What an excellent approach and an art to live happily adopting a positive attitude. It is by accepting the fact that all positives and negatives in life crop up to keep a person busy and pass time in action. A life of indolence is the one ridden with worry and the worst punishment. Why not then to accept the reality of life that every negative aspect or individual has the positive feature? It has education, guidance, help and hints for life. Trace them, accept what befalls and act enthusiastically, do not lament or brood over. Do not take it an onus or loathsome, it will weigh heavily and difficult to perform. When you realize that work is worship and life passed in work is certainly better than that which languishes in idleness you will enjoy life and its responsibilities. If so, then good and bad persons, events and situations come in life to keep you busy. If so, take them pleasingly and trace the positive in them. You will live a better and tension free life.

Deficiency Evokes Action

Deficiencies are indispensable to life. If there were no deficiency in one's professional, family and social requirements, there would not have been any action in the world. A world devoid of action is a nonentity. No one in the world is quite perfect. Perfection of body, beauty and brain is perhaps no one's privilege. It is this need of perfection that keeps action alive and human beings animated. All good and bad deeds are the products of action for an achievement to fulfill a deficiency. The lust of perfection and supersession incites jealousy and hence there is evolution of trifles, squabbles, arguments, fights and foeships. This is one aspect of humanity. The other is that of suavity and sobriety. With the evolution of positive and negative, that is good and bad, the doers who are saints and Satans continue their respective jobs to comprise a world mingled with happiness and grief. These two groups are always in quest to create their co-taste companions to augment their respective strengths. In good times the group of saints that is ruled by solemnity of action exceeds while in the bad times the one led by Satans and ruled by roguish and rowdy people remains in vogue. The former is a good luck of a society and a generation because it generates peace and pleasure while the latter creates an atmosphere of acrimony, tension and stress in society. A peace loving person obviously opts to espouse the former while the one gone astray or led astray in life falls in to the latter camp. The immediate achievements of latter group may seem tempting and fetching fast results, but the ultimate is quite disgusting leading to psychopathic ailments of an obscure nature. Illiteracy and ignorance about and agony of such ailments quite often create suspicion of some hoo doo, which has bewitched the person behaving in a strange manner. Some suspect the victim spell bound by apparitions and approach an occultist to get rid of the fetish effect. The claimants of emancipation from the evil spirits' spell and enchantment exploit those believing fetishism as the cause of unusual actions and gestures of the victim. Some others find cure in narcotics and sedatives while the erudite and more exact people prefer going to a psychotherapist. When adverse effects exceed the bearing capacity of one's brain, it leads to suicide to get rid of this life and the agony due to conglomeration of tension, depression and frustration. Why not then to learn the art of living by knowing the realities of life and accept deficiencies as complimentary to action in life. For a life of peace and prosperity a positive and virtuous approach should be preferred while fulfilling the deficiencies and necessities and abstain from material lust and concomitant wickedness.

18

Sagacity to Deal Necessary Evils

Necessary Evils

A person, place, position, purpose or a proposal can be a necessary evil. The adage' What can't be cured must be endured' applies when any thing from amongst these becomes a necessary evil. Question is how to endure this unavoidable evil so that the tension and disturbance effect of such reluctantly accepted positions is minimum. A discerning approach is the best respite from the mental agony that entails such compulsions. When we talk of telling ways of a peaceful living it does not mean renunciation of the worldly responsibilities. He is brave who faces the vicissitudes of life and living peacefully while performing duties and confronting unwanted situations. Thus living in the world means facing the troubles and tribulations. Try to pass through them or learn to live with them with composure of mind and maximum peace and pleasure. Resignation or running from challenging events tantamount to cowardice. If endurance is the only way left, then it is possible only by mustering attention on the positive aspects and ignoring the negative part. Every person howsoever abhorrable, has positive qualities which if attended can enhance forbearance for the unwanted.

Nature in all forms is moving with the synchronizing positive and negative aspects and no person or position is without either because both are complementary to each other. It is only a matter of search and intention that matters. For acquiring maximum possible peace when one has to live with the necessary evil, only the positives present in the person or position should be observed. Pleasure and patience to bear should be mustered and the negatives ignored. If negatives reckon the brain there will never be acceptance and consequent endurance. When it is concluded that cure of the negative is not possible and it has to be endured, concentrate on the care of the positive deriving power from it to nullify the effect of negative. While doing so must keep in mind that the disliking position has also a fixed length like the position that you liked. If those are not having an eternal endurance even the unwanted can't loom large. Nature has its set principles and the person or a position of your maximum disliking today can be the one of maximum liking tomorrow. Times change and with that change the other parameters and hence your options. Likings or dislikings will change with the change of time but the utterances and attitudes of the disliking moments for the necessary evils of that time, cannot be obliterated. That will affect the positive mind-change of the present of both sides. It is therefore advised that composure of mind, control of speech, and constraint on actions is required to accept a necessary evil. To be more lucid we can conclude that sagacity to deal with necessary evils and leaving the desired actions, attitudes and expectations to time factor is the best course for those aspiring maximum possible peace of mind. This can help a person live a life of reconciliation and pleasure while accomplishing the worldly responsibilities.

The Astute and Sagacious

Dexterity, wisdom and prudence is not destined to every one. There are some fortunate people who are gifted with the art of understanding the subtle realities of life and adroitly accomplish their duties assigned by their respective fortunes. Suppose there are two characters A and B. Mr. A works wisely in a planned and poised style without any type of inner conflict or haste to embrace all pleasures at once. He has imbibed the subtle reality that honest and dedicated efforts for an achievement are the prime factors expected from a person. Thus A, peacefully carries on his responsibilities enjoying fully what he earns, saving something from it for contingency and eschewing any immoral act to augment his earning. This style of life keeps his brain and mind free from tension, his conscience upgraded because he has not resorted to wrong acts for the so called betterment, avoided self degradation and demoralization. This way he has endeared himself to all and maintained peace in the family. The combined effect of all these actions is that he is having a sound sleep and a health that is free from little ailments getting aggravated because of his 'cutting the coat according to the cloth'. Mr. B on the other hand who is an absolute flaunter making ostentatious display, an agile and over clever person who wants to control the entire material prosperity at once adopting any means right or wrong. The apparent achievement at that moment is far more in the case of Mr. B but he cannot save even that much for the family necessities from his wrongfully earned income what Mr. A could, despite comparatively smaller income. Mr. B couldn't give that time and attention to his family, social and professional responsibilities as Mr. A could. Mr. B's mind was replete with stress and tension due to the hypocritic steps he preferred for affluence. He has sleepless nights, nuisance in his family and a bunch of ailments that are breeding in his body due to his careless approach to the realities of life and his not efficiently performing the art of happy living. It is wise to do little, do well in a planned manner so that the entire output is utilized, whether it is the utility of time or labour. What generally is seen today is that people are creating rush in life due to their rash approach to life and a rubbish comprehension of its realities. The light, easy and a charming life is being converted into a loathsome, complicated and repulsive form due to lack of an astute and dexterous performance of activities of life. First they create fire and then become busy in extinguishing it. Can such approach leave any scope for a balanced and desired effort for the necessities? When we have started relishing wantonness and creating nuisance jobs, when we prefer investing our energies and resources to futile and purposeless acts of flaunt, ostentation, hypocrisy and call it nimbleness, smartness and signs of prosperity and advancement, the plight to be and the consequence of such thinking is obvious. Such trend of people reminds me and makes me mention another instance. An artisan who didn't know his job well was called to see why the newly purchased high priced machine was not working. The smart but hollow engineer remained busy for a pretty long time dismembering all vital parts of the machine and perspiring himself too giving a feeling to the on looking owners that he was very sincere with the job and possessed the necessary skill. It was good fortune of the owners that an engineer of actual ability came, he was surprised with the jumble that the imposter created and spoiled the new machine which required little clamping of a screw. Similar is the state of affairs if a patient is wrongly diagnosed or a wrong route is chosen for a journey or an ignorant physician happens to treat a patient. Isn't the chaos and confusion all around, day to day increasing stressful situations, hue and cry all around and the clamour of materialism and progress are the products of a mindless modernization? Tensions are increasing and the life that should have been free from complications is getting embroiled into increasing intricacies day by day. It is all the consequence of an immature approach to life and ignorance of its subtle realities by some people who are first creating defect in a right thing, then horrifying its defects before the owner and ultimately making that item of utility an onus on the owner. Same practice is being applied on the charming life that is so simple but subjected to the policy of creating a fire and then making a show and ado of extinction. Similarly these immature bosses of humanity are first creating tensions and depressions, then making lives difficult to live with and ultimately going out in quest of peace. This makes them quite often renounce all material effects or renouncing the world by committing suicides or occult suicides in the form of brain strokes, cardiac failures because of hypertension and stressful conditions that preceded the ultimate anecdote. Obviously it was all due to lack of astuteness and dexterity to carry on life comprehending its subtle realities.

19

Luck is Life Companion

It is Positive Thought and not a Frustrated Note

Complacence is declared a cowardice by some modern enthusiasts flaunting their achievements in the name of toil, wisdom and planning. They are right in doing so till their rail of acquisition is going well. The dictum 'Nothing succeeds like success' holds good here. These so-called progressive elements try to justify their every act progressive and do not stop till stagger at some point. They realize the worth of other things like health and peace of mind when get afflicted by some torment. Till this stage they jeer at any one advising them restraint on over exertion, as that would forfeit the purpose of any success or achievement. One strives for affluence and achievements to enjoy and feel the pleasure of having them. If during this effort one exhausts one self to the extent of some irreversible mental agony or nuisance, what is the fun of such acquisition? These agile moderns call their blind materialistic race an effort for surmounting joy. If the body and brain become unwell what is the fate of that surmounting joy? It is this stage that makes them realize the advice of the savants sermonizing restraint and abstemiousness from excess and blind race and whom these neo moderns were hitherto teasing, joking and declaring their conclusions the proverbial grapes are sour? A blind thought that never lets a person review his action till it mentally affects and improve dietary till it affects their health deleteriously. Sagacity therefore lies in observing precautions of thought and diet before manifestation of any ill effect. We must analyze, improve and decide our attitude in the light of past experience and trend of luck? An instance of Harry will make the things more comprehensive. Harry was a very nimble, smart, diligent and intelligent gentleman and had nurtured high ambitions in life but impediments at every step would not let him achieve cherished aspirations. He was thus scrambling for success till fatigued to accept the supremacy of luck and the will of nature. His childhood and youth passed in pain and penury but he hoped fulfillment of his aspirations through his sons whom he nourished with all pains and provisions in possession. Luck however would not let him enjoy the fruit of his toil here too and he became an absolutely broken person having no purpose for any action or dream of any ambition becoming true. The only purpose left with the Harry couple was to pass the remaining years of life. However an anxiety of succour during disease and dusky days was disturbing the couple every minute. But positive thoughts invigorated Harry. What were the positive thoughts in these dejecting moments is worth knowing. He **first noted** the hitherto observed trend of luck towards his toil. He recollected five or six occasions in life when he recklessly worked for something but deprived of the fruit of his labour. If remained deprived with the pleasures of childhood during parents' domain, if could not heave a sigh of relief and faced protracted professional and other nuisance during youth and prime years of life, why expect fulfillment of all desires and ambitions from sons? Why not yield to the will of destiny and accept all that is lotted? **Second** he did his duty and paid debts due by upbringing his sons, getting squared up from debt that in itself was not a little achievement. Getting return of duty done towards sons was to get indebted again. 'Moreover' he thought, 'my target in life was to see my children settled and smile. My smile lies in the smile of my children, why should I gloom with their bloom'? Parents' best cooperation lies in accepting the condition that keeps congenial the couple and must eschew any action creating discord or disharmony in the young couple. Since the birth of children parents sacrifice everything for the pleasure of children, why should not the same practice be maintained? **Third** living of the parents with the married children is a cumbersome management because of the wide gap of temperaments, thoughts, feelings, sentiments, circumstances, wants and abstentions, likings and disliking of their respective stages. For such joint living set up to survive, lot of sagacity and discipline is required. Today social circumstances are abruptly different. A deliberately or inadvertently caused rift amongst the children because of parent' interference or a defiance and apathy shown for the parents' needs and sentiments by the children, become a permanent anguish. In short any joint ship requires sacrifice in many respects by the potential partners. They must do introspection of this fact before deciding such deal or coveting for such arrangement. **Fourth** he analyses his own nature, circumstances, the delusions that prevailed his mind, the prudence and astuteness desired of an elderly status. Reviewing all such factors reveals the feasibility and sustenance of such proposition succeed and expectations fulfilled. **Fifth** the Harry couple preferred observing restraint, avoiding ado, fuss or taken in by the abetment or misguidance of family rivals, **Sixth** and the last, leaving normalcy to the favourable time and the will of fate when even the most complex situations get instantaneously solved. Time is a great healer, teacher and reformer. If it can make Harry review faults and acquire maturity of new responsibilities, it will mature the young couple's thinking, relaxing the novice conjugal charms and reviving recognition for value of relations. Now here again some people may conclude the foregoing thinking as the one of pessimism, frustration, defeatist's attitude and synonymize it with 'Grapes are sour' saying. It is worth asking such thinkers whether their meaning of progress is aimed at progress for pleasure or progress for sheer measure? A measure that becomes meaningless when tension and depression prevails, nuisance rules the temperament, everything around seems worthless. A need is felt for peace of mind through the palliative tranquilizers which is temporary and the permanent solution of peace. A possible by meditation and abstemiousness. Why not to control, check and monitor your actions and activities before getting afflicted to some psychosomatic troubles invited and engaged in the name of progress, smartness, over alacrity, agility and ostentations or to satisfy ego and arrogance or merely due to a corrosive lust of emulation for excess accumulation of material means?

The Three Mysteries of Nature

We generally do not admit them and conclude by hackneyed utterances like ' by chance', 'incidentally', 'fortuitously'. It is so because we don't want to accept the role of luck in life. Also because we pretend to be more scientific logical and bear an argumentative and action based approach to life. The strangeness of these three types requires review as it may help to know the mystery and ways of nature. Such review can conduce way to less tension by accepting certain realities of life. This realization can prevent a person from lamenting own troubles or blaming nature as if it has done some thing with him out of prejudice. **The First** when we see some people emerging alive and successful from fatal and horrible conditions but succumbing to minor event of least care or consideration, someone returning safe from an adventure or an expedition but getting hurt by a minor stumble to suffer protracted bed confinement and sometimes even more. Someone getting through a tough competition or selection or completing a tremendously important professional achievement but meeting an accident exactly before enjoying that success. Some other gentleman building a bungalow investing entire monetary and physical power, waiting to enter but dying immediately before entry into so hardly built dream house. Whole life earning of someone or the aspiration of some other getting duped due to the devilish doer, the most trusted people betraying, an erudite person with profundity of knowledge loitering in quest of two square meals while a nincompoop rolling in an all type abundance, an ingenuous man's son so hopefully and strivingly made a professional snatched even sentimentally by spewing venom in his ears and cunning tactics by the robbers of relations. These are the types of torments that keep humanbeings worry worn and tension torn. Such multiplicity of anguish breeds stress however relaxation possible by accepting the reality that lies in front. **Second** strangeness of the acts of nature is seen when the verity of the proverbial 'Silver shining behind a dark cloud' is observed so frequently in life. There are frequent mishaps that seem to vanquish the person but the ultimate is a good fortune. Like an achievement after toil and acquisition of spiritual powers after penance, the advent of fortune quite often precedes an agonizing and awful situation. On the 21st July 2006, 6PM a five year old son Prince, from a nearby hutment of a village near Kurukshetra(India) fell into sixty feet deep pothole. This boy could get injured by the fall or die because of suffocation or getting buried because of scarcity of resources with the guardians and little rescue arrangements available. But this child emerged as a national hero and considered reborn after his safe excavation fifty hours after remaining alive and active in that narrow cell. For these fifty hours his position was like a child in the uterus before birth. His poor parents remained scared till his survival but found their fate absolutely changed afterwards. They became parents of a son symbolizing national unity, because of joint humanitarian action, prayers from the entire country and abroad from all sects, ages and places of worship and for which all the state, army and national resources were deployed to save. This was far more than silver shining after a cloud that was definitely very dark. Sometimes a kick feels very painful and fatal to the onlooker but it is found to cure the hump of the kicked hunchbacked person. An embroilment in some false case proves a boon to expose and appreciate some quality in a person that till date remained obscure. So the implication in a false case or a dark cloud in these instances are the preceding causes of the silver shining that is, bringing the person from obscurity to limelight or changing his condition from penury to plenty. The advent of a windfall fortune quite often precedes appalling circumstance. Many times during life tranquility precedes tempest. Perfect peace and normalcy precede disturbances of a level never contemplated. A rich man's child kidnapped and nourished like a beggar or a beggar's child taken by a rich from a child care centre, A rich man's daughter married to a richer who dies after sometime and she has to pass time in penury when remarried to a poor person. People wept on the death of husband of that poor lady but fate and circumstances had arranged her remarriage to an affluent person. What such strangeness of nature reveals? What is the lesson for the human beings? It is, that a windfall change, good or bad, of fortune is quite often preceded by the contradictory effect. Nature has got its own ways to act in a mystic manner which when gets manifested or comes to light should be accepted with a pleasing disposition, no one knows when the will of destiny takes one to which side. However they remain evergreen who are docile to Almighty's will. **Third** strangeness of nature is seen when we see someone killing an innocent and the slayer getting the news of fortune due to a lucky draw. On the other side a philanthropist and virtuous man returning home after doing an act of charity and getting the news of his son's murder or kidnapping or meeting an accident. Can it be construed that the slayer has been rewarded due to murder in the former case and the philanthropist punished due to charity in the latter case? No, it is never. This strange behaviour of nature has got an explanation. All good and bad deeds of human beings are entered in their respective lists and these lists remain revolving for settling scores or rewarding to the committers. When a good deed is being done in the present, it may be that some bad deed of the past is to take its turn resulting in the same way and when a bad deed is committed say a murder as in the above case, it may be turn of some good deed of the past that has been paid accordingly. Decidedly however the balance sheet of deeds moves in a very accurate way, one must never confuse that committing bad acts prove prolific. It should be an endeavour to register as many good deeds as possible so that it is turn of some good deed every time in this life and the new life after death due to transmigration of soul.

They Differ Overtly and Covertly

Like nature's bipolar theory in other aspects of life, even the attitudes and deeds of human beings differ overtly and covertly. With the increasing rapacity and materialistic bias, the proverbial 'Face is an index of mind' seems to have lost credibility. People seem to be justifying the Shakespearean theory that this world is a stage where human beings are actors. He succeeds most who acts best. Hypocrisy prevails in every action, utterance and behaviour of people showing an alarming increase in clandestine deeds and cunning acts. Sometimes in our daily life we observe such contradictions in nature's contributions to human beings that it seems as if there is injustice. We forget that the omniscient nature knows the actual deeds of a person and rewards accordingly. Some overtly looking sage may covertly be committing satanic acts. The balance sheet of deeds of previous lives and the reality of actions in this life decide the plight of a person. The supreme power, the omnipotent and omni present judge who decides peoples' fates is quite judicious and seldom bothers what people think or speak about its decisions. Man under such circumstances must act ideally, adopt a virtuous style of life, and strive hard for an achievement in life. One should leave no scope for blame of 'lack of labour and action' and accept with pleasing disposition that what follows. Lamentation over own luck and vying with that of others proves least conducive to change of condition of such cawing crow that burns his blood. When one is not aware of the good or bad deeds in someone's balance sheet, he shouldn't feel surprised at the sight of zero people becoming heroes and heroes becoming zero. This world is full of such surprising situations that are on the basis of deed balance sheet of an individual lying with the destiny maker. Criticizing the decisions of the Almighty is committing a sin. Many surprises and consequent comments will only enhance the number of sins. Best way therefore is to concentrate more on the self-deeds, actions and ways of life and imbibe its realities. Ideal ways of service and sincerity for all should be adopted leaving the rest of worries and anxieties to the 'All Powerful Regulator' of the world who decides destinies on the basis of over and covert deeds of human beings.

Sheer Labour is Not Luck

As money is not the exclusive requisite of happiness in life, labour is not the only factor that makes people fortunate. Successful people or those with a rewarding and prolific present boast about their being very diligent, having toiled day and night and then meeting success of the present level. They seem to sneer at the struggling people as if they are all indolent or sullen, shirk toil and hardship. 'That is the cause of their not meeting success', these wizards of luck conclude. Infact these fate- rich nincompoops are sneering and finding faults in their own selves by such assertions. They are in a prolific possession today and attribute this success to hard work; do they mean they were idler or nincompoops whole life that has preceded the present? Obviously they will reject such inference. What is then that else labour and hard work that takes the same person from penury to plenty? It is the fortune, luck, destiny and propitious time. The role of luck in enacting destiny is a universal truth. Innumerable hard workers are hankering after success, which is so difficult that it remains evasive throughout their life. Happiness in life is possible with money, satisfaction, knowledge about the realities of life and laws of nature plus many things more. Similarly success requires wisdom, favour of time, a sincere mentor and guide, circumstances, environment, ambience of birth and nourishment, luck along with hard work and labour. Neither all successful people are the icons of hard work nor the scrambling people represent lack of labour and toil. Why not then to accept the reality and truth of life that sheer sagacity and labour do not earn. Also it is not sheer foolery that loses. There are many allied factors. One must keep this fact while striving for success. Those who are enjoying success and prosperity must not become blind folded to the facts of life and also the truth that they never remained the same in the past nor there is a guarantee of their present position getting perpetuated. Good times and good lucks can be stayed by good utterance, good deeds and good actions and not becoming snobbish, coxcomb or delusive as the luck makers of others and judges of their efforts and struggle. Such lowlessness pricks and pains the soul of a striving and struggling person. Any irresponsible, hasty or arrogant utterance of the successful person can prove injurious. A sigh or sob of the scrambling person at this stage can shorten the span of success and achievement of the afflicting person. One must therefore continue doing best to ones capabilities while trying to achieve. No heed should be paid to the utterance of successful people of weak digestion. Such low contained people utter and conclude this way because of their weak mind that cannot digest success and achievement. They deserve more sympathy than those who are combating adversity and struggling for headway in life. It must be kept in mind that there are as many natures and behaviours in the world as are the number of human beings. This vast number is not entirely wise. No utterance or assertion of such vain fools should impede fight for success and invite undue tension or stressful conditions. 'Don't care never mind' attitude is the best course to become 'Happy go lucky man' type of an animated person whose absence is conspicuous at every occasion and whose need is felt by everyone of any status or stature.

'Why and What for' Theory to Sift Worries

Sometimes a person worries for things without knowing the purpose. It is just like follow some people and stand in a queue lest we miss something that so many people are yearning for. A worry is thus created only by imitating others and not own judgement. Such created worries need sifting. Once this sifting of worries by introspection becomes a habit, life feels light and easy. Some worries or the matters being worried are simply worthless having no bearing on one's life but the blindness about the importance of that matter or thing and consequent anxiety, create their importance in our life making matters to be deferred and ignored as matters to be cared and bothered. For example Worrying for two square meals is comprehensible but worrying for the reality that life has an end, is a funny creation of some brains. Some people look worried about matters of national importance as if they are the people to decide the fate of nation or holding the reins of administration. The poor fellows may be loitering in quest of two ends meals but they look worried about the entire world. Similarly some people in your relationship will be found as if they are worried about the affairs of all families irrespective of their having any alliance or acquaintance with them. Why? Obviously due to their vicious habit of spewing venom in the ears of one against the other. Such people deserve no sympathy and nature gives them the first punishment in the form of worry habit for their misdeeds. It is therefore advantageous for a person remaining scared or worried due to many problems, to sift his worries, their cause and the bearing of that cause on their life. When a person questions himself why I am worrying or what is that what worries me. The causative factor will come forward. Now the consequent effect of worrier if not bothered, cared or complied with should be examined. When prepared for the worst and also ready to face its effect in the event of not conforming to what is desired, one gains confidence and moral boost. Therefore the effect of a single worry or a jumble of worries can be diluted and even vanquished by sorting out the worry type and its cause.

How to Live (when Expectations Duped)

There is an adage advising humanbeings to do good and forget. No doubt one sows to reap or one invests to earn or get the credit of having done. Can it be advised that when we do something we must expect the return? Very often you receive the return immediately but you do not feel having got and cherish hopes or nurture expectations of return in the future. This becomes a very painful aspect. Whenever you feel anguished due to no return of your toils or obligations by someone, you must introspect and explore the actual factor that made you work or toil for the other or oblige other. Suppose it is a matter of rearing your family, you did so not for them but for your own self and the satisfaction that you got after doing for them is a return of your action. Further expectation to fulfill is a matter of chance and not a claim. When you love someone's child, you cannot feel obliging the parents of that child and cherish some return in lieu of your loving their child. You loved the child to please your own self and should rather feel obliged to the child's parents that they allowed you to kiss, embrace or hug their child. Remember, if you are emotionally or sentimentally weak you have to incur some cost to appease your soul and that cost or action cannot be considered an obligation for others to be returned at a later stage. He who does not analyze the cause of an action or seldom feels doing things for his own self but feels obliging others by his every action, remains anguished because of such obsession. An unprejudiced thought will reveal that most of your actions centre round your own pleasure, satisfaction, fulfill a purpose or assuage some personality weakness including emotions and sentiments. He who gives up futile expectations like the return of an action, help or guidance and performs all such acts as an overture of duty or service to society, is free from remorse-based-tension and lamentation. When however some unexpected return comes, it proves enthralling and gives pleasure more than what could have been given by fulfilment of an awaited expectation. One of the best ways to live a happy life is to do an act of help, charity, service, guidance, physical toil or financial assistance as a grace of god, which enabled you to do something for others. Such grace of god that makes a person capable to perform not only his own worldly duties or responsibilities but also those of his fellow beings, is endowed in the few favourites of the Almighty. It should never be exploited by becoming egoist or arrogant. The all-powerful gods feels pleasure in doing so much for the humanbeings however most of them still complain deficiencies and seldom thank the Almighty. These people themselves expect so big returns for the little acts they happen to do for their fellow beings. Such ironical state obviates one major cause of tension namely expectation, a freedom from which leads to a happy life.

Avoid Inquisitiveness to Know Future

There is a desire in many people to know their future. When it is said that Lotted cannot be blotted, what remains in the aptness of such curiosity? When the importance of present is stressed, that obviously makes futile any inquisitiveness to know future. When it is said that 'Work is thy duty reward not thy concern', what is the fun of knowing what is going to happen in the ensuing times? An Indian astrologer argued that by knowing the ensuing effects one can make shelter arrangement or take some prevention against the misfortune to come. Scriptures arc replete with the events of misfortune that fell on the great men and even the deities who knew about their future but they could do nothing to avert the event to occur. When the prophets and astrologers cannot control the events of their own life, what fun is left in their claiming to become saviour or physicians of others' misfortunes? They themselves are wise to obey the truth to 'Act in the Present', which they do by convincing some credulous people, and get the reward of handsome earning .The best saviour in life that generates power in an individual to fight adversity is to do good deeds, live life by good means of livelihood, serve the needy and those in trouble to the maximum possible. These convictions however must not be misused as strong tools of logicians to repudiate even the bonafide and hard realities of life and declare them sheer superstitions of the illiterate, orthodox, conservative and dogmatic characters. That will encourage the disgruntled neo moderns who would feel as if their approach to life, attitude and material inclinations is justified. The consequence of such approach is amply discussed in the preceding discussions. Similarly a thought that prevails in some minds about some times and days being ominous or ill ominous deserves review. All times and days are the creations of the creator of universe or if it (ominous or ill ominous) exists, it is unknown to anyone and if known, it is unavertible or unchangeable. What is the fun of diffusing the self in pursuing such time wasting techniques of betterment rather than action and duty that an individual's present demands?

20

Compassion

Prodigality is Money Wastage, Worry is Time Wastage

Both are busy in wasting things that are vital to existence. While the former wastes precious money in wanton acts the latter wastes precious moments of life in anxiety and tension. Who can afford all this? Obviously the one who is either ignorant of their worth or have them in exuberance. Prodigal of time is he who forgets that life is gifted for a limited length. It is meant for action for the welfare of mankind, perform duties with a pleasing disposition and sow the crop of good deeds, which can be reaped at the time of need during this life. Deeds accompany a person even afterwards. A person of sagacity cannot afford wasting even few moments of this limited life time for worry and despair .Man is so calculative that he keeps even minor account of pecuniary profit and loss but is prodigal in regard to the limited wealth (span of life) given to him. How much wise it is to waste this precious life in squabbles, skirmishes, fights, debates, hatching conspiracies against persons about whom one nourishes the feeling of own ness? Such tendencies are both way harmful. On one side they spoil your deeds i.e. the crop to be reaped in future and on the other side they breed fear, apprehension, acrimony, tension and stress in the present. One wrong committed drifts you in a row of stressful situations imposing tension and depression. Thus the victim develops a habit to worry and fear. Mr. X could not remain without worrying something or the other. Worry had become indispensable to him and he would always have something or the other to worry. Matters, which were meaningless for others, were the subjects of his worry and self invited tension. Fear and worry are complimentary. Scaring situations and apprehensions create worry. Whenever there is fear or apprehension worry is a concomitant. It means a person inculcating the habit of worry becomes a coward. Thus day-to-day condition of a coward is quite obvious. While the brave dies once, a coward dies every moment of fear and worry during life. Mr. X started worrying before embarking on a journey lest there should be some untoward incident. The nearer would be the journey day the more was X's worry. He would worry about the plight of his family due to his being on tour. Sometimes when he got awakened at midnight some matter of the previous day or the next morning would create tension and worry in his mind to keep him sleepless for the rest of night. Some times he would worry about the antidotes against some scaring situations another time some apprehensions or imaginary fears about future matters would worry him. Worry and Mr. X had thus become synonymous and those friends and well-wishers who abhorred worry, started shunning his company and even sight. A conversation with him would create demoralization and his swollen grumble-some face would spoil the mood. Such despicability only due to a habit is enough to show the effects generated by such personality traits. It also highlights the wastage of precious life moments incapacitating Mr. X to do his duties competently, not to speak of doing something memorable and beneficial for others. This is an apt instance of a person who is prodigal with the precious life and its moments that are being wasted in self-imposed anxieties and worry without any achievement

The Gutsy Man Deserving Compassion

He was considered shrewd by his colleagues because he collected money and material beyond his status by cunning tactics and exploitation of his status. All his relatives and friends were jealous of him and nurtured complaint of one type or the other. But the clever and smart gutsy man wouldn't bother anyone's attitude and go on augmenting wealth. For this he would alienate all decency, gentleness and not hesitate going to any depth of wickedness or moral turpitude. He is thus a big pot who has amassed money and means for the son. There was no doubt in his mind that his son would consider him the best father who has done the best for his son. But the cleverness of the gutsy man demands everyone's compassion. He is weeping because the son for whom he alienated all well wishers, for whom he listened to sarcasm from all circles, for whom he committed deeds that will erode him internally; still curses father for not having done much for him. The son alludes several fathers who have done far more for their sons. The man is ruing his sins committed in the stray thinking of 'my son, my love and my succour' that entirely seems duped. He lies in deep anguish for such heartbreaking result of his avidity and intrepidity. The great deeds of the gutsy man receive disheartening result.. There is another such like man who remained busy mooting plans to loot his parents for his own welfare and also for the welfare of his children. He was the eldest in the family and the best bet and hope of his father. But the poor father was duped. Destiny didn't let that mighty man of magnanimity remain capable even for the school fee of his intelligent youngest son. It was so because the eldest was busy all the time concentrating on the self-ends and never bothered for the father or his family. The man is successful in giving sound professional standing to his sons and also enabling them have big bungalows to live in. His father died in penury and pain and the wretched son didn't feel any compassion on the widow mother after father's death. He would like and conduce circumstances for the mother to die shelter less and support less. No feeling for the parents or brothers and sisters. The man did all sins for his own family comprising his children and wife who are made by his sins at the cost of father's dignity that the wicked son staked by a fraud in business. Where this man stands when becoming old and his sons who also have their own families and it is his turn to feel the taste of his concept of 'own family'. His sons are fighting for their father's assets and property. There is a condition of chaos and clamour amongst his children who nurture doubt about their father's intentions. The sons are full of wrath for the father whom they call as an all time idler and gossip master who has spoiled their lives. The wicked man's parents died in pain and penury because of the pangs inflicted by this great son. His brothers and their families, for whom the eldest successor had left no power and prestige of father, were at the mercy of luck and grace of god. The children for whom he committed all these excesses are complaining the worthlessness of their father. The shameless wicked man flaunts amongst the people having made his sons rich and resourceful. He would collect some women and children around him to tell contrived tales of his sacrifice and contribution for father's family and other relatives. He is doing so to hide his deeds, as it is his turn to face result of his deeds from his sons. But these are the self-praising events that cannot cover the deeds that man committed and which he will have to repay. The children for whom he committed all these acts are in search of an opportunity to show him his real place and worth.

Avoid Increasing Enemies by Introspection and Substitution

With increasing animosity tension too increases. Some situations are beyond one's control but some are within absolute control. Those which develop either by misunderstanding or due to one's utterance or attitude which doesn't feel abnormal to the doer but feels pinching to the person whom words said or attitude shown. The adage 'Think before you speak' can be extended even to one's action. It can be said, 'Feel before you act'. Question arises, how can one feel an action before doing? What effect it will have on the other? There is an easy method for that. It is the method of substituting self in the place of your victim. First think whether the attitude you are going to adopt is appropriate. If you feel that it is indispensable, substitute yourself in the place of the bearer (victim) with the thought if I were in his place and faced this attitude, how would I feel. Your attitude can be considered right if its introspection favours it and the person deserved it. There shouldn't be any weakness or feeling of guilt or bothering for the effect of action. You remain bold and have the courage of conviction even if the hearer feels humiliated or nurtures some malice or minds your action.. It must be told here that when we advise about peaceful living that does not mean cowardice or yielding to any excess to any extent. Suppose a debtor neither returns money on the promised date nor heeds numerous gentlemanly reminders, there is no help left but to show him some objection against his callousness and dishonesty. Lender must not bother debtor's minding his rigid attitude. Lender's leniency is the cause of the debtor's indifference to pay back. Excess if committed without having examined the facts could create animosity and tension. Substitution however provided strength to the aptness of action and there is nothing to feel guilty. Here leniency and gentleness is the cause of that callous creature whose apathetic attitude is creating tension for the lender, there is no help left but to act and not leaving to luck. To be fortuitist is justified after having acted for some thing in the best possible manner, never in one's interest to be a sheer fatalist and wait fortune, sitting idle and refraining action or duty. Tension reduction has not been advised without action. It has no doubt been advised to be sagacious and well posed but cowardice or abandonment of desired action and prefer idleness or leaving to luck without having acted best, is not advised in our lectures. It has been repeatedly advised that the purpose of our thought and action should be to avoid multiplicity of troubles that may crop up due to lack of prudence causing subsequent tension. However to act as per the need of time and the type of confronting person one has to spur to suitable action. When wisdom to restraint is construed weakness by some rowdy, rogue or cheat and becomes cause of tension, an effective remedy action is introspection and substitution.

21

Man's Perception of Happiness

Man's Perception of Happiness

Every one born on the earth feels that he or she is happy only when the people amongst whom he lives and interacts with should think and speak in the same way as he does. Any contradiction will cause irritation. I should have my own options to work or to rest; any compulsion or reluctantly done act will be a displeasure. I should have everything I desire, others may or may not have it and my aspiration may be infeasible but if it does not mature, it is a bad luck. I should never have a disease or discomfort and no adversity should ever come in my life. I should be in a position to dictate others and defy others'. Such concept of happiness in one's mind is quite difficult to be achieved or fulfilled. What is the result then? Such people are always found grumble-some. Where lies the remedy? It obviously lies in the rectification of thinking. If a person is advised by a doctor to see all green. If he tries painting or changing everything green something rather many things will be left unchanged despite his having done the best. A sagacious thought will laugh at such an effort to see all green by changing green all the material objects. Is there a possibility that the man should see all green in an easy manner? Yes, it is there, very easy, very short. Wear a green specs and everything around you will be green. Similarly one cannot be happy and peaceful in aspiring one thing after the other. This is a never-ending fission of the atom of avarice that continues incessantly irking the rapacious person to the extent of frustration. Does it mean a person should abjure his desire to achieve more or sit complacently after some acquisition? No, it does not stop a person from aspiring more however he must do so up to a limit where he can remain composed and not burning in the inferno of emulation. If he does not control that voracious appetite of blind accumulation of wealth he can get dejected and enjoy neither an achievement in the offing nor those already in possession. If you become oblivious about your possessions and achievements and never try to derive power from them, what for and what is the fun of all that which in fact is weighing on you and make you moan and groan when mortality knocks the door. Be sure therefore that man is given a length of life and a schedule of duties. It should be kept in mind that deeds are done to pass time in a constructive happy way by remaining busy in work, to fulfil duties and to leave behind a good name and performance for the progeny to remember and feel proud of, doing such deeds of welfare that the doer is missed even after death.

Happiness Means Adjustment and Habituation

Adaptation and adjustment to circumstances is happiness . It is the feeling of comfort that provides pleasure and not the high cost or luxurious status and atmosphere. Unless one enjoys an environment and ambience from within, all ostentations and glitter is useless. An instance of it is the comfort that one feels in one's humble cottage to others' palatial lodge. One may see any type of luxuriant living and enjoy material amenities to any extent in other's place but a return to own shanty habitation even, gives the pleasure of a different quality making one realize the dictum 'East or west home is the best'. Similarly the right-minded people of integrity and self-respect love their little possession and prefer it to an indebted profusion or the one belonging to others. For them, little of self-respect and affection is better than profusion of detestation and disparagement.. It means it is not the magnitude or material quantity that makes one enjoy a thing, person or circumstance; it is the feeling of self respect and a dignified adjustment with a place or person that proves soothing and tension free. There is an obvious instance to prove it. The initial stage of adjusting in a room with dim light is difficult; once you get accustomed to it the more lit room feels uncomfortable. If a sensitive stomach gets disordered with the coarse meals, the strong stomachs get lose with the light meals meant for the delicate people. If wearing a suit is loathsome today, wearing something else (after getting adjusted to suit wearing) will be an onus after few days. If some aspects of consort's habits look unlikeable the missing of it will pinch when get accustomed to that. If a vegetarian person becomes horrified at the thought of eating nonvegetarian diet a nonvegetarian gets disturbed at the sight of vegetarian diet. It is the adjustment and habituation that matters. It may be a case of adjustment with a person, place, circumstances, diet or dress. Even in professions, a good boss for one may be bad for the other. Why? It is a matter of mutual understanding, adjustment and intoning. All this discussion means that material value or status doesn't matter that much in providing peace of mind as much matters the adjustment, understanding and intuning. Even otherwise it is obvious because every action in the world is done for the peace and pleasure of mind. If mind remains unpeaceful or unhappy, the basic purpose of any achievement gets forfeited. Thus it is unwise on the part of arrogant people to flaunt their effluence and try to belittle the self-reliant people whose best pleasure and achievement lies in maintaining self-respect at any cost and not to hanker after little benefits at the big cost of loss of self-respect. The ignoble, egoist, arrogant and snobs try hard to hurt this respect of the self-reliant people and enjoy their hurt feelings. People who actually want a tension free life of pleasure and charm must bother for their mental inclinations; least bothering the conventional or customary trends. All individuals have their individual inclinations of mind and there cannot be a parity of tastes, temperament and circumstances. One must therefore act according to ones own trend of mind and capacity to adjust with the persons and circumstances. Basic pleasure lies in this adjustment and not in battering of mind because of taking decisions unacceptable to the individual's mind.

The Precious, The Nectar and The Sweet

Generally a costly thing is considered **precious** and several other factors like feelings, sentiments, circumstances and effect are ignored. When we talk of cost we must remember that more cost means something that provides more pleasure. A needle or a safety pin financially costing too little become too precious when save a person from humiliation in a function by proving utility. A menial worker or a relative becomes too worthy when comes to succour at a time when the expected rich well wishers turn face and leave someone in the lurch. A gift prepared with own hands by investing day and night labour, remembering the person and the purpose; becomes too precious in comparison to a costly gift arranged through a servant and delivered through a servant or a courier. Gabble means cheap, meaningless and useless talk but wisdom and sagacity means precious words, speech or advice that quite often saves or serves millions' worth. Similarly the positive effects of a little man in solving big problems that hitherto failed big men and big money bags; elevate his stature because of his worthy and precious wisdom status. However it depends upon the beneficiary to understand and appreciate the person and provide preciousness to his emotions, sentiments, deeds and circumstances. **Nectar** is not necessarily the drink of the gods. A very pleasant thing is also nectar. Nectar of flowers is the sweet essence of flowers. When a person is very thirsty in the scorching heat that parches body, a draught of cold water gives the feeling of nectar. When a person is groaning with pain that evades even confirmed palliatives, a home remedy or an indigenous decoction that alleviates trouble is not less than nectar. Some people relish and enjoy some soothing song or a sermon to the extent of nectar. When there is a drought situation, people pray and worship for rain. A consequent shower on the parched soil is the nectar rain. In life therefore, nectar exists in several forms, the best being the nectar of pleasant and peaceful life, which gives very soothing and satisfactory effect and a justification to come to life. This is possible only by learning the art of living. **Sweet** is considered a thing with admixed sugar (sucrose, glucose or fructose). It is not only a thing to eat or drink which is sweet, even a thought and a speech can be sweet. What cannot be achieved by lots of financial investments and physical toil is achieved quite often by sweet words. Sweet song proves the best soporific. Cows give more milk under the influence of sweet music and sweet songs besides making one to sleep, dissolve the sins of mind turning in to tears that weld up from the eyes leaving a clean mind. Habits are also sweet. Some people behave obnoxiously and treat bitterly while some others are remembered and missed because of their sweet habits and temperament. Even looks and figures are sweet. Beautiful and charming people are called endowed with sweet features. Some people especially rival and adversaries see each other with bitter looks while some friends and well-wishers see so sweetly that they win endearment. Their absence in a get-together or a meeting is conspicuous. Naturally they become the special attractions and cynosure of all eyes. In life one must try to talk sweetly and behave sweetly live a sweet life replete with pleasure and happiness. Wear sweet, look sweet, and talk sweet to enjoy the sweetness of living. One aspect namely the diabetics are advised to abstain from sweetness (of sugar) in their diet, that too however is an effort to enable them live a sweet healthy life.

Happiness is not Vendible

If it were so, there would have been its dearth for and denial to the poor. But it is the reverse here in the world. The number of poor with all types of paucity but feeling happy exceeds that of the rich with full affluence. The rich people are more dejected and anguished despite all amenities of pleasure at their disposal. Happiness cannot be procured by pecuniary profusion. It is the profusion of knowledge about the realities of life that leads to a happy life. When that light of knowledge kindles within, there is happiness all around. Try to reach these beautifully decorated sites of happiness in you. Visit these sites that are hitherto deserted because people have not been properly guided to these sites thus diverting their paths. Misguided humanbeings are groping in the dark and splashing the mud of materialism to the best of their individual capacities. They are vying with each other, indulged in material emulation with the delusive thought of finding happiness but getting fatigued and frustrated. Glimpse within and search within, delve deep into the realities of life, come out of the falsehood of searching happiness in material profusion. You will start feeling the taste of life, the fruitfulness and not the futility of coming to this life. It will make you realize that abandonment of jealousy, emulation, snobbery, false egoism and the big fives that is, Anger, avarice, amativeness, arrogance and attachment is the real path towards a life of peace and pleasure.

Internal Dirt and Disease on the Increase

These days it is noted that the external blemishes on the skin namely cracked hands, fissured heals, rough skin, anal worms, pediculosis(the symptoms produced by lice or pediculus) are getting replaced by the neat silky hair, soft glowing skin and hands and also the sophisticated and soft spoken young people. Are they actually so or it is a sheer pretentiousness under mental pressure? The increasing tension and alarming psychic irregularities irrespective of age, betray something wrong at the bottom. That wrong is the dirt and disease that is increasing in the minds and hearts of people in the form of jealousy, emulation, anger fear, suspicion, conspiracy, callousness, cunningness, robbery, rancour, rapacity and least care for moral values or fear of god and conscience. These are the modern ailments that have sickened human brains under the familiar brand names; tension, depression, mental stress or the psychic disorders. Today skins and speech have become soft and delicate no doubt but the brains are shameless and callous and hearts have become very cruel and selfish. They are wise who avail today's trend of external neatness and hygiene but do not abandon the golden gems of internal beauty by refraining from or keeping at length the modern internal diseases namely jealousy, emulation, rancour and others of that category. As it is elaborated in the aforesaid 'grumble and boast', full life length of none is woeful or gayful. It is a changing circle that shows every taste and colour to every one. Thus there is nothing to boast during rise or grumble during fall for an astute person. Only the low contained and ignoble people exhibit such changing trends or get affected by the momentary changes. Such gullible people who do not use their own wisdom suffer anguish during fall and face jealousy during rise. Sinful deeds are collected in bits but repaid in bundles. Keeping these realities in mind, an approach to life that combines the modern external glow (scientific approach) and the age-old internal brilliance (spiritual philosophy), is the one that can impart peace and pleasure to live a life of progress and prosperity.

Basic Cause of Woefulness

As discussed earlier that it is not one's own plight that troubles a person, it is the thought and sight of others which affects one's own life. This thought and sight of others may be an absolute delusion. Why not attend your own self and peep into the self instead of peeping in and attending others? No one on the earth is trouble free. It is the type of trouble that changes and no one, howsoever worldly powerful, enjoys the privilege of freedom from trouble. The rich and powerful have troubles and worries of a type that may not be even thought by a person of limited means. Only he is happy who has derived it from within. Only he is happy and specially privileged by the Almighty who imbibes the realities of life and channelizes his thinking accordingly. This thought and sight of others' superficial happiness is one point of human torment. The other point is their delusion about the life itself namely; Ignoring, forgetting or deferring the naked realities and remaining apathetic to the purpose of life. The general feeling abinitio that pervaded many minds was that life is meant to eat, drink and enjoy. These days its enlarged form includes accumulation of wealth by any means, degrading to any extent alienating all morality, forgetting the actual needs and also the facts that life is a limited length game, the people for whom you are collecting are in kinship with you for that limiting length, the life length or the age of a person after which the entire material accumulation will remain here in the world. He will get disconnected from any concern with his material collection and accountable all alone for the deeds done and the ways adopted for that material enhancement. It is the deeds alone that are to be carried forward for deciding the shape and type of next birth for the transmigration of soul. Some moderns may argue that such thought is a message of lethargy, indolence and inaction. It is frustration of a defeatist. It is such misconception that needs clarification. They must not mistake their agility as activity and over cleverness or cunningness as the hallmarks of intelligence and success. In fact such versions and beliefs are responsible for the everyday increasing suicides, strokes and separations in society due to dismal decline of respect for the elders or their advice and indifference for the cultural and moral values. It is creating an occult fatigue in brain, malaise in body and discord in relations. The purpose of life is not exclusively selfishness and deployment of or adherence with immorality. It is not even burning body and brain, the precious gifts of god, in pessimistic thought or emaciating them in futility in the name of god's worship. It is said that human life is a valuable gift of god to a soul and also they say that god inhabits in every body. Humanbeings are endowed with a precious brain to think and a body to act. It is not advisable to misconstrue the term worship as if it means deliberate and self invited decay of body. A person who rightfully performs the duties of life keeping in mind its realities and also the creator of universe, prays for the welfare of all humanbeings , helps the needy to his best ability and capability, adopts a routine and life style of rightful earning , does not humiliate, torture, exploit, cheat or misguide his juniors or inferiors and weaker people and keeps his thoughts and actions sublime, he starts feeling a natural happiness emanated from his soul. It is the best worship of the creator the reward of which is seen in the smile, satisfaction and sagacity of such saints, yes, they deserve to be the real saints who enjoy and justify their life in the real sense.

22

Self Sacrifice

To Secure one Benefit you have to Sacrifice some Other

How fortunate seems the pet dog of the rich man in comparison to a poor humanbeing, wandering for two square meals? Its meals, milk, breads, pats, hugs and so delicate laps of the rare beauties are, enough to feel anyone jealous on the lot of that pet dog. Is it actually happy and never feels the pinch of something missing? Yes, it does. What is that what this so fortunate animal feels missing? It is that freedom to breath in the open and pass an untamed and untethered life or traits inherent to it. For the sumptuous meals and so temptuous treatment of the masters it had to abjure the idea of willfulness in every aspect. Similar is the case with human beings who expect everything of their desire and are never ready to accept even a bit of inconvenience, abandon or afford sacrificing even a bit of what they already possess, in lieu of the new achievement. They enjoy the goodness as their right earned by no grace of any authority but acquired by their self-efforts and toils. About their woes they shriek and wale and attribute that unwanted situation either to the human beings around, the Almighty or their luck. It means such people feel that they are infallible creatures and their miseries are either due to errors by others or the prejudiced Almighty and the pleasures of life are their own making. This delusive thought makes one agonize with what we call tension, anxiety, worry and depression. One must first try to understand the basic realities of life, one of which is that there is nothing and no one in the universe is flawless. Also to achieve a thing of choice, one has to sacrifice some other of liking and convenience. If one feels that he can pile up pleasures only, one is inviting depression and stress. It is like a person ignorant of the fact of mortality and lamenting luck when told or comes to know that life is a journey and everything whatsoever is piled up will remain here along with the relations for whom all sins and crimes have been committed. It was better for a person to remain acquainted with this fact of life and earned something for his own self too in the form of good deeds, passing life in action while performing its duties and responsibilities in a virtuous way. If one wants to reduce worry he must imbibe the fact that life is reposed on two opposite poles, the North and South, the Protons and Electrons, the Cathode and the Anode, Cations and Anions the bright and dark, the day and night, the rise and fall, the bitter and sweet, the gain and loss, give and take, achieve and deprive and so on. Therefore to achieve or gain something, be ready to lose some other thing in lieu of the gain. It may be due to error of observation or feeling that one mistakes feeling getting something without foregoing another. The principle of nature however never allows it. Any achievement demands the sacrifice of willfulness and wantonness. No achievement possible without sacrificing the ease and freedom. Now when one gets prepared for this situation and mentally accepts this fact he gets ready to sacrifice one thing in preference for the other. The thought of achievement of preference should compensate the potential investment (abandoning or foregoing something else) for that. When such stage is reached one enjoys even the act of renunciation or abandonment. Suppose you want to help a poor. Is it possible to help him physically without striving yourownself or to help him financially without reducing the pennies in your pocket? It is never possible, but if you decide your preferable option, say helping the poor the mental satisfaction derived compensates the pecuniary deficit that occurred .A sagacious thought will provide pleasure even in leaving and parting that what pains today. Try therefore to understand the realities of life and reach such stage of maturity of thought that even the seeming loss of yesterday becomes a pleasure of today. To achieve a preferred thing therefore be ready to leave some other in lieu there of

Moment Not the Material Value that Matters

When attending a function one's pent is torn, a safety pin becomes valueless. Similarly timely help to a dying patient, a draught of water to the fainted person, shanty shelter in the torrential rains, all these things become very important and supersede their material value. 'A drowning man catches at a straw'. This straw is the saviour and it is ungratefulness to see it from its material or physical value when the moment of need is passed. 'A stitch in time saves nine', any subsequent attempt to compare its physical entity, namely the numerical number namely one (stitch in time) or more, tantamount to ingratitude which if inculcated and gets matured in one's nature, manifests itself at all levels in life. A meagre salary father making his son a doctor or an administrator or a professional, loses entire zest and enthusiasm if the son on getting settled starts comparing the material value of father's sacrifice and dedication and tries to repay the little numerical cost of expenditure father spent to enable son earn big amounts. This is the depth of ignobility and the consequence of today's ungrateful people devoid of attachment, affection, emotions and sentiments and concentrating exclusively on material gains for selfish ends. Ingratitude may be momentarily feeling beneficial but it breeds tension in mind sooner or later in an indirect manner. The cause of prospective stress may be attributed to the trouble points of that time. However the ingratitude shown for some one's courtesy or kindness and that which has now become a part of personality, is one of the major causes of alienation, animosity and consequent stress brewing in the self centred human beings. For a person desiring less tension in life, ingratitude and selfishness are amongst the major deficiencies of personality, which have to be abnegated. It must be remembered that it is the need of the moment that is important and cannot be evaluated or repaid by numerical value at a later stage. A thing that comes to our rescue or utility in the hour of needs ranks very high and invaluable. Similarly a person that succours or saves physically or morally from the crucial moments is above comparison and evaluation. Any attempt to materially evaluate, repay or return is not only an act belittling the big overture but also betraying the ungrateful and ignoble nature of the former beneficiary namely son in the above instance. It also discloses the extent of one's moral turpitude and petulant nature obviating plenty of stress and tension in such personality.

How to Live (Attachment)

Like fear and expectation that make one's life wretched, attachment with the worldly things, charms and relations also generates tension and stress. He who is over attached and over caring about a thing or a person, has to pay through the nose in the event of such thing or the person going a little away. When you are over attached with a person or a thing a thought of its loss always scares and keeps tense. There is a dictum ignorance is a bliss and we must add to it that negligence and indifference also prove beneficial many times. The over caring and over possessive parents especially mothers are becoming tension torn or depression victims because they remain apprehensive of the child's security, safety and feel concerned about the child's performance in exams and competitions. Some parents remain scared from the child's company or friends lest he goes astray. Most of the disputes and tensions in the mediocre families crop up after marriage of sons. It is due to the scaring parents especially mothers who do not realize the post marriage realities and feel themselves as the exclusive well wishers while the new coming wife wouldn't bear interference or command of anyone as she entered into a fiduciary relationship, the conjugality bond and hence in the superior most position. People forget the mortality theory of nature. Nothing is eternal. Partings and losses are inevitable. If a person ignores this reality he is responsible for self invited mental torture. The one, who is mentally ready and awakened about such realities of life, gets recuperated after some preliminary shock in the event of a loss or departure of the beloved things or persons. Like ignorance with the facts of life, even personal deficiencies are responsible for an aggravated tension. A sceptic, whimsical, cynic or a person ailing from some other mental deficiencies remains more apprehensive about the things or the persons of attachment. An over attachment even with the own self keeps a person apprehensive of a mishap and makes him timid. It means attachment is a major source of fear. He is happy who is attached more to his soul and conscience and less to the physical body or worldly interest. Thus an attachment with or anxiety for the mortal physical factors should be avoided to the maximum. If this holds well even on the own self, what will be achieved by worrying about those with whom you feel blindly attached? No one is competent to worry about the physical entities of one's own liking and attachment. Of course maximum toil and help for the welfare of those worldly attached with you in a relationship is a must. Do best and toil maximum for your own physical well being to keep fit for the worldly responsibilities but not get attached to the extent of inviting fear or worry if and when some abnormality is seen. If this fact holds good on the own self, other well-wishers, relatives or persons and things of attachment are no exceptions to it.

23

Moderation is not a Folly

Avoid Excess of Anything

Any thing and everything, good or bad goes well if performed within limits of suitability, fitness, aptness, decency or propriety. Anything, whatsoever, a habit, manners, diet, dress, entertainment and love or regard; excess of everything proves harmful. Not to speak of the notorious habits, even etiquettes, manners, instincts, costumes or consumables, what so ever; excess in any matter leads quite often to undesirable results. Let us start with **thinking** which is always advisable before any action. What then when this thinking exceeds normalcy and there is no action but only thinking? It is brooding and may point some psychological disturbance. It will no longer remain a quality but become a fault of personality. **Speech** is a virtue that enables expression. It pays to talk pertinently, succinctly and lucidly. Orator is an ornament of an institution however exceeding the limits leads to nuisance and grave troubles. Elocution and rhetoric are the marks of speech-distinction however exceeding the limit makes it chatter. A speaker is eloquent till he feels the limits and avoids his eloquence becoming gabble. **Vitamins and tonics** are good for health till they are taken in limits or to replenish the deficiency. Their excess and unwanted use leads to toxicity and ill effects. It is good to be **Hygienic and Health conscious** but an excess attention may make and keep one an all time patient making hell of his life by over observation of the so called hygienic and health related precautions, such persons suffer from health complaints of psychosomatic genesis. It is good to be **Clever** but an over dose will make the person over clever and cunning making him despicable and a scare for the ingenuous class. **Wisdom** is a positive requirement. A wise person with sagacity, and prudence is a great succour for all well wishers but an excess of it can turn him an egoist, nagging and a self opinionated person whose astuteness becomes unacceptable to the hitherto beneficiaries. To be **sensitive and sensible** are the salient features of gentleness however excess may lead to psychopathic manifestations. In today's world of unscrupulous and callous people the excessively sensitive that is 'touch me not and talk me not' personalities are always in trouble and grumble for something or the other whenever they meet. Even a poison in little dose may act like a medicine but the excess of even butter or milk show adverse effects. **Vigil and care** are the basic necessities to live with life these days but that too to a reasonable extent. Even this tendency exceeding the limits leads to a person's becoming a cynic, sceptic or a paranoid. All this excess is discussed in regard to the positive aspects. Excess done regarding them too proves detrimental. Excess of negative aspects is undoubtedly harmful. Similarly excess in the matter of eating, drinking, sleeping, toiling, running, resting, bearing are all deleterious to health. Chronicles are testament to the fact that excess **patriotism** like that of Hitler proved harmful to humanity. Excess **love and attachment** proves highly painful in life due to children leaving parents in the lurch or settling away from them or preferring their own options for relations. Excess of anything or any aspect good or bad proves detrimental to peace and prosperity. It breeds stress and worry in life. Avoiding excess in any respect means a sincere wish to pass a life free from tensions that brew due to attitude.

The Easy Way

If you want to see green all around, it is very cumbersome to change everything around you to make it look green. The easiest way is to wear green glasses so that everything looks green. Similar is the position in dealing with the people during life. There are as many natures and temperaments in the world as are the number of people. Every individual has his own qualities and drawbacks. While dealing with the people, you may not find many of them akin to your taste and temperament. Their way of thinking, talking, dealing and their manners or behaviour may not suit your nature. This creates a rift and tension for you. However none can afford antagonizing or remaining aloof from many people only because they do not suit one's nature. Man is a social element and cannot remain alone or isolated. What is then the easiest way to live with the people bearing their varying natures? That way is reconciliation or changing the self. It is very difficult to change every person as per your liking or to remain engrossed in stressful situations but it is not so to change the self, to develop patience and tolerance for others' attitudes. In short, it is easy to change the self instead of trying to change everyone. A person who inculcates this habit of changing the self finds himself in a comparatively better position than those who fight and argue in an endeavour to change others. Variety being the spice of life, all people and their natures or behaviours may not be alike. The fingers of a hand are all having individual utility despite their varying size. Similarly is the case of humanbeings having varying natures and behaviours. The best way therefore to remain tension free is to avoid unnecessary debates, arguments and clash due to difference of nature and wherever possible an attitude of compromise, composure and accommodation be adopted. It is advisable to adapt yourself to the nature of the confronting person for amicable and tension free life and avoiding argument, debate and squabbles to the maximum possible extent.

Index